YOUTHTRENDS™

YOUTHTRENDS™

CAPTURING

THE

$200 BILLION

YOUTH

MARKET

Lawrence Graham and Lawrence Hamdan

ST. MARTIN'S PRESS
NEW YORK

YouthTrends, F.L.Y.E.R.S., and Fun Loving Youth En Route to Success
are registered trademarks of F.L.Y.E.R.S. Services, Inc.,
and are used with its permission.

Design by M. Paul

Library of Congress Cataloging-in-Publication Data

Graham, Lawrence.
    Youthtrends : capturing the $200 billion youth
market.

    1. Youth as consumers—United States. I. Hamdan,
Lawrence. II. Title.
HC110.C6G67   1987   658.8'348   87-4426
ISBN 0-312-00704-3

First Edition
10 9 8 7 6 5 4 3 2 1

FTW
ADS9737

To Our Parents,
Betty and Richard, and Dorothea and Ali

To Our Brothers,
Richard and Allen

CONTENTS

ACKNOWLEDGMENTS

*B*ecause we are consultants on the youth market for many major American companies, we have often been described as being both in the business of selling young people to corporate America and of selling corporate America to young people. Originally, we saw ourselves as only performing the latter, but our point of view has changed somewhat since we began writing this book.

Nearly three years ago, we created the term F.L.Y.E.R.S. (an acronym for *Fun Loving Youth En Route to Success*) as a name for the thirteen-to-twenty-five-year-olds who spend $200 billion each year on products in this country. When we founded our firm, F.L.Y.E.R.S. Consulting, we were well aware of the significance of this consumer group. Our service, therefore, was to help companies develop marketing and advertising strategies to capture these 50 million young purchasers. From the enthusiasm of our clients, it was clear that they also knew the value of winning over the F.L.Y.E.R.S. generation.

But something happened during the two year period of researching this book: We realized that not everyone had opened their eyes to the financial clout of this audience. Fortunately, most of the more than 200 company chairmen, presidents, and marketing executives that we interviewed for *YouthTrends* were already aware that the F.L.Y.E.R.S. market was important. Their primary concern was learning how to develop strategies that would capture that market.

There were, however, many others interviewed who had never considered targeting the F.L.Y.E.R.S. because they were already fixated on the much smaller yuppie (*Y*oung *U*rban *P*rofessionals, aged twenty-five to thirty-nine) market. In the following pages, we will share statistics, conversations, and information about marketing campaigns that have been used to reach the young consumer. In addition, through the polling research of our firm's network of student testers, we will provide the reader with a look into the minds and popular attitudes of young people. Much of this will better explain what goes on in the business of selling to young people.

At this time, we would like to thank all of those who have contributed to this book and who continue to contribute to our monthly *YouthTrends* marketing newsletter. We are most grateful to the corporate, advertising, and marketing executives listed separately at the beginning of this book. We are also grateful to our editors, Thomas Dunne, Betsy Williams, Margaret Schwarzer, and Pamela Hoenig, who worked so diligently on the manuscript.

We also thank our network of student testers, Baker Library at Harvard Business School, New York City Public Library, White Plains Public Library, Scarsdale Public Library, and the Library of the Princeton Club of New York. Special appreciation goes to our classmates in Harvard Business School's Class of 1988 section H, Harvard Law School's Class of 1987 section 2, and our professors at the Law School and the Business School for allowing us to run in and out of our classes when we had to conduct an interview.

For the technicalities that they have had to endure, we thank our trademark lawyer, Paul Blaustein, and our publicists, Karen Mender, Maryanne Mazzola, and Diane Mancher. Very special thanks goes to Naydeen Hamdan, Nina DeLuca, Teresa Nevola, Searcy Grahame, Dauna Williams, Bruce Felton, Bill Haney, Jack Bowen, Jordan Horvath, David Jones, James

Grasfield, Adam Gottlieb, Teresa Clarke, Carl H. Michel, Jay Ward, Leslie Fagenson, Pamela Thomas, and David Schwartzbaum.

For always believing in us—in spite of our age—thanks to Elliot Hoffman.

And finally, we thank our parents, for everything.

EXECUTIVES INTERVIEWED AND CONSULTED

*T*o produce the information in this book, the authors conducted more than 200 interviews with executives at the country's leading corporations, marketing research organizations, magazines, television networks, as well as advertising and public relations agencies.

The authors would like to thank the following executives who gave their time to be consulted and interviewed for *Youth-Trends:*

Martin Davis, chairman of Gulf + Western Industries; August Busch, chairman of Anheuser-Busch; Frank Mancuso, chairman of Paramount Pictures; Reginald Lewis, chairman of McCall's Patterns; Jeff Katzenberg, chairman of Walt Disney Studios; Roger Enrico, president of Pepsi–Cola U.S.A.; Brandon R. Tartikoff, president of NBC Entertainment; Robert Pittman, president of MTV Networks; Brian Dyson, president of Coca–Cola; Luciano Benetton, president and founder of Benetton; Max Imgruth, president of Swatch Watch; Earle Angstadt, president of McCall's Patterns; William Howell, president of Miller Brewing Company; Andrew Kohut, president of the Gallup Organization; Alan McDonald, president of Nestlé; Jay

Darling, president of Burger King Company; Tom McBurney, president of U.S. Foods Group for Pillsbury; George Miles, Jr., chief operating officer of WNET Public Television; Martin Lerner, president of the American List Corporation; Lester Rand, president of the Rand Youth Poll; Frank Zazza, president of Advertising in Movies; Jerry Welsh, executive vice-president of American Express; Francesco della Barba, executive vice president for Benetton Services Marketing; Edward Meyer, chairman and president of Grey Advertising; Burt Manning, chairman and chief executive officer of J. Walter Thompson/U.S.A.; Jack Bowen, chairman and chief executive officer of D'Arcy Masius Benton & Bowles Advertising; Keith Reinhard, chairman and chief executive officer of Needham Harper Worldwide; Stuart Upson, chairman of Dancer Fitzgerald Sample; Paul H. Alvarez, chairman of Ketchum Public Relations; Jack Porter, chairman of Needham Harper Porter Novelli Public Relations; Byron Lewis, chairman of Uniworld Group; Frank Mingo, chairman of Mingo–Jones Advertising; Gary Susnjara, chairman of Dancer Fitzgerald Sample/New York; Barry E. Loughrane, president and chief executive officer of Doyle Dane Bernbach Group; Jerry Siano, president of N.W. Ayer/New York; Jane Maas, president of Muller, Jordan, Weiss; Edward Stanton, president of Manning, Selvage & Lee Public Relations; C. James Schaefer, president of Needham Harper Direct Marketing; Bill Weed, director of international accounts for Ogilvy & Mather and director of the Ogilvy Group and of Ogilvy & Mather Worldwide; Richard McLoughlin, publisher, vice-chairman of *The Readers' Digest;* Christopher Whittle, publisher of *Esquire* magazine, founder of Whittle Communications; James Spanfeller, publisher of *Newsweek on Campus;* Milt Franks, publisher of *Young Miss* magazine; Doug Ranalli, publisher and editor-in-chief of *Dorm Magazine;* Robert MacLeod, publisher of *Teen* magazine; Bob Guccione, Jr., editor and publisher of *Spin;* Warren Guy, publisher of the 13–30 Magazines; Richard Robinson, president of Scholastic,

Inc; Leslie Zeifman, associate publisher of *Rolling Stone* magazine; Felice Arden, associate publisher of *Spin* magazine; Midge Turk Richardson, editor-in-chief of *Seventeen* magazine; Amy Levin, editor-in-chief of *Mademoiselle* magazine; Phyllis Schneider, editor-in-chief of *Young Miss* magazine; Phillip Moffitt, editor-in-chief of *Esquire* magazine and founder of the 13–30 Corporation; Barbara Coffey, managing editor of *Glamour* magazine; Ed Chenetz, vice-president of Scholastic, Inc.; Lyn Langway, editor for *Newsweek On Campus;* Nancy Lipton Hessel, fashion director for *Seventeen* magazine; Carol Lott, senior fashion editor for *Seventeen* magazine; Wendy Gavin, fashion editor for *Young Miss* magazine; Jim Rainsford, advertising director for *Seventeen* magazine; Wanda Bolton, director of career & college competitions for *Glamour* magazine; Diana Holtzberg, vice-president of marketing for *Spin* magazine; Kathy McGrain, director of public relations for Scholastic, Inc.; Dottie Enrico, assistant to the publisher of *Rolling Stone* magazine; Liza McAlister, assistant to the editor of *Esquire* magazine; Joseph T. Murphy Jr., advertising sales representative for Scholastic, Inc; David Williams, director of public relations for BBD&O; Bruce Felton, D'Arcy Masius Benton & Bowles Advertising Corporate Magazine; Stan Stein, Pontiac account at D'Arcy Masius Benton & Bowles Advertising; Lisa Wasser, public relations for BBD&O; Julianne Hastings, corporate communications associate at N.W. Ayer; Dale Walton, assistant to the chairman at Doyle Dane Bernbach; Peggy Turner, assistant to the chairman at D'Arcy Masius Benton & Bowles Advertising; Brad Lynch, assistant to the chairman at N.W. Ayer; Diane Rosin, assistant to the executive vice-president at Ted Bates Advertising; Nancy Nolan, assistant to director of Ogilvy; Judy Halloran, assistant to president of Muller, Jordan, Weiss; William Pritchard, senior manager of corporate affairs for Panasonic; Lana Ehrsam, manager of corporate affairs for McDonald's; Kenneth T. Russo, retail marketing manager: womenswear for J.C. Penney; Gerry L. Shores, retail marketing manager: menswear for J.C. Penney; Ed Meell, director of the Time Magazine Education Program and president of Media Management Services; Rhonda Gainer, advertising director of Daniel Hechter Paris; Steve Rechtschaffner, creative director of Swatch Watch; Richard Blossom, vice-president of marketing for Pepsi–Cola U.S.A.; Robert Levin, vice-president of marketing for Walt Disney Studios; Thomas Sawyer, vice-president of marketing for Burger King; Robert J. Niles, vice-president of marketing for NBC; Robert Boyer, vice-president of marketing for Borden Foods; Kent Mitchell, vice-president of marketing for General Foods; Robert Altschuler, vice-president of marketing for CBS, Records; Jan Van Amerongen, vice-president of marketing for CPC Corporation; James J. Klein, vice-president of U.S. marketing for Avon Products; Jim Cawley, vice-president: sales and distribution for Arista Records; Mike Martinovich, vice-president: merchandising for CBS Records; Steve Demeritt, vice-president of marketing services for General Mills; Michael Sobel, vice-president: advertising sales for MTV Networks; Gail T. Hamilton, vice-president: advertising and sales promotion for McCall's Patterns; A. Courtney Shepard, vice-president and general manager for Colgate–Palmolive; Dan Clark, vice-president of new business development for Pepsi–Cola U.S.A.; Bill Dennis, vice-president of licensing/ancillary rights division of Metro–Goldwyn–Mayer; Lois Sloane, vice-president of licensing/ancillary rights division of Metro–Goldwyn–Mayer; Janet Pines, vice-president of graduating seniors division for American Express; Randy Gretz, vice-president of the Emerging Investor for Merrill Lynch; Bruce M. Ley, vice-president of Wendy's International; Steve Forsythe, vice-president of Miller Brewing Company; Robert Toledo, vice-president of Miller Brewing Company; Betty Hudson, vice-president of NBC; Bill Rubens, vice-president and director of research for NBC; Gerald Jaffe, vice-president of research projects for NBC; John Moorehead, vice-president of corporate affairs for Pepsi–Cola U.S.A.;

George F. Schweitzer, vice-president of communications and information for CBS Broadcast Group; Joseph McCann, vice-president of public affairs for PepsiCo; Tony Tortorici, vice-president of public relations for Coca–Cola; Ted Regan, chief creative officer of N.W. Ayer; Penelope Queen, executive vice-president and member of the board of directors of Dancer Fitzgerald Sample/New York; Larry Light, executive vice-president of Ted Bates Advertising; Eric Weber, executive vice-president and executive creative director of Dancer Fitzgerald Sample; Roger Pisani, executive vice-president and supervisor of the Colgate–Palmolive account at Ted Bates Advertising; Mary Churchill, executive vice-president of Grey Advertising; John Eighmey, senior vice-president of Young & Rubicam; Bill Haney, senior vice-president and executive assistant to the CEO of D'Arcy Masius Benton & Bowles; Louis A. Tripoda, senior vice-president and corporate director of public relations for Needham Harper Worldwide; Mike Vaughn, senior vice-president and group director of the Hershey account at Ogilvy & Mather; Denny Wilkinson, senior vice-president of Foote, Cone & Belding; Pat Doody, senior vice-president and management supervisor D'Arcy Masius Benton & Bowles Advertising; Albert Shapiro, senior vice-president of Bozell & Jacobs; Jane Barr, senior vice-president of Burson-Marsteller Public Relations; Burtch Drake, general manager of Foote, Cone & Belding; Scott E. Marshall, vice-president and management supervisor of the American Express account at Ogilvy & Mather; Bob Gleckler, vice-president and supervisor of the Dr. Pepper account at Young & Rubicam; Ed LeBar, vice-president and supervisor of the Gillette account at Young & Rubicam; Peter Barnet, vice-president and supervisor of the General Foods account at Ogilvy & Mather; Stephen J. Centrillo, vice-president and supervisor of the Nabisco Brands account at Bozell & Jacobs; Valerie Graves, vice-president and associate creative director for Uniworld Group; Sheila Hackett Thomee, vice-president of Burson-Marsteller Public Relations; Alice

Goldberg, vice-president and director of research at D'Arcy Masius Benton & Bowles Advertising; Celia Visconti, senior account executive for the Andrea Cosmetics account at Bozell & Jacobs; John Garment, senior account executive for the Lee Jeans account at Bozell & Jacobs; Susan Harris, account supervisor at Manning, Selvage & Lee Public Relations; Mark Gjovik, management supervisor of the Pontiac account at D'Arcy Masius Benton & Bowles Advertising; Michael Moore, director of media planning for D'Arcy Masius Benton & Bowles Advertising; Clifford Merriot, director of news relations for General Motors; Bill O'Neill, director of public relations for General Motors' Pontiac Division; Syd Havely, director of public relations for Subaru; Linda Ury-Greenberg, director of market research and analysis for CBS Records; Michael Weisberger, director of market research and analysis for CBS Records; Thomas W. Evans, deputy director of advertising and sales promotion for the U.S. Army Recruiting Command; Steve Backer, director of college marketing for CBS Records; Donna Alda, director of promotions for MTV Networks; Eileen Morrow, director of the Bucknell University Bookstore; Dorothy S. Lofland, general merchandise manager of the University of Delaware Bookstore; Sally Fisher, Benetton Services Marketing; Patricia Norman, Columbia House Record Club; Mike Hogan, Alan Weston Communications; Carole Orgel, Licensing for MGM; Ann Stillwagen, Artistic Design for MGM; Anne Reilly, assistant to the chairman of Paramount Pictures.

YOUTHTRENDS™

1

*T*HE *N*EW *Y*OUTH *G*ENERATION

> If you are on target with youth and have something
> else to appeal to adults and children, you can be a hit.
> To be successful, you have to make it trendy, chic and
> cool.

> —Brandon R. Tartikoff,
> president of NBC

*T*his book details the marketing strategies of this nation's
most innovative companies to reach the often overlooked $200
billion youth market. Based on the work of our own consulting
firm and our interviews with hundreds of corporate, marketing,
media, advertising, and public relations executives, we show
how companies are reaching out to young people. We review
why some succeed and why others fail. We examine how almost
any company can take advantage of this market's potential.

But these campaigns do not only reach young consumers. As
Roger Enrico, president of Pepsi-Cola explains, "We can appeal
to the broader audience through the eyes of youth. We put a
youthful mindset on the product emphasizing vitality, excitement, being on the cutting edge." In fact, our firm,
F.L.Y.E.R.S. Consulting, has developed a highly effective marketing strategy called YouthTrends (The term, *YouthTrends* is
a trademark of F.L.Y.E.R.S. Services, Inc.). Based on six general models (the "American Express Approach," "MTV Approach," "Snickers Approach," "Pepsi Approach," "Swatch

Approach," and "Newsweek Approach"), it centers on one basic concept: The trends and attitudes of today's youth have a pervasive effect on American society. This influence extends beyond the 20 percent of the population that is young to an even larger "youth-oriented" or "youth-conscious" adult market.

Successful marketers realize that each new generation has its own new trends, sense of humor, and lifestyle. They know, that in order to remain successful, they must understand the generation, capitalize on its trends, and incorporate their product or service into the preferred lifestyle of that generation.

In the 1960s when "hippies" were in, both the hippie character and the hippie attitude appeared in print ads, commercials, TV shows, and movies. Marketers and creative teams knew that putting a hippie in their ads or commercials would make their products seem current. It didn't matter whether the hippie used the product or just appeared somewhere in the backdrop of the commercial. His mere presence let the viewers and buyers know that this commercial was "hot" and representative of popular trends.

The same thing has been done with the "yuppie" of the early 1980s. More than just a name for a group of ambitious, city-living lawyer and MBA types, the term yuppie (for *y*oung *u*rban *p*rofessional, aged twenty-five to thirty-nine) came to identify a particular lifestyle and attitude as well. Not surprisingly, the yuppie description expanded to include not only a certain type of individual, but also certain types of products used by these young professionals. For instance, the Swedish-built Saab inadvertently became the car for the yuppie; and Reebok found itself the yuppie brand choice for running shoes.

Soon Michelob, Volkswagen—and virtually everyone else— was incorporating yuppies in their commercials and ads in order to grab a share of this popular group of consumers. The ads showed ambitious young, blond-haired, conservatively dressed executives bounding out of corporate offices and heading out to their weekend hideaways in the country after a rough week on Wall Street.

But not only were non-yuppies repulsed by these privileged, callous junior executives, even the *real* yuppies came to shun their own image and name. Nonetheless, while the label has taken on more of a negative connotation than it had when it was originally created, it has remained an important symbol of our times. The yuppie's mere presence in an ad or a TV commercial lets the public know that the product being sold is really one that belongs in the 1980s.

F.L.Y.E.R.S.—The New Generation in America

With yuppies on the wane, attention has begun to shift to a new generation—the roughly 50 million young people between the ages of thirteen and twenty-five. For a while there was no name to describe this vast age group which spends over $200 billion each year on everything from records, cosmetics, and clothes to fast food, cars, and computers.

Our consulting firm was helping Fortune 500 companies and others to understand and to market products to this age group, so we had pinpointed the qualities that make it special. Unlike the twenty-five- to thirty-nine-year-old yuppies, this younger group wants to get more fun and enjoyment out of life, yet at the same time, expects to be successful.

Considering these characteristics, we developed a name to describe the group: *F*un *L*oving *Y*outh *E*n *R*oute to *S*uccess, or F.L.Y.E.R.S. (The term *F.L.Y.E.R.S.* is a trademark of F.L.Y.E.R.S. Services, Inc.).

Before creating the label at all, we used our nationwide network of student testers to poll several hundred young people around the United States on their likes, dislikes, heroes, lifestyles, favorite foods, songs, clothes, movies, etc. The data gathered allowed us to understand what today's young people are truly like. And we had another critical advantage that helped us identify the unique qualities of this new generation—we belong to it ourselves.

A newly targeted market, F.L.Y.E.R.S. are now making their presence known to the public. *Fortune* magazine and *Advertising Age* were two of the earliest to recognize the trend we cited, followed by such newspapers as the *Boston Globe* (calling F.L.Y.E.R.S. "a new socioeconomic class"), the *Los Angeles Times,* the *New York Daily News,* the *Houston Post,* the *Dallas Times Herald,* the *Seattle Post-Intelligencer,* the *Detroit News,* and the *San Francisco Examiner.*

Cable News Network and over fifteen hundred other U.S. TV and radio news programs have reported on the new F.L.Y.E.R.S. generation. General Mills and the Pillsbury Company underwrote one of our own speeches on today's youth generation. National Public Radio broadcast the hour-long presentation throughout the country. Recently, the trend has been picked up by Canadian news shows and even by West German and other European media.

Corporations are beginning to respond as well. Burlington Industries, Lorillard Tobacco, and ArtCarved Class Rings have sponsored our public presentations on the new trends of young America. Daniel Hechter, America's largest manufacturer of men's fitted clothing and Swatch Watch have created direct promotional tie-ins to the F.L.Y.E.R.S. trend. Metro-Goldwyn-Mayer has stepped outside the film industry to develop a line of F.L.Y.E.R.S. brand products aimed at the high school, college, and early-twenties market. These include T-shirts, pullovers, porcelain mugs, beach towels, posters, as well as stationery and such school-related products as calendars and notebooks—all featuring our trademarked F.L.Y.E.R.S. name and logo designed to look like a college seal.

American industry is finally waking up to the new F.L.Y.E.R.S. demographic group!

2
TEN REASONS WHY THE YOUTH MARKET IS IMPORTANT

Young people are an extraordinarily important consumer group both for setting trends and for influencing many of their parent's brand choices. Although the head of household pays the bills, companies must not miss the interaction which occurs in a household between parents and children, especially in the growing number of single parent households.

—Robert Pittman,
president of MTV Networks Inc.

1. ALL CONSUMERS ARE AFFECTED BY THE TRENDS AND MIND-SET OF YOUTH.

Recently, Ted Bates Worldwide, one of America's largest advertising firms, conducted a study to determine the age about which people felt best. Individuals were asked the question: "If you could be any age, how old would you be?" The poll found that more people chose the early- to mid-twenties (ages twenty to twenty-five years old) than any other time of life. Teenagers looked forward to more independence and opportunities, while older adults looked back favorably upon the excitement and freedom of those days.

This study only confirms what companies have known for years and have applied in creating their advertisements. Even for products aimed at the middle-aged consumers, companies choose models in their early twenties. Why? Because people want to be vigorous and energetic—and, naturally, they identify these characteristics with young people. This preoccupation with remaining vital, strong, and aware helps stimulate even older adults to keep abreast of youthful trends. What's hot among young people today can often become the rage for all Americans tomorrow—from fashions to fast foods, from music to movies. Hence, the youth market affects hundreds of billions of dollars of spending each year.

2. THE YOUTH MARKET INCLUDES FIFTY MILLION CONSUMERS—TEN TIMES THE NUMBER IN THE YUPPIE MARKET.

The early 1980s saw the rise of the yuppie (the young urban professional baby-boomer, aged twenty-five to thirty-nine). But the concept had negative connotations—yuppies were seen as driven, ruthlessly ambitious, selfish conspicuous consumers—that led many to reject the label.

Furthermore, despite their strong media presence, according to *American Demographics,* there were only some 4.2 million yuppies (with annual incomes over $30,000)—less than 2 percent of the U.S. population. Clearly, yuppies were too small a group to establish pervasive trends or to hold really significant market influence.

The group we've defined—the often overlooked thirteen- to twenty-five-year-old (F.L.Y.E.R.S.) market—is far more important, in sheer numbers alone. Figures from the U.S. Bureau of the Census show that, in 1985, this group comprised 22.5 percent of the total U.S. population. This includes 23 million teenagers, most of whom are high school students; more than 7 million college students and recent graduates; and 21 million young adults, aged eighteen to twenty-five, who are not in college.

Through our research, we've been able to identify the special tastes, sensibilities, and purchasing patterns that unite these young people into a new, visible, powerful generation of consumers. Throughout this book we use the words *youth, young people,* and *F.L.Y.E.R.S.* interchangeably to define the members of this crucial market.

Census projections indicate that the number of F.L.Y.E.R.S. will move from today's 50 million to 44 million by 1990, and then rise again to 47 million by the year 2000. Thus, despite the end of the baby boom, the size of the youth market is not destined to spiral downward; instead through the end of this century and for decades beyond, it should hold steady at 45 to 55 million consumers—representing at least 20 percent of the U.S. population.

3. ANNUAL INCOME OF YOUNG PEOPLE IS CURRENTLY $200 BILLION.

Young people have incomes totaling nearly *$200 billion annually,* according to data from the Census Bureau, studies by *Business Week, Newsweek,* and *Advertising Age,* and figures from the Simmons Market Research Bureau and the Rand Youth Poll. Teenagers have $50 to $55 billion to spend; college students, $35 to $45 billion; and noncollege young adults, $100 to $115 billion. Thus, F.L.Y.E.R.S. directly control *12.5 percent of the total income in the United States.*

Moreover, most of their income is discretionary. Unlike yuppies or adults, young people pay little or nothing for housing or taxes. The Conference Board reports that in 1985 an adult aged thirty-five to fifty had discretionary income of only $2,904; although Conference Board figures for young people are not available, $200 billion spread among 50 million F.L.Y.E.R.S. makes for an average per capita income of $4,000—certainly comparable to the discretionary income of the average middle-aged adult.

Hence, young people are able to purchase a wide range of products, from the inexpensive to the costly. The youth market controls billions of dollars to spend on any product it decides it wants.

4. YOUNG PEOPLE HAVE AN INCREASING INFLUENCE ON $500 BILLION OF ANNUAL FAMILY SPENDING.

F.L.Y.E.R.S. (including teenagers, college students and young adults) possess significant personal income, but they also wield enormous power within the larger, adult markets. More than 95 percent of all teenagers and 50 percent of those aged eighteen to twenty-five live with their families. These 34 million young people certainly influence, if not choose, the brands of the products purchased by their parents. These products include foods and snacks, cosmetics, household and personal care items, etc.

Census data show that young people live in households accounting for $497.8 billion in annual income, or about one-third of the national total. Moreover, with the rapid changes in the family structure over the past two decades, the influence exerted by young people over family purchases has risen significantly. For example, the Census records that, due to rising divorce rates, 22 percent of teenagers live with only one parent, up from 14 percent just a decade ago. In addition, 60 percent of all teenagers have mothers who work, up dramatically from 39 percent in 1970. This percentage is projected to grow to 75 percent by 1990.

With more single-parent households as well as households with two working parents, it is not surprising that young people are becoming more involved in making brand selections and actually doing the shopping. Families are more "factionalized" than in the past, with each member going his or her separate way, rather than having a single individual, traditionally the mother, provide for the needs of all. The fact that most single-serving food products are actually sold to families, not to single-person households, is just one indication of the growing influence each family member, including the young ones, has over family purchases.

Marketers have always known that they cannot sell a product if the family member doing the shopping is opposed to its purchase. Clearly, at the very least, marketers must work to "avoid the veto" of millions of young people who live with their families. In the more brand-conscious and less-structured family of the 1980s, it is especially important not to estrange the actual consumer, whether that person is old or young.

5. YOUNG PEOPLE HEAD TEN MILLION HOUSEHOLDS—FIFTEEN PERCENT OF THE U.S. TOTAL.

It is a mistake to assume the youth market is consuming only a limited range of "young person's" products. Census records show that there are 3.8 million households headed by fifteen- to twenty-four-year-olds; these households account for $52.4 billion in annual income (or a median income of $12,669). However, the Census figures exclude both the 4.4 million students living in college housing or apartments and the fifteen- to twenty-four-year-old spouses who share purchasing decisions with older "head of household" spouses.

When college students living on their own are included, young people head over 8.2 million households. Add to that at least 2 million women aged eighteen to twenty-four who are living with spouses outside that age bracket, and the number of youth-controlled households rises to 10 million or more than 15 percent of all the households in America.

Clearly, it is not just the stereotypical middle-aged housewife who goes to the store to buy food, appliances, cleaning and washing solutions, medicines, and so on. Young people, running more than 15 percent of the total households in the country, are a significant market for a full range of household products and services.

6. YOUTH ARE MORE WILLING TO TRY NEW PRODUCTS.

F.L.Y.E.R.S. are a significant "fresh" market, without established buying patterns. Unlike adults, young people are just beginning to develop loyalties to particular brands and products; and a Simmons Market Research Bureau poll supports what common wisdom would hold: Young people are more likely than adults to try something new. Thus, advertising and promotion targeted at youth are especially effective in influencing their brand selection, compared to efforts aimed at adults. Since, to the young consumer, all product purchases are new product purchases, F.L.Y.E.R.S. offer companies a greater opportunity to establish product loyalty—an especially important consideration for companies whose products are not market leaders with adults.

Moreover, the same Simmons poll indicated that adults were only slightly more brand loyal than young people. In fact, a *Seventeen* magazine study of women's brand preferences indicated that at least 30 percent of the twenty-five- to thirty-five-year-olds still use the first brand of cosmetics and packaged goods they tried as teenagers. Hence it is a mistake to view young people as "fickle" consumers; rather, they should be seen as consumers attempting to determine which of several similar products most satisfies their needs—a new, unclaimed breed of consumers.

7. TEENAGERS ARE INDEPENDENT PURCHASERS AND THE PRIMARY MARKET FOR MANY PRODUCTS.

There are 23 million teenagers in the United States, representing a total income of $50 to $55 billion annually. Although the number of teenagers has declined over the last decade, their purchasing power has doubled. Teenagers are the primary consumers of a wide range of products including movies, snack foods, soft drinks, record albums and cassette tapes, new fashion products, and cosmetics. Teenage girls spend over $5 billion just on cosmetics and $16 billion on their wardrobes.

In just ten years, the percentage of teenagers owning cars, motorcycles, televisions, telephones, calculators, tennis rackets, skis, and even securities has more than doubled. Most own their own stereos, cameras, watches, radios, and bicycles.

In addition, they *control* certain areas at the market. Various studies by pollsters and advertising firms indicate that teenagers have all or most of the say in determining the brand selection for products as diverse as records, shoes, stationery and school supplies, jewelry, radios, snack foods, health and beauty aids, sporting equipment, and movies. Most polls also show that teenagers choose the stores where purchases will be made. These results are indicative of the greater independence of young people. This is certainly due, in great part, to the increase in the percentage of teenagers who work, and the increasing number of teenagers with two working parents.

8. COLLEGE STUDENTS ARE THE ELITE OF THE FUTURE ADULT MARKET.

College students have incomes of $35 to $45 billion annually. Of all eighteen- to twenty-four-year-olds, 42 percent now go to college, up from just 26 percent in 1970; this percentage is expected to increase to 48 percent by 1990. Unlike the youth market as a whole, the number of college students is continuing to grow rapidly, increasing by about 200,000 annually.

According to the census, of the 12.4 million people in college today, 7.2 million are aged eighteen to twenty-four and 4.5 million are full-time, four-year students. Nearly 60 percent of them have part-time or full-time jobs during the school year, while 90 percent have summer jobs. College students are also likely to come from upper-middle-class families: 46 percent come from families earning $40,000 or more, with only 19 percent from families earning less than $15,000. Given these income statistics and the tendency of parents to try to shelter away-from-home college students from economic hard times, the spending of these young consumers is almost recession-proof.

With almost half of all young people attending college and with college graduates having higher current and future incomes than nongraduates, this group certainly represents a critical target market—and one with very broad needs. Since many college students are setting up their first "households," they need to purchase many or all of the same household items as the family at home. Hence, the college market presents a significant growth area for companies selling virtually anything—both immediately and in the future.

9. YOUNG ADULTS ARE AN ENORMOUS AND OVERLOOKED GROUP—CAPABLE OF SUBSTANTIAL PURCHASING POWER.

There are more than 21 million individuals eighteen to twenty-five years old who are not in college, representing a total income of over $100 billion annually. Since half are employed full-time—with 30 percent earning more than $10,000 a year—they have money to spend on the full range of products and services available to the adult market.

Even so, marketers rarely attempt to reach this group specifically and instead simply target them with the same advertisements and promotions used for the adult market. This neglect is a mistake because these individuals have buying habits more similar to those of other F.L.Y.E.R.S. than to those of adults. Like college students, they need the same types of products and services as the typical adult household, but not surprisingly, marketing strategies aimed at the middle-aged housewife or the stereotypical family with 2.2 children will not appeal to them. Later in this book, we'll discuss various effective techniques for reaching this group while maintaining the appeal to older customers.

10. COMPANIES MUST LOOK BEYOND SHORT-TERM MARKETING PLANS; THE YOUNG CONSUMER WILL SOON BE THEIR PRIMARY CUSTOMERS.

Now that young people head some 10 million households and account for $200 billion in annual income, there are few products that are too expensive for them or of no interest to them. It is essential, then, for a company to establish its product's value with the youth market, even if it has made a strategic decision not to focus on nonprimary markets. Negative impressions formed in adolescence and young adulthood may carry on into later years, simply because a competing company consciously focused on the youth market or a rival product was used by young consumers' parents. The college-student and young-adult markets, just a step away from adulthood, are especially important.

Recognizing the perils of neglect, smart companies are starting to make direct overtures to young consumers. For example, both *Reader's Digest* and *Newsweek,* which do not depend on the youth market at all for subscriptions, have developed programs to enhance their visibility on college campuses. On the other hand, the coffee industry, which ignored the youth market for two decades while it was the nation's largest selling beverage, now faces the sobering fact that a whole generation of young adults has grown up preferring soft drinks to coffee.

Even if youth is not a company's primary market, young people, as they grow older, will soon become the principal market. If a company has any interest in medium-term marketing strategies, it should care a great deal about creating an image attractive to youthful consumers, who are just beginning to establish their buying habits and preferences. After all, if a company can't serve them, its competitors certainly will.

In the next four chapters, we'll debunk some persistent myths and provide some insights into young people's thoughts and concerns.

3

THE YOUTH MIND AND THE FOUR COMMON MYTHS ABOUT THE YOUNG CONSUMER

To be successful at reaching the youth market, we need
greater sensitivity to that customer than to any other.
If our advertising offends them, they will simply buy
from our competitors.

—Keith Reinhard,
chairman and CEO of Needham Harper Worldwide
Advertising

*A*s the founders of a consulting firm that advises companies on the youth market—and since we are young ourselves—we are often invited to present lectures to corporate
executives or to students on college campuses. Most of these
lectures are focused on topics that relate to young people or the
young consumer.

But the subject which we have found to be the most helpful
to audiences is one we call "The Youth Mind." It is a discussion
of what today's young people talk about, how they view their
friends and their parents, what they like to buy, what they don't
like, and how they hope the rest of the world will treat them
or perceive them.

Surprisingly, few business people carefully consider young

people's attitudes, motivations, and orientations, even in developing products and marketing techniques aimed at youth. It simply isn't enough for marketers to know the youth slang or the popular youth-oriented celebrities and singers. In order to be fully in touch, these marketers must try to understand the mind-set that underlies the youth culture. It is this sensitivity that will allow them to create marketing campaigns that will most effectively appeal to the current youth generation.

It is a grave mistake for sixty-, fifty-, forty-, or even thirty-year-old executives to think that memories of their own youth can shed light on the attitudes of young people today. Tastes have changed dramatically—not to mention the fact that it is very easy to forget why certain things were appealing ten or fifteen years ago. Some executives consult junior people in their firms or talk to their own children, forgetting that these "advisers" have often led lives very different from the average young person's. In talking to privileged children or to junior executives, they are more likely to learn about tastes cultivated in private schools, around country clubs, and on wealthy college campuses, far outside the mainstream of current youth culture.

Savvy executives have learned to look beyond their own worlds to keep up with young people and their lifestyles. Barbara Coffey, managing editor of *Glamour* magazine, says, "In order to keep up with the current trends of today's culture, I make sure to look at the newest movies." Bob Guccione, Jr., publisher of *Spin* magazine, agrees adding, "With all the different cable channels covering sports, health, music, and movies, I can stay in touch with what young people are talking about."

Other executives such as Eric Weber, executive vice-president of Dancer Fitzgerald Sample Advertising, and Burt Manning, chairman of J. Walter Thompson Advertising, also track youth trends successfully by watching MTV and attending concerts. Our firm's monthly newsletter, *YouthTrends,* attempts to keep busy marketing executives up to date on these and other current topics of interest to the young consumer.

This chapter will attempt to explain the mind-set of youth today, by outlining their major concerns: their need to be "different" yet to fit in with certain groups; their need to appear independent to their friends yet to feel loved by their parents; their need to complain about their parents and to rebel against institutions (even when they don't want to); and their need to create a public image for themselves. Then we'll take on some of the more persistent myths about youth, discussing why each has survived, how it affects marketing decisions, and why it should be discarded.

Understanding the Youth Mind

WANTING TO BE DIFFERENT AND WANTING TO FIT IN

Young people want to be "different," to be anything but what parents or the ruling institutions (that is, school) want them to be. While growing up, they have had to say yes to everyone—to parents, to teachers, to bosses. Having the chance to say no, to reject the direction of their elders, makes them feel in control of their lives. Usually the chief things they *can* control are their clothing and their language.

So young people not only dress and talk in special ways to be like their friends, but also to feel different from their parents and teachers. Even if a young person is not sure what kind of car he wants, he knows that he certainly doesn't want the kind that his parents or teacher would drive. To young people, being different from their parents (or other symbols of authority) is an essential feature of the popular culture.

While teenagers want to feel separate from their parents, they generally do want to belong to *some* group. Whether that group is made up of three people or ten, young people want to feel that they are not alone. In order to fit in with peers, they want to conform—to wear the same clothes and speak the same language as their peers. These are the first and easiest steps toward being accepted.

The secondary steps to fitting in are the more difficult ones. They include developing a sense of humor and a personality acceptable to the peer group. One aspect of developing the "right" personality is learning the "right" topics for discussion. Depending on the group involved, these topics could include music, sports, clothes, girls, boys, sex, school, drugs, money, movies, and TV. And to make matters even more complicated, there are specific attitudes that peers expect their group members to have about each one of these topics.

In developing these alliances, most young people quickly recognize which peer groups they fall into. The nerds know that others call them nerds, the jocks know that they are the jocks, the greasers know they are greasers, the beautiful people know they are considered beautiful, and so on.

Still, while young people might use these terms to describe other groups, they would never use them for their own group, saying, "Yeah, we're nerds" or "Yeah, we're jocks." While the adult world might rate one group above another, each of these groups considers itself just as good or better than the next. The jocks might be willing to admit that the nerds are smarter, and the beautiful people to admit that jocks are stronger. But beyond those minor (and rather obvious) admissions, one group is not likely to praise any of the others.

REBELLING AND COMPLAINING ABOUT AUTHORITY

One important rite that binds young people together is complaining about their parents: "My parents are always nagging me about something." "Can you believe what my parents want me to do?" "My parents never stop asking me questions. . . . They're so clueless." The remarks go on and on. While there certainly are some hateful parents out there, many young people simply want to outdo their friends in telling my-parents-are-so-bad stories. All young people are expected to come up with tales about how old-fashioned, unreasonable, pushy, or nosy their parents are. Whether or not these complaints are valid, young people know that it is "in" to complain about how ridiculous their parents are, a way to feel "different," to be accepted.

Another time-honored young people's ritual is rebelling against authority, a practice often attributed to the so-called generation gap. But, in fact, young people don't rebel because of their parents' actions or misunderstandings; they more likely rebel because of their peers' expectations.

Friends at school talk about how they refuse to obey their parents. Classmates brag about how often they skip class. Many young people rebel or pretend to rebel against authority figures because they believe that their peers will accept them faster because of it. Claiming to resist authority makes them seem more daring, more independent.

BEING INDEPENDENT YET NEEDING LOVE FROM PARENTS

To most young people, independence does not mean what it means to their parents. It does not mean having jobs that pay for their food and electricity. It does not mean washing their own clothes and cooking their own food. More than *being* independent, young people want to *feel* independent. They want the benefits that independence is supposed to provide.

They want their own rooms. They want to spend their money the way they want. They want to leave the house without being asked where they are going and when they are returning. They want their parents to say, at least occasionally, "Well, it's up to you. Whatever you decide."

Just as important, they want to appear independent to their friends. Even a son or daughter who enjoys living at home will say, "I can't wait until I move out." A young person would be committing social suicide if he admitted that he got along with his parents so well that they were friends.

Our student polling research shows that *appearing* to be independent is just as good as *being* independent, suggesting that young people are happy to settle for these signs that create that impression, such as owning a car, having a separate telephone number, or having a late curfew.

Despite these bids for independence, young people continue to want and to need love from their parents. To begin with, all young people realize that society dictates that there should be love between parent and child. Young people, therefore, expect that their parents will love them. They can admit this fact to themselves, and they can sometimes discuss it or admit it to friends.

Complications begin when a young person does not feel loved by his parents. While he can say things like, "My parents and I really don't get along," he can almost never admit, "My parents really don't *love* me." To young people, *like* and *get along* are not serious terms. *Love* on the other hand, is a very serious—almost dangerous—word when used in reference to parents. So, while it's cool sometimes to say, "My parents are such jerks," it is far too threatening to say, "My parents don't love me; they just don't care about me." Being unloved is too big a problem for them to share with their peers. Most young people just don't want to hear that from friends.

IMPORTANCE TO MARKETERS

Clearly, in targeting products or marketing campaigns at youth, it is essential to be sensitive to the peer and parent relations that are young people's major concerns. On a more practical level, it is also important not to fall prey to the pervasive myths about young people today. Some of these myths falsely characterize young attitudes and lifestyles, while others underrate youth's economic power. *Rolling Stone* magazine, with its wide young readership, confronted these perceptions head-on in a recent ad campaign.

As Leslie Zeifman, *Rolling Stone*'s associate publisher, explains, it was essential to dispel some of the mistaken notions that advertisers and the public, in general, held concerning young consumers. "We called it our 'perception–reality' campaign because the ads ran in pairs. There were five pairs. One pair contained: a picture of a long-haired hippie underneath the word *Perception,* and a picture of a well-groomed college student, with a blazer, underneath the word *Reality.*" The message was that *Rolling Stone*'s audience had changed. Today's young people are a different breed from the entrenched stereotypes of the baby-boom generation.

"In another perception–reality advertisement," Zeifman continued, "we showed a photo of forty-eight cents (three pennies, two nickels, one dime, and one quarter) underneath the Perception banner; underneath the Reality label was a photo of an American Express charge card." Research has shown that young people are no longer an insignificant market force but a group of sophisticated consumers—something to be reckoned with.

Companies can no longer afford to ignore these lessons. The second half of this chapter will focus specifically on some of the popular myths that companies have held (or are holding) with regard to the young consumer. We will also explain how these myths conflict with reality.

Four Myths About the Young Consumer

MYTH NUMBER 1: YOUNG PEOPLE THROUGHOUT THE COUNTRY SHARE YUPPIE GOALS AND CONCERNS.

The media has made the yuppie lifestyle seem universal. But as we mentioned in Chapter 2, young people today hold twenty-five- to thirty-nine-year-old yuppies in disdain, perceiving them as a personification of the selfish 1970s "Me" decade. The surest way to scare young people away is to imply that a product is the choice of the yuppies.

Anheuser-Busch, with its Michelob beer campaign, was only one company that learned this lesson the hard way. Michelob's "You can have it all" campaign told of Wall Street-types who were able to move gleefully from the fast pace of a trading floor to the excitement of a fast-paced squash court to the intimacy of a glamorous restaurant without ever breaking stride.

Not surprisingly, this commercial did little to enhance the sales or the image of Michelob. What turned off the under-twenty-five audience was the unforgivably aggressive yuppie attitude which pervaded all of these "Have it all" commercials.

MYTH NUMBER 2: YOUNG CONSUMERS DO NOT CARE ABOUT A COMPANY'S PUBLIC IMAGE OR ITS "SOCIAL RESPONSIBILITY."

The people who believe this myth might be wise to talk to the executives at Nestlé Foods, Dow Chemical, and Union Carbide. These are three companies that have been fighting to improve their images, damaged by public criticism of their conduct in foreign countries.

Nestlé was threatened with a nationwide boycott spear-headed, in many places, by students on college campuses. It all started due to Nestlé's advertising of baby food formula in developing countries. The formula was to be mixed with water, but sometimes the water used in these countries was impure. Nestlé was soon made aware of this fact, yet refused to halt advertising the formula in these areas. The limited education of the purchasers and, thus, continued use of the tainted water brought about many infant deaths.

High school and college students organized groups and clubs to study the reports on Nestlé's wrongdoings and on the alleged deaths that resulted. Our consulting firm has found that many young people were concerned about Nestlé's image when making a purchase decision. Naturally, Nestlé has had to address this potential loss of the youth market. "We are very concerned about our company's image," says Alan McDonald, president of Nestlé Foods. "We ran a huge public-relations effort to inform people of what happened with the baby food formula controversy. The college audience was a major concern."

Dow Chemical, too, has suffered image problems as a result of producing the poisonous, defoliant napalm during the Vietnam War. Recently Dow has also tried to redeem itself in the eyes of youth with an innocuous ad campaign on TV and in print. The ads showed young people about to graduate college, to accept a job at Dow, and then to save the world from starvation. While it missed the mark—the commercial was too heavy-handed in its attempt to make the company appear socially responsible—Dow deserves credit for realizing that a bad image will stick in the minds of the youth population for a long time.

Union Carbide's image is still suffering because of its connection to the chemical poisonings that occurred during December of 1984 in Bhopal, India. More than 2,000 residents of this residential community died when lethal gases escaped from a Union Carbide chemical insecticide plant. In a failed attempt to demonstrate its social responsibility, Union Carbide sent its chairman to visit the site in India. Upon his arrival in Bhopal, he was arrested and then told to leave the country. Not surprisingly, many students throughout the United States began to take sides against this corporation and publicize the atrocity that occurred.

The importance of a company's image among youth was underscored by Valerie Graves, vice-president of Uniworld Group Advertising. She says that many companies are starting to use nonproduct, corporate advertising to improve their images. "The purpose of today's corporate advertising," Graves explains, "is to make consumers feel good about the company's image. Many companies are becoming very ambitious in that they are beginning to target their corporate ads. Before they had one ad for everyone, but now they have special ones for young people and other consumer groups. We design special corporate ads for General Foods, and they are aimed specifically at young people."

MYTH NUMBER 3: YOUNG PEOPLE DON'T REALLY CARE ABOUT A PRODUCT'S QUALITY.

More than their parents, today's young people have grown up during a time when fraud has been publicly exposed. They also have much greater media savvy than older generations and are much quicker to question the quality of products, or even to *look* for flaws in items that are specifically marketed for them. Because they expect deception, they feel no shame in challenging a store salesperson or a manufacturer if a product disappoints them.

In fact, Scholastic Inc., one of the leading researchers and magazine publishers for the youth market, has rated product quality as youth's second most important concern when purchasing items for themselves or their families.

MYTH NUMBER 4: THE ONLY COMPANIES THAT
SHOULD BE AIMING FULL CAMPAIGNS AT YOUNG
PEOPLE ARE THOSE THAT SELL ITEMS LIKE CANDY,
FAST-FOOD AND SOFT DRINKS.

As we discussed earlier, young people *directly* control some $200 billion per year—a fact that is coming to be recognized by such big-ticket companies as Merrill Lynch, IBM, DeBeers Diamonds, and American Airlines. Many are surprised to hear that such large corporations as these have developed special youth marketing campaigns.

Still, this myth persists, sustained by aging executives' visions of the stereotypical children they saw twenty years ago on TV's *Leave It to Beaver* or *Father Knows Best.* The teenager, then represented on TV was one who could buy only candy and soda. He had to ask mom and dad for everything. Today, not only are young people more independent than the TV children of yesteryear, but those old portrayals were never factually sound. Even in the 1950s, young people had much more money than they could ever spend on just candy and soft drinks.

Another reason why this myth is perpetuated is that many companies are unaware that IBM, Merrill Lynch, and other non-fast-food corporations are out there courting the F.L.Y.E.R.S. These forward-looking companies have begun to create special promotions—or even special, small departments—to serve high school and college students. Merrill Lynch, for instance, has its Emerging Investor Division, which helps young people make their first investments.

IBM offers a special discount program for students on selected college campuses around the country. DeBeers Diamonds runs ads in teen magazines, a place that would surprise many fifty-year-old parents who think of diamonds as being a very "grown up" item. And American Airlines runs special youth promotions, such as low fares to encourage people under twenty-five years old to fly more often.

Unfortunately, there are dozens of major American companies that continue to ignore the evidence that young people are significant purchasers. One shocking example is Borden Snack Foods. Robert Boyer, vice-president of marketing at Borden for such salty-crunchy snack products as Cheez Doodles, says that his ads are aimed at the mother in the house. "We want to appeal to the twenty-five- to forty-nine-year-old housewife because the mother is the one who buys the potato chips to reward dad for fixing the kitchen door or to reward the kids for a high grade." Ironically, Boyer quite readily acknowledges that Borden's primary competitor, Frito-Lay, aims many ads at young people.

Statistics noted in Chapter 2 indicate that young people not only influence their households' purchasing decisions, but that young people are often the ones making the grocery lists and pushing the shopping carts. In spite of the research, companies like Borden seem to hold onto myths about young consumers. As we examine in the next chapter, it is certain that these myths will create problems for similar companies and industries in the future.

4

Nine Industries That Need Youth Marketing

People begin to shop for themselves and form their
brand impressions during their teenage years. If you do
not begin early to form attitudes about a brand or
store, you will have a harder time changing those
attitudes later.

—Jerry Siano,
president of N.W. Ayer Advertising/NYC

*F*rom a strictly economic point of view, the youth market
should be of great significance to any business person," according to New York investor Reginald Lewis, chairman of the
TLC Group, a company that has acquired such businesses as
the McCall Patterns Company. "When I look at a company, I
know what type of potential it has—and young people are
generally a part of that untapped potential."

Still, some industries refuse to see the evidence that the youth
market is critical, both for the present and for the future. Here,
we'll examine some of the most intransigent industries, debunk-
ing their long-held myths and suggesting new directions. The
nine industries that are in the greatest need of youth marketing
strategies are:

1. Brand Name Foods

2. Personal-Care Products

3. Household Products

4. Appliances

5. Home Furnishings

6. Travel

7. Department/Discount Stores

8. Supermarkets/Convenience Stores

9. Financial Services/Credit Cards

Although they have taken little initiative in approaching young people, each stands to benefit substantially from recognizing its growing market of young consumers.

The Nine Industries That Need More Youth Marketing

1. BRAND NAME FOODS

With the increase of working mothers and single-parent households, teenagers are doing a growing share of the family shopping. Out of such major-brand food companies as General Foods, General Mills, Dart & Kraft, Beatrice, Borden, Consolidated Foods, CPC, Dean Foods, H.J. Heinz, Kellogg, United Brands, Quaker Oats, and Pillsbury only a few have taken account of this phenomenon. In fact, most of the brand name food companies continue to assert that the youth market is of no interest to them.

Still, a few have taken the leap. Campbell's Soup, for example, has a rock-videolike commercial that runs regularly on MTV. Castle & Cook Foods, producer for Dole canned goods, has run several promotions for teenage girls, including a poster giveaway and the sponsorship of Olympic marathon gold medalist, Joan Benoit. Unfortunately, few of the other corporations that have invested promotional dollars toward reaching the youth market have had notable successes. While these failures serve to reinforce the industry's prejudices, most can be attributed to poor and/or inconsistent executions.

2. PERSONAL-CARE PRODUCTS

Most young people do not depend on their parents to choose the brands of personal-care products they will use. Moreover, 10 million young people run their own households and select these products for themselves. But except for the makers of acne preparations and a few cosmetics firms, other companies, including Colgate–Palmolive, Gillette, Johnson & Johnson, Chesebrough–Pond, Richardson–Vicks, Schering–Plough, Scott Paper, Avon Products, and Bristol Myers do not regularly undertake advertising or promotional efforts aimed at consumers from fifteen to twenty-four years old. Unfortunately for these corporations, many brand preferences for personal-care items are formed during these years.

3. HOUSEHOLD PRODUCTS

Household-product manufacturers, including such corporations as Procter & Gamble, Clorox, and American Home, have yet to capture the potential billions of youth dollars—despite the fact many young people, like college students, are setting up personal households for the first time. These young consumers are strongly inclined to favor the products used by their families, but when setting up their own homes, are open to new ideas. This market presents a significant opportunity to companies who can create new brand preferences that may remain steady for years to come.

4. APPLIANCES

Rarely, do such companies as General Electric, Black & Decker, Hoover, Magic Chef, Maytag, Whirlpool, or Zenith market to anyone but the middle-aged homemaker or head of household. These firms virtually ignore the 10 million young people who head their own households, as well as the new graduates who begin to establish their own homes each year. They do so at that peril—not only do younger consumers need to buy appliances, but their first brand selection helps confirm their long-term preferences for a wide range of products.

5. HOME FURNISHINGS

As with the makers of appliances, such manufacturers as Corning Glass, Fieldcrest Mills, and West Point-Pepperell fail to recognize the number of young people with their own households. Moreover, the makers of home furnishings ignore the influence that young people have over the choice of furnishings for the homes they share with their parents. Young people have strong feelings about how their homes should look and they usually make these feelings known to their parents.

6. TRAVEL

Although some airlines offer student discounts, rarely is this fact communicated to the student market. Aside from this unadvertised effort, airlines such as Northwest, Delta, Texas Air, Pan Am, United, and TWA have not taken any special steps to capture the student travel market. Bus lines, such as Trailways, or railroads could, but do not try to convince students or young adults to try less-expensive modes of travel. Any of these companies could run targeted advertisements or special promotions to woo the student traveler during spring break or summer vacation.

7. DEPARTMENT/DISCOUNT STORES

Stores such as Sears, K-Mart, and other large department store chains know that young people are important customers. But the larger chains have not been able to provide the same type of atmosphere in their youth departments that is found in many smaller specialty retail stores such as, for example, Benetton, the Italian clothing manufacturer. Moreover, it is only recently that the larger chains have begun to try to show the young consumer that they carry stylish, quality merchandise.

8. SUPERMARKETS/CONVENIENCE STORES

As has been noted, there are growing numbers of young people shopping for their own households as well as for their families. There are also millions of college students, living away from home, who use local supermarkets. Therefore, supermarkets and convenience stores could, profitably, present promotional events to attract these new shoppers, but again, most do not.

9. FINANCIAL SERVICES/CREDIT CARDS

Apart from American Express, financial services firms such as Sears' Dean Witter, E. F. Hutton, and Paine Webber, along with credit card companies such as Visa and MasterCard have not been receptive to the youth market. F.L.Y.E.R.S. Consulting's studies have shown that, generally, financial services firms are unwilling to deal with the investment and financial-planning needs of young people, even young people with several thousand dollars to invest annually.

Despite the fact that college graduates will soon be the primary market for their services, these companies do not reach out to the college campus. Nor have other credit card companies made any major efforts to challenge American Express's position on the college campus, despite the fact that both Visa and MasterCard are more widely accepted.

There are tremendous opportunities for companies in all these areas. Seizing the opportunity to become the most purchased product in a given category among youth as well as among youth-conscious adults, can boost present profits and also contribute to the product's longer-term strength.

5

THE SIX YOUTHTRENDS*
APPROACHES: TARGETING YOUTH
WHILE ATTRACTING ALL
CONSUMERS

The program we have developed, YouthTrends, helps companies link their products to what is truly contemporary, exciting, and positive—the trends of young people—while maintaining or increasing their appeal to *all* consumers. Our program is based on six fundamental strategies:

1. The "American Express Approach"
2. The "Snickers (Mars Inc.) Approach"
3. The "Pepsi Approach"
4. The "MTV Approach"
5. The "Newsweek Approach"
6. The "Swatch Approach"†

*The term YouthTrends is a trademark of F.L.Y.E.R.S. Services, Inc.
†"American Express" is a registered trademark of American Express Company; "Snickers" of Mars Inc.; "Pepsi" of PepsiCo, Inc.; "MTV," of Viacom, Inc.; "Newsweek" of Newsweek Inc.; and "Swatch" of Swatch Watch U.S.A. In using these terms, which we ourselves have created for the sake of easy reference, we do not necessarily imply that any of the companies named here, or elsewhere in this book, have or would describe their marketing approach(es) in the same manner as we have.

When our firm, F.L.Y.E.R.S. Consulting, assists a company in developing a youth-oriented marketing plan, we begin by determining which of these six basic strategies, or which combination of them, will be most useful. Whether a product or service is principally aimed at the F.L.Y.E.R.S. market, whether youth is an important secondary market, or whether young people represent a fringe market with potential for an increase in market share, at least one of these strategies is always appropriate, and all can be tailored to a marketing budget of any size.

Of course, there are reasons why some firms decide not to try to appeal directly to the youth market:

- They have had no experience or no positive experiences in reaching the youth market;

- Attempting to appeal to young people might hurt their products' positions among their primary consumers, who are adults;

- Most importantly, their returns on any marketing, advertising, or promotional expenses aimed at young people may not be sufficient to warrant the effort.

But these companies fail to appreciate that, for a wide range of products (many more than marketers currently recognize), creating a youthful appeal can boost sales among all consumers, young and old. For example, as will be described below, by using the "American Express Approach" or the "Newsweek Approach," a company can maintain its present image among the adult market while reaching out to young people. Similarly, the "Pepsi Approach" or the "MTV Approach" can help minimize advertising and promotional expenses by reaching out to *all* potential consumers.

Thus, the six YouthTrends approaches can provide the strategic framework for any youth-oriented campaign. They are described below, along with appropriate uses:

1. The "American Express Approach"

The "American Express Approach" is often the first way that a company begins to reach out to the youth market. Simply put, the "American Express Approach" involves market segmentation—providing distinct advertising and promotional campaigns for young people and adults.

Scott Marshall, vice-president and supervisor of the American Express account at Ogilvy & Mather Advertising, explains that American Express runs several ad campaigns simultaneously: one for the general adult population; usually, one for young professionals and/or women professionals; and one for college students on campuses. For the adult market, American Express uses its longstanding "Do You Know Me?" campaign, in which individuals with extremely well-known achievements but less-than-familiar faces explain that even they need "The Card."

The "Interesting Lives" campaign is for young professionals or women professionals. The purpose of this campaign is to show that the American Express Card is not just for the established businessperson—that it can also serve young, up-and-coming professionals. Specific commercials in this campaign include "Reunion" (a group of friends reunite at their alma mater) and "First Date" (a young male banker and a female geologist go out on their first date).

But Janet Pines, manager of the Graduating Students Program for American Express, notes that American Express does not depend on these television commercials to reach youth. Nor does it use national magazines, or even local radio. Instead, American Express reaches the college market by going right to the college campus with special promotions and specifically targeted advertisements. It places displays in the college bookstores and puts student-oriented ads both in college newspapers and in magazines that are distributed exclusively to college students. Moreover, these ads are specially designed to make college students realize that "The Card" is relevant to their needs, present and future. All the ads emphasize that career-oriented students can receive the American Express Card even before graduation. Recent ads have featured celebrities, such as musician Clarence Clemons (saxophone player for Bruce Springsteen), who have a strong following among college students.

A large number of companies employ this "American Express Approach"—from Anheuser–Busch and Nissan/Datsun to Daniel Hechter menswear and ArtCarved Rings. Many companies, including some of those named above, combine this "American Express Approach" with others, especially the "Pepsi Approach" or the "MTV Approach," (as will be discussed below). By using the "American Express Approach", companies create specifically targeted advertisements and promotions to attract teenagers, college students, and/or young adults. Unfortunately, there are no synergies between the general market campaign and the campaign aimed at the youth market.

Thus, the "American Express Approach" is efficient only when a firm believes that a special emphasis on the youth market will produce sufficient increases in sales to the young, whether the purchases occur now or in the future. A company might also elect this approach when:

- Young people are not considered the core market for a product, and so wholesale modification of the overall marketing strategy would be inappropriate;

- F.L.Y.E.R.S. have different reasons for purchasing a given product product than the general population;

- The youth market is less aware of the product's value and attributes than the general population is.

2. The "Snickers (Mars, Inc.) Approach"

The Snickers bar, manufactured by Mars, Inc., is America's best-selling chocolate candy. Although children and young people are the largest consumers of chocolate confections, Snickers appeals to a wide range of consumers, both young and old. Thus, the "Snickers Approach" involves the use of a single advertising and/or promotional campaign but with different executions for the youth and the adult markets.

Larry Light, executive vice-president of Ted Bates Advertising, who has worldwide responsibility for all Mars, Inc., brands, described how the single-campaign strategy works: Snickers is positioned as a candy that satisfies hunger; its advertising message is "Snickers Satisfies You." No matter what age group the ad is trying to reach, this line is used. However, a different spokesperson is used to attract each market: a teenager playing in a school band, a college student relaxing between classes, a teenage girl working on her high school newspaper, a mother buying candy for her children, and an executive working on a construction site. (Of course, none of these spokespeople would be considered completely unappealing to a viewer of any age.) There are also slight modifications in the wording of each commercial, but the message is always the same. Thus, Mars found a quality of its product—"hunger satisfaction"—that would appeal to its primary market, children and young people, but still can target *all* consumers.

There are, however, some difficulties with the "Snickers Approach." It is expensive to prepare each ad, and since they all have the same theme, the company is spending extra money without getting the chance to promote any other special features of the product. Then, too, potential consumers may ignore some of the presentations since they may not identify with some, or all, of the spokespeople.

But there are important benefits of the strategy. All the ads reinforce the same general message, which is directed toward all consumer segments. In addition, each execution is more precisely targeted at a particular segment of the market, thus increasing the impact of its message.

Thus, a company might choose the "Snickers Approach" if:

- The product has one attribute that can attract all consumers;

- The product's potential consumers have such disparate tastes and values that a single advertising or promotional pitch would be ineffective;

- The expected sales increase in each market is sufficient to make the special pitches cost-effective.

3. The "Pepsi Approach"

What we describe as the "Pepsi Approach" has been utilized successfully by manufacturers of cigarettes, beer, fashionable clothing, cosmetics, and, of course, soft drinks; it could benefit an even wider range of consumer products. As was noted in Chapter 1, the "early-twenties" lifestyle is one with which people of many ages identify positively. This is the central premise of the "Pepsi Approach": to position a product for youth and simultaneously to attract the adult market. Roger Enrico, president of Pepsi-Cola, U.S.A., explains, "We appeal to the broader audience through the eyes of youth. We put a youthful mindset on the product, emphasizing vitality, excitement, being on the cutting edge."

Therefore, the "Pepsi Approach" in advertising is more likely to be lifestyle advertising rather than brand advertising; that is, the ads focus on the types of people who use the product rather than on the brand attributes. Thus, the "Pepsi Approach" advertisements portray exciting, energetic lifestyles, while the promotions involve "youthful" associations, events, and contests.

Richard Blossom, vice president of marketing at Pepsi–Cola U.S.A., summarized, "Youth is a communications tool—it shows us what is hot, in tune, and current. Adults can relate to these best qualities of young people." This concisely states the recent advertising efforts of Pepsi–Cola. The "Choice of a New Generation" theme that runs in all of its commercials, is an overtly youth-oriented pitch. The company's most spectacular, memorable commercials feature celebrities who have their earliest and strongest following among youth: Michael Jackson, Lionel Richie, Don Johnson, and Michael J. Fox.

Of course, Pepsi's youth-conscious marketing efforts have been exceptionally successful in attracting young people to its product and away from its competitors. But its approach has a much broader goal: to simultaneously reach consumers from the pre-teenage years all the way through middle age with a single advertising campaign focused on the most appealing characteristics of youth. The result of this attraction to youthfulness, among all Americans, has been to make Pepsi–Cola the best selling beverage in the nation's stores.

For similar reasons, cigarette companies (though they argue that they do not target their advertisements toward young people) present youthful, sensual images in their print ads. Salem ("Salem Spirit") and Lucky Strike ("Light My Lucky") are two of the most obvious examples of this strategy. Clearly, these and other cigarette companies believe that a "young" image will attract adults to their product.

Unlike the "Snickers Approach," the "Pepsi Approach" aims all advertisements and promotions at a wide range of consumers, not only those specifically targeted. Of course, with the "Snickers Approach," each "shot" is better focused on its target audience, but more "guns" and more "shots" are needed to attain the same number of bull's-eyes. This implies greater costs to get the same effect as the "Pepsi Approach." Moreover, the "Pepsi Approach" doesn't depend on sales from a particular market to support a given ad or promotional event.

In summary, the "Pepsi Approach" is best used when:

- Consumers of all ages have the same reasons for using the product (unlike in the "American Express Approach");

- The image of a product or service can be portrayed as youthful, vigorous, active, athletic, trendy, stylish, chic, or contemporary;

- A lifestyle can be associated with a product that is attributed to all consumers, regardless of age.

4. The "MTV Approach"

The "MTV Approach" is unlike all the other YouthTrends strategies. First of all because there are few, if any, restrictions on the types of products it can benefit; and, secondly, because it is a strategy only for advertising, not for promotional campaigns. The "MTV Approach" is *not* based on how this music-video cable channel advertises itself. Rather, just as MTV has revolutionized the performance of popular songs, the "MTV Approach" *revitalizes brand advertisements,* whether on television, on radio, or in print. Simply put, the "MTV Approach" is audio/visually-appealing brand advertising, designed to attract young people, as well as those who prefer youthful, exciting presentations—that is, most consumers. These ads do not necessarily feature music; they *communicate facts about the product* in a "visually hip" way. As Robert Pittman, president of MTV Networks and one of its masterminds, has noted,

"MTV has shocked advertisers into seeing that old-style commercials are not effective. It has shown that the best way to communicate on television is through strong visual impressions."

But the "MTV Approach" differs from the "Pepsi Approach" because it is appropriate even when lifestyle advertising is not desired or appropriate. Already, this approach has been used to sell products from corn chips to automobiles.

Recent ads by Colgate toothpaste are a good example of the "MTV Approach." Colgate introduced its new pump dispenser with a commercial called the "Colgate Pump Dance." It was the first rock video for a toothpaste and it included the same copy points as a traditional toothpaste ad would have—that the paste is dispensed by a pump, that mothers and fathers are confident about its effectiveness, and it contains fluoride. But while Crest and the other toothpastes were still trying to target housewives with spokespeople who explained that their brands prevent cavities, Colgate reached out both to the young person (the end user) and to parents (also users) with a commercial that distinguished it from all its competitors. Using the music of the English rock group Madness, this colorful and energetic ad had scores of young people singing and dancing. As a result, Colgate made major inroads against the top seller, Crest, without changing its toothpaste formula or even the points made in its advertisements.

Thus, with the "MTV Approach", the points made in the advertising copy are still written to target the core market, but it is then developed to take full advantage of the intended medium whether it is television, radio, or print. As in the "Pepsi Approach" (as opposed to the "Snickers Approach" or the "American Express Approach"), one presentation is made to appeal to consumers of different ages. The primary purchaser/user is targeted but a youthful appeal is added through the use of music, humor, visually attractive images, and so on.

The 1980s have brought about a revolution in what most

consumers, especially the F.L.Y.E.R.S. market, expect both to hear and to see in advertising. Regardless of the type of product, a company can certainly benefit by taking advantage of developing technologies to produce more attractive and stylish ads.

5. The "Newsweek Approach"

Young people do not represent an important market for *Newsweek* magazine. Nevertheless, Newsweek, Inc., has created a separate magazine called *Newsweek on Campus* that is distributed free to 1.2 million college students, six times a year. It recognizes that graduating students in both high schools and colleges will eventually be setting up their own households and purchasing a wide range of products and services. Hence, the "Newsweek Approach" is the development of youth appreciation, to cultivate an audience for the future.

Newsweek is particularly interested in college students because, as is true for many products and services, the news magazine their parents purchase is likely to be the one that they prefer. *Time* magazine is older and has a circulation approximately 50 percent greater than that of *Newsweek,* so *Newsweek* looked to the college campus as a way to expand its share of the market over the long-term. Moreover, as James Spanfeller, publisher of *Newsweek on Campus,* indicated, "People are at the peak of trying new products in college. They also are beginning to try brands different from their parents."

Cover stories in *Newsweek on Campus* feature topics of special interest to college students: "The Revival of Fraternities," "The Conservative Student," "The Crackdown on Drinking," "Ron Howard and Young Filmmakers," and "Cheating in College Sports." Since the articles are written and edited by the staff of *Newsweek* itself, young people can begin to appreciate the value and quality of the magazine.

Our consulting firm has given advice to several corporations, such as financial services firms, that would not ordinarily think of young people as their customers; certainly, young people are not large investors. But when they do begin to invest, in the near future, they will likely turn to a familiar firm. Targeting the youth market is a long-term strategy that most corporations neglect, but it is extremely important to their future strength. Many products, especially those that are not the largest sellers in the adult market, could benefit from the "Newsweek Approach."

It is useful to compare the "Newsweek Approach" to the "American Express Approach":

- Like the "American Express Approach," the "Newsweek Approach" does nothing to supplement or to jeopardize a company's general market campaign;

- Unlike the "American Express Approach," it aims for future, not present, purchases of a product. As a result, its "sell" is much softer. Thus, the company must be willing to accept present expenses in exchange for future sales.

- Like the "American Express Approach," it communicates a special message to young people that is distinct from the pitch to the general market.

6. The "Swatch Approach"

Swatch is the manufacturer of those wildly colorful, plastic Swiss watches as well as of sportswear, sunglasses, and other fashion accessories. Swatch revolutionized the watch industry when it established itself as the watch of choice among young people. As Max Imgruth, president of Swatch Watch, puts it,

"Although we aimed ourselves at the youth market with colorful and funky styles, we found that the older population enjoyed the youthful appeal of the watches."

Swatch introduced its watches with many wild colors and styles, turning them into an inexpensive status symbol among young people. Incredibly, through word of mouth, the watches became so popular with the F.L.Y.E.R.S. market that they spread to the larger, fashion-conscious adult market. Then the company was able to develop other fashion items from watch guards to sunglasses to sweatshirts—all sporting characteristically bright, splashy colors.

Hence, the "Swatch Approach" develops a trend among youth and then transfers it to the larger population. For example, "Swatch Approach" describes the phenomenal growth of blue jeans: The product was principally identified with young people, but by the 1970s jeans were considered casualwear for all Americans, from children to senior citizens.

As in the "Pepsi Approach" or the "MTV Approach," the "Swatch Approach" emphasizes the product attributes that appeal to young people in order to attract the adult market. Although this approach is not appropriate for all products, it does offer potential benefits for many industries. In particular, the "Swatch Approach" can be best used when:

- A company manufactures fashion items, entertainment/leisure products, athletic/health-related goods, or any so-called image products.

To summarize, the six YouthTrends approaches are:

1. The *"American Express Approach,"* or market segmentation—distinct youth and adult campaigns;

2. The *"Snickers Approach,"* or presentation modification—one campaign for all consumers, but with different executions for youth and adults;

3. The *"Pepsi Approach,"* or lifestyle advertising and promotions that emphasize youth, while appealing to consumers of all ages;

4. The *"MTV Approach,"* or audio/visually appealing brand advertising to attract any consumer;

5. The *"Newsweek Approach,"* or development of youth appreciation;

6. The *"Swatch Approach,"* or extension of a trend among youth to the larger population.

Using the YouthTrends Approaches

In recent years, manufacturers of a wide range of products, including automobiles, clothing, snack foods, cosmetics, and beverages, have dramatically improved their images among young people and youth-conscious adults. Here we'll use the six YouthTrends models to analyze some recent, successful campaigns in various industries.

COSMETICS: L'OREAL

L'Oreal has always had a more expensive, elegant, and refined image among consumers of hair-care products; this image is reinforced by its ad line, "It's More Expensive, But I'm Worth It." But L'Oreal, too, has been trying to attract younger consumers, using the "American Express Approach." In 1986, it unveiled its Studio Line, including sculpting mousse, hair spray, and styling gel that can be used to produce wild, elegantly defined, or ultra fashionable styles that are funky and youthful. Consistent with the "American Express Approach," the line has a distinct name, so as not to alter the perception of the L'Oreal trademark among its older customers. But this

Studio Line ensures that the company can also take advantage of new hair trends among young women.

MOVIE INDUSTRY: PARAMOUNT PICTURES

Frank Mancuso, chairman of Paramount Pictures, explained that the popularity of a movie among youth, who purchase half of all movie tickets, can be extended to reach the adult viewer using the "Snickers Approach": "We change the advertising throughout a film's release to get a broader audience. We can start by targeting young people and then can move the target older."

Mr. Mancuso illustrated this development with Paramount's smash hit *Flashdance*. This movie, which portrayed the struggles of a young woman to become a dancer, was on the cutting edge of the video explosion; it conveyed the look and style of this new generation in both fashion and music. Not surprisingly, the initial target for the movie was young girls and then young boys. Due to the strong endorsement of the movie by these groups in the home, it encouraged adults to go see the movie. To supplement this endorsement, using the "Snickers Approach," television commercials were altered to interest the adult viewing public, including giving more attention to the less "hard rock," more easy-listening sound of the theme song "What A Feeling." The ad changes were based on information, gathered through exit polls, on what people of different ages and sexes enjoyed most about the film. Thus, by placing different emphases on a movie's advertisements, such as adding youth appeal or certain attractions for adults, the distributor is able to help support and increase a film's success at the box office.

AUTOMOBILES: GENERAL MOTORS' PONTIAC DIVISION

To rejuvenate its image, Pontiac utilized the "Pepsi Approach." Mark Gjovik, management supervisor of the Pontiac Account at D'Arcy Masius Benton & Bowles Advertising, and Bill O'-Neill, director of public relations at General Motors' Pontiac Division, discussed with us the efforts begun in 1983 to rejuvenate the Pontiac image. The division's new philosophy was to manufacture automobiles having "innovative engineering and styling, with superior roadability and performance." In addition to these technological improvements, the division produced contemporary, sporty designs for its Fiero, Firebird, Sunbird, 6000 STE, and Grand Am.

Moreover, the division's new marketing strategy for these cars was to attract the first-time buyer as well as the so-called "New Values Buyer," who is younger, affluent, and tends to buy foreign cars. Consequently, to support the technical innovations, "Pepsi Approach" advertisements were created around the "We Build Excitement" theme. Television, radio, and print ads were developed to appeal to car buyers who are young or who feel young.

Then, in a major "Pepsi Approach" promotional effort in 1984–1985, Pontiac sponsored the sixty-five-city concert tour of the rock group Hall and Oates, the most popular duo in musical history. The urban contemporary sound of Hall and Oates was a perfect way for Pontiac to reach out to eighteen-to twenty-five-year-olds while also attracting twenty-five- to thirty-five-year-olds. At each concert site, Pontiac cars were displayed, and Pontiac also created a sweepstakes to publicize its tour sponsorship. In each concert city, local radio stations and Pontiac dealerships awarded free concert tickets, T-shirts, and Hall and Oates records.

With its new, youth-conscious image, Pontiac has the lowest median age for its car buyers within General Motors as well as the lowest throughout the automobile industry. The Pontiac

Division now accounts for 18 to 20 percent of all of GM's annual revenues. Specifically, Pontiac's annual sales rose from 500,000 cars in the early 1980s to 900,000 cars just four years after beginning its YouthTrends revitalization.

SNACK FOODS: NABISCO'S BABY RUTH AND BUTTERFINGER

Nabisco has been attempting to improve young consumers' perceptions of its Baby Ruth and Butterfinger candy bars and has done so using the "MTV Approach." As Steven Centrillo, vice-president at Bozell & Jacobs Advertising and supervisor of the Nabisco Brands account, explains, in the chocolate business, "image" is the principal differentiator among products. In 1985, various chocolate confection companies spent approximately $165 million on image advertising. Since the top-selling candy bars are, for the most part, made of many of the same ingredients (chocolate, peanuts, caramel), each manufacturer tries to emphasize a particular feature that distinguishes its product from the others. For example, as previously noted, the Mars' Snickers bar is known as the "hunger satisfier," while Baby Ruth and Butterfinger, under their previous owner, Standard Brands, had traditionally been promoted as providing more peanuts and caramel.

However, in the early 1980s, when Nabisco Brands purchased Baby Ruth and Butterfinger, the company discovered that consumers, especially teenagers, complained that the bars were stale when purchased. Since, on average, teenagers consume nine candy bars per month while the rest of the population eats about four bars, the dissatisfaction of teens was clearly a serious consideration. Nabisco determined that the freshness problems stemmed from cost-cutting changes in the recipe by Standard Brands. So Nabisco returned to the original, high-quality formulas and picked up the old, stale products from retailers.

Then it developed a new advertising campaign, "Guaranteed Fresh," that began airing in late 1983. The company offered a money-back guarantee that both Baby Ruth and Butterfinger bars would be fresh when purchased. Of course, this campaign was not without risks, as the ads had to admit that the product had been stale in the past.

Thus, using the "MTV Approach," the new commercials noted the improved quality of the candy bars and offered the money-back guarantee, but did so using a contemporary musical theme, attractive young models, and extremely appetizing presentations of the candy bars. Since the improved formulas ensured that the products lived up to these claims, the ads were effective at changing the young consumers' viewpoint. As a result, sales of both bars began to rise steadily. After regaining teenagers' confidence, the campaigns took a further step to attract greater youth purchases by using the same commercial style, but now emphasizing that the candy was "better than ever" and had a "richer chocolate taste."

COFFEE INDUSTRY: GENERAL FOODS' MAXWELL HOUSE

As we discussed earlier, the coffee industry has suffered some setbacks in recent years, at least in part because of its failure to attract the youth market. A few of the major producers have tried to revitalize flagging sales by developing appeals to young people, with varying degrees of success.

Peter Barnet, vice-president at Ogilvy & Mather Advertising and supervisor of the General Foods account, reviewed some of these industry-wide efforts, as well as the particular campagns of Maxwell House Coffee aimed at the youth market.

The first approach the coffee industry used was an advertising campaign called "Coffee for the Young Achiever." The ads showed young celebrities in very stressful, competitive situations, nervously drinking coffee before a big interview or performance. Unfortunately, the commercials highlighted the aspects of coffee drinking most negative to young people; that is, that people who drink coffee are tense, compulsive, and overly aggressive.

General Foods' Maxwell House Coffee, however, approached the problem from an entirely different direction using the "Newsweek Approach." Their campaign, titled "Young Comedians," uses contemporary humor to focus on the concept that drinking coffee is a badge of becoming an adult. The humor often hinges on the idea that when people are young they look at coffee as something forbidden, with a taste that only adults could enjoy. Thus, these soft-sell ads attempt to break down the negative coffee stereotypes and to make coffee drinking a part of a contemporary lifestyle—hopefully capturing the long-term loyalty of this new generation.

TELEVISION INDUSTRY: NBC

As Brandon R. Tartikoff, president of NBC noted to us, "If you are on target with youth and have something else to appeal to adults and children, you can have a hit." As the "Swatch Approach" would indicate, when a show is popular among F.L.Y.E.R.S., its popularity can begin to spread up and down: that is, up to their parents and down to their younger brothers and sisters. Cited as an example is *Facts of Life,* NBC's longest running sitcom. The comedy centers on the school life of four teenage girls; thus, this story line principally seems of interest to teenagers, especially teenage girls. But Charlotte Rae (now Cloris Leachman) has been added as a mother figure to give the show greater attraction to older viewers.

Mr. Tartikoff also pointed out, "You don't set out to make a show that appeals just to fifteen to twenty-five-year-olds. But this group is responsible for the success of alot of slow growth hits like *Happy Days, Hill Street Blues,* and even *Miami Vice.*" Hence, a youthful appeal sometimes can create a trend that can turn a program into a hit. Mr. Tartikoff's efforts in programming hit shows certainly have been successful, since NBC won the Nielsen ratings race for the 1985–86 season for the first time since Nielsen started measuring ratings back in 1960–61. Moreover, in 1985, NBC led in youth ratings, having eight of the top ten youth programs.

Thus, even with a mass medium like television, youth appeal can serve as a bridge to connect older and younger viewers to a program, or can even help establish the success of a new show.

CLOTHING: AMERICAN HOME SEWING, J. C. PENNEY, AND BENETTON

Below we examine how three different organizations within the clothing industry have successfully utilized different youth-oriented approaches.

The American Home Sewing Association represents textile and sewing machine manufacturers, retail outlets, and makers of sewing patterns. Earle Angstadt, president of McCall Patterns, in discussing the work that the association is doing to revive home sewing, noted that the pattern business hit its peak in 1976 and has been on a decline in the United States for the last ten years. In 1976, 170 million patterns were sold in the United States, but by 1985 the number had dropped to only some 60 million patterns. This decline is due, in part, to the growing feeling among young people that sewing is an outmoded skill. Moreover, teenage girls do not believe fashionable clothing can be home sewn.

To reverse this trend, the American Home Sewing Association determined that it had to change these perceptions. To begin with, each pattern company has initiated its own programs to interest teenage girls in learning to sew. For example, McCall Patterns now features collections licensed by model Brooke Shields, actress Shari Belafonte Harper, rock singer

Appolonia, or produced by such trendy fashion lines as Camp Beverly Hills.

But the association, as a whole, has made a bold attempt to reach out to young women. In 1986, it aired a rock video–type commercial on MTV titled "Be an American Original." Using a sexy, upbeat musical theme, the ad made two central points: (1) that a hand-sewn outfit is "one of a kind," and (2) that it is possible to make stylish clothing, not just old-fashioned dresses, at home. Thus, using the "American Express Approach," the American Home Sewing Association is presenting a special message to young women without the fear that it will alienate its older, more traditional consumers.

J. C. Penney, America's third largest retailer, combined the "Pepsi Approach" and the "Snickers Approach" to redefine its image completely.

As K. T. Russo, retail marketing manager of Womenswear, and Gerry Shores, retail marketing manager of Menswear, explained, beginning in the 1980s, J. C. Penney decided to move out of hard goods like paints and tires to become more of a department store. Taking a cue from the "Pepsi Approach," the company spent over $1 billion in store refurbishing and now utilizes more appealing, exciting point-of-purchase displays. Further, it has dramatically improved the variety and quality of its clothing stock, now carrying a wide selection of popular brand names, including Levi-Strauss, Sasson, and Halston, as well as its own private labels (Fox and Hunt Club).

With the first stages of this transformation complete, Penney is trying to convince fashion-conscious young adults that the store has changed and now features the most up-to-date apparel. Since young people begin to form their impressions about clothing and where to shop for clothing at an increasingly early age, it has become essential for Penney to create positive attitudes about its chain among teenagers. To do so, Penney hired NW Ayer Advertising. Jerry Siano, president of NW Ayer/New York (who in fact wears stylish three-piece suits from J.

C. Penney) says that Penney now spends $30 to $40 million annually on image advertising and has increased its presence in youth-oriented magazines such as *Glamour, Mademoiselle,* and *Seventeen.*

J. C. Penney has used the "Snickers Approach" to reach out to the youth market. To revitalize its image among all consumers, it employs the appealing slogan, "You're Looking Smarter Than Ever." In its efforts to attract young consumers, it uses the same slogan, but runs special ads for young people on television and in magazines, especially at back-to-school time, showing attractive, popular young people wearing the styles of the trendy clothing they desire.

Unlike both American Home Sewing Association and J. C. Penney, Benetton has used the "Swatch Approach" to popularize its clothing line.

Luciano Benetton, president and founder of the Italian–based Benetton, spoke with us (fortunately, through a translator) about the tremendous international growth in the sales of his company's clothing. Benetton manufactures a line of sweaters, jeans, and other casual apparel in characteristic bright, bold colors. With over $500 million in 1985 worldwide revenues, the company is the world's largest maker of knitwear with 5,300 outlets in 54 countries. The clothing line was introduced to the United States just in 1979, but already Benetton has U.S. sales of $230 million from its 400 nationwide outlets.

Its "United Colors of Benetton" ads, which run worldwide, feature groups of teenagers of different races and from different nations, all wearing the fashionably colorful clothing. This trend-setting casualwear is affordably priced and exceptionally popular among youth. But Mr. Benetton noted that his customers range from from teenagers to Princess Diana and Jacqueline Onassis to any fashion-conscious adult. Thus, as with many fashion items, the connection of the Benetton product to youth only enhances its attractiveness to the entire buying public, even the most elite adult consumers. Thus as these examples show, the six YouthTrends Approaches, carefully selected and effectively implemented, can help rejuvenate a product's image among young people. A new, more current image can increase sales, both to young consumers and to the youth-conscious adult market.

6
YOUTH TRENDS CASE STUDIES OF THREE MAJOR INDUSTRIES

Although we aimed ourselves at the youth market with
colorful and funky styles, we found that the older
population enjoyed the youthful appeal of the watches.

—Max Imgruth,
president of Swatch Watch

Given the high percentage of youth-oriented campaigns
within these industries, it is probably no surprise to hear us say
that the clothing, fast-food, and entertainment industries are
both leaders and innovators in youth marketing. They have
managed to make themselves appealing to both the adult and
the F.L.Y.E.R.S. generations by making use of the six Youth-
Trends Approaches discussed in Chapter 5. Here, through separate case studies, we will see how the three industries manage
to both stay on top of the youthful trends and hold the interest
of this young generation of consumers.

The Youth Market and the $80 Billion Clothing Industry

The clothing industry has long been sensitive to youth trends because young people are so conscious of fashion as a mode of expression. More than anything else, buying the right kind of clothing is the first step to fitting in with their peers.

Because of its bold advertising, its creative promoting—and because fashions change constantly—this industry manages to attract a major chunk of the youth population's income each year. The $80 billion clothing industry realizes that the F.L.Y.E.R.S. market is buying sportswear and designer items, as well as expensive accessories, at a rate that far exceeds that of their parents.

Here we'll present a collective case study on an industry, focusing on those companies that have succeeded or failed in capturing the young consumer. From our own experiences of launching a successful line of clothing, as well as interviews with the presidents, executives, and advertising agencies of such companies as Benetton, J. C. Penney, Swatch, Levi-Strauss, Daniel Hechter, Sears, McCall Patterns, and Wrangler, we will consider the ways that the clothing industry has provided for and marketed to the youth population.

We will also look at such youth-oriented clothing companies as Lee Jeans, Esprit, Calvin Klein, Ocean Pacific, and the Gap Stores, as well as the way that the licensing industry has helped clothing businesses attract more young buyers to their products.

As companies like Nike and Adidas attempt to extend their product lines from athletic footwear into "athletic wear" and from there into "sportswear," it is becoming increasingly evident that the business world realizes how much money young people will spend for clothing labels. The question is, What makes a label matter—or makes a company successful?

WHO SETS CLOTHING TRENDS?

Who exactly dictates the trends in young people's clothing? Are they decided by a select group of designers in New York? By some young trendsetters on a beach in California? By the fashion magazines? By such popular TV shows as NBC's *Miami Vice?* Or by the average high school or college shopper who suddenly decides each week that whatever is on sale at the mall is fine? (The last choice is most unlikely, as most young people avoid the stigma of buying from sale racks and choose the higher-priced name brands.)

According to Amy Levin, editor-in-chief of *Mademoiselle* magazine, "As a well-respected lifestyles magazine that emphasizes fashion, we are able to both predict and create the trends. I like to think of *Mademoiselle* as a magazine that, more than anything, reinforces trends that are just about to begin among our young readers." Levin believes that the clothing her fifty-one-year-old magazine features is what has just begun to appear at the popular dance clubs or to be worn on the streets by trendy young people.

Midge Turk Richardson, *Seventeen* magazine's editor-in-chief, says that magazines set trends—and so does California. "There is no question that strong magazines like *Seventeen* and others can both reinforce and set clothing trends. As surprising as it may sound, we not only launch new styles, but we are capable of making a particular color popular for a given period." Richardson adds, "A very important force, though, is California. The youth-oriented fashions are definitely coming out of southern California. Just as the roller-skating and yogurt crazes started there, so are the clothing styles."

Certainly today's female youth-oriented media focuses heavily on the clothing industry. Young people do not have to wait until they're twenty-five and reading *Esquire* or *Vogue* to become aware of which fashions are being worn by their generation.

Such magazines as *Seventeen, Mademoiselle, Elle, Young Miss, GQ, Teen,* and *Glamour* run many pages on clothing in each issue. Along with articles on various fashion trends, they offer editorial layouts featuring stylishly dressed models promoting swimwear, footwear, underwear, jeans, sweatshirts, sportswear, and accessories (sunglasses, earrings, bandannas, hats, scarves, and so on). And over the past few years, the youth generation has become more accepting of clothing articles and advertisements aimed directly at young men. There are many more men's clothing ads and features in such previously non-fashion magazines as *Rolling Stone, Us,* and *Spin.*

Many in the magazine business know that, each month or week, when these magazines are published, several million young people flip through the thousands of editorial and advertising pages, waiting for some piece of clothing to catch their eye, one that conveys an image they are willing to accept for themselves and to present to others.

Burt Manning, chairman of J. Walter Thompson Advertising, says the advertising and publishing worlds have a more limited role in setting trends. "The popular culture is what creates a trend." He explains, "After that, the advertiser takes advantage of the trend. Levi-Strauss didn't create a blue jeans trend. They simply were clever enough to capitalize on something that was becoming popular within the culture."

Manning adds that the clothing styles are also dictated by youth-culture celebrities. "The cast-off clothing look has been popularized by several people at several times. At one time Barbra Streisand did it; then came Bette Midler's turn. Most recently, the cast-off look was popularized by Madonna's and Cyndi Lauper's clothing styles."

NBC Entertainment president, Brandon Tartikoff, believes in the trendsetting impact of television. Citing his own network's shows, such as *Miami Vice, Saturday Night Live,* and *Friday Night Videos,* Tartikoff says, "When young people like a certain TV program, they copy the fashions and turn both the show and the clothing into a trend. The viewers determine what is right and what will spread further throughout the youth culture."

So it is obvious that the clothing trends among young people originate from many different sources within the youth culture—popular television shows, new musicians, lifestyle magazines, etc. It is, thus, up to the clothing companies to remain abreast of the changes taking place in these areas. So far, the industry has managed to do that.

Review of Youth-Oriented Clothing Companies

Whoever initially sets the trends, companies can certainly benefit by pursuing them. Here we'll look at the strategies and the track records of some of the major ones.

Benetton. With stores in over 50 countries, Luciano Benetton, founder and chairman of the clothing company that bears his name, told us that the fifteen- to twenty-five-year-old F.L.Y.E.R.S. market was originally—and still is—his company's primary target.

One of the most innovative labels to arrive in America in several years, Benetton is special because of its clothing and also because of its unusual store design. The clothing line, which originally concentrated on sweaters, became popular in this country in the early 1980s because it was unisex and very colorful. The styles were loose fitting, with an unstructured look that attracted those who wanted comfortable sportswear.

The physical environment of Benetton stores was just as appealing. According to Benetton's executive vice-president, Francesco della Barba, "We do not like to use counters in our stores because we want to create more of a personal relationship with customers." Benetton also told us that he dislikes seeing barriers between products and consumers: "My store encourages people to pick up whatever they like." And this is true. The clothes that line the walls are fully accessible to the customers, allowing them to unfold and to touch every item that is on display. Young people like the open, nonthreatening design, so different from the intimidating atmosphere in so many shops that only pretend to invite young buyers with rock music and popular posters. The bright green displays and large windows that adorn most of the Benetton shops are also eye-catching for sidewalk shoppers.

Esprit. Producing somewhat of a cross between Benetton and funky teeny-bopper styles, Esprit distributes its popular line of sportswear in department stores throughout the country. Retail sales for this California–based clothing company reached $800 million in 1986. Known for its unusually appealing "personality" ads with semi-pretentious biographies for its models, Esprit offers bright colors and never hesitates to put its logo on shirts, jackets, and totebags. Very quickly, Esprit is becoming more than just a youth "label"—it is becoming a youth boutique. Stores like Macy's and Bloomingdale's are opening complete sections, specifically for Esprit designs.

Ocean Pacific and Santa Cruz. These two firms can best be described as California companies. Along with many other clothing companies and licensed designs, Ocean Pacific and Santa Cruz are capitalizing on the trend for lightweight sunwear, beachwear, and sportswear. Adorned with palm trees, surfboards, pineapples, and beach scenes, as well as colorful dots, stripes, and patterns, their California–styled clothing has gained national popularity. These two companies were quick to pick up on the trendiness of California—both by their styles and company names—but they may lose out when the California style is replaced by the preppy or European styles that seem to return every few years.

Because such companies as L.A. Gear and the fourteen-year-old Ocean Pacific sunwear company are also in the business of licensing, their names have popularized many types of clothing accessories as well. Ocean Pacific licenses its name to more than ten different manufacturers (of ski jackets, umbrellas, etc.) and receives a 5 percent royalty on those licensing sales.

Calvin Klein Jeans and Guess! Jeans. Eric Weber, executive vice president of Dancer Fitzgerald Sample Advertising praises the bold creativity of Calvin Klein's ad campaign: "He is definitely the genius of the decade. He was conceited enough to realize that others would identify with their creativity." The jeans company that shocked the world with its provocative TV ads has made itself *the* symbol for the fashion-jeans craze that swept the country in the 1970s. More than the clothes themselves, the marketing approach of selling a sexy image in printed TV ads is what made the Calvin Klein name so appealing to young people and to those who wanted to look young.

One of the few other companies that has displayed such creativity is Georges Marciano's Guess! Jeans. Guess quickly began to put its name on other items, such as sweatshirts, watches, and pens. Considering Swatch Watch's success in marketing similar items, Guess! had made a clever move, further solidifying the trendy nature of the Guess! name.

The Gap Stores. At one time the most popular blue jeans store among young people, the Gap began to lose its popularity in the early 1980s. It was known for selling Levi-Strauss products and, eventually, its own name-brand leisurewear. Now the 600-store chain is making a comeback from its once hippie-like image. It has created a more upscale image for itself, no longer using its well-known slogan, "Fall into the Gap." Now its clothes emphasize more color and many more conservative styles, including a wide selection of sweaters.

The Gap stores are beginning to look more organized and hi-tech, like the Benetton shops. They have changed their Peter Max–style design and layout, which had been appealing to the youth of the 1970s, and are now toning down their once multicolored racks to more acceptable muted tones.

Levi-Strauss, Wrangler, and Lee Jeans. They call it the

American look. Responsible for clothing nearly all young Americans, these three companies are the major manufacturers of denimwear in the United States.

Levi-Strauss is the world's largest manufacturer of brand name apparel. Its jeans division, alone,—famous for its popular 501 brand jeans—has annual sales that exceed $1.5 billion. Denny Wilkinson of Foote Cone Belding Advertising explains that Levi's core consumer is aged twenty-five and under: "After the designer jeans craze, we worked very hard to get those young consumers back to the basic denim jeans." According to Wilkinson, the designer jeans trend has almost disappeared for male consumers, who have indeed returned their loyalty to Levi's.

In comparing the advertising for Levi's, Wrangler, and Lee jeans, there is no question that Levi's is more innovative. It uses women, minorities, and the handicapped in its ads, which are also well-executed. The Lee image comes across as sexier. The ads use pretty male and female models who throw smoldering sexual glances at each other. Wrangler, by contrast, comes across as being more athletic and male-oriented. As Gary Susnjara, chairman of Dancer Fitzgerald Sample explained to us, "Wrangler has a very Western image. It makes sense for the brand to use such slogans as 'Live It to the Limit in Wrangler.'"

Many companies within the clothing industry are successful at capturing the enthusiasm of the young consumer for two reasons. First, they are adept at watching the trends that are created by popular magazines, movie stars, TV shows, and musicians. Second, there is a desire by many clothing companies to not only keep up with the trends, but also to *create* trends. Unlike the nine industries we discussed in Chapter 4, the clothing industry is unafraid to gamble its marketing dollars on outrageous or funky advertising. These companies have long considered themselves innovators so they feel no compunction about dictating the styles and trends to their potential consumers.

While less aggressive than the clothing business in creating trends, the fast-food restaurant industry is still extremely competent in applying the YouthTrends Approaches in their efforts to capture the F.L.Y.E.R.S. consumer group.

Youth and the Food Industry

"Not enough food companies are taking the young consumer seriously. More of them should be aiming advertisements and commercials at this age group," said Jim Rainsford, advertising director of *Seventeen* magazine. While Rainsford has attracted General Foods, Hershey Foods, and a few other companies to his impressive roster of advertisers, the industry has generally not accepted the importance of the youth market.

Leslie Zeifman, associate publisher of *Rolling Stone,* faces the same problems. "We haven't been able to get food advertisers," Zeifman says, "but we are working on special ad supplements and projects that should interest some of the nontraditional food companies." Following an extensive study on teenage food shopping, Richard Robinson, president of Scholastic, Inc., concludes, "The food industry is our newest target of potential advertisers. The facts on young shoppers are overwhelming." Scholastic's Ed Chenetz adds, "We're telling Kraft, General Mills, Kellogg's, and others that young men and women are in the supermarkets making decisions for their families."

The absence of food advertisements on MTV is a clear sign of the industry's misperceptions about young people as food purchasers. Only a handful of companies, including Campbell's Soup, Kraft, and General Foods, are attempting to reach young people through MTV and other youth-oriented media. Chenetz credits MTV for having raised the consciousness of marketers about the spending habits of young people.

And, indeed, the figures support the claims of these media executives. A food and nutrition study performed by Scholastic, Inc., and *Food Processing* magazine focused on teenage shoppers (a group that spends less than twenty- to twenty-five-year-olds). The study found that:

- More than eight out of every ten (82.4 percent) teenagers shop for food.

- 72 percent of all young males participate in food shopping; 85.7 percent of young females participate in food shopping.

- 68 percent of the teenagers polled frequently do *all* their families' food shopping.

- 74 percent of the teenagers polled prepare *their own* meals a few times each week.

- 53 percent of the teenage respondents prepare *the whole family's* meal at least once each week.

These figures are surprising to many executives who grew up during a time when all mothers were housewives, food shoppers, and meal preparers. Because so many women now work, many of their previous responsibilities have been delegated to their children.

What should *not* be surprising is that young adults aged nineteen to twenty-five are taking on even more food shopping responsibility than teenagers. When young people move away from home, many make their own grocery lists and cook in their own apartments or dormitory kitchens. This group relies on a combination of frozen dinners, fast foods, and regular meals they prepare themselves. The myth is that all college students live in dorms and are fed in the dining halls. The fact is that most students do not live in dormitories. While many schools can provide housing for most of their freshmen, the next three years are generally spent off the campus, where one lives and eats in a private apartment.

THE MENTALITY OF THE FOOD COMPANIES

Many food marketers are playing a dangerous game by overlooking the youth market. They may risk suffering the coffee industry's fate of several years ago. Peter Barnet, senior vice-president at Ogilvy & Mather Advertising, described how the coffee companies ignored the youth market and then lost the group to the soft drink industry. "The coffee people were not just in the coffee business," Barnet explained. "They were in the beverage business. Because they didn't look at themselves this way, they never realized that young people would shun coffee and turn to another beverage like soft drinks."

One expects that the recent mergers of food companies with other experienced marketers (such as the unions of General Foods and Philip Morris and of Nabisco and R. J. Reynolds) food companies will be encouraged to take note of the youth shopper. It is an idea whose time has come. Alan McDonald, president of Nestlé Foods, for example, cites his company's new plans to pursue the young consumer. "While we aim confection at young people, we are making plans to do more with our food and coffee products."

THE FAST-FOOD/RESTAURANT COMPANIES

It is no secret that the fast-food companies are talented at projecting youthful images for promoting their goods to young people. Their commercials feature popular music, young models, and the latest youth-oriented fads.

These companies are intent on increasing the size of the $47 billion fast-food industry, unlike the conservative food producers who avoid aggressive promotions and controversial ads. Wendy's eccentric "Russian Fashion Show" TV ad, which compared the lack of choice in the Soviet Union with the choices available in other fast-food restaurants, is just one of the more ambitious efforts fast-food companies are making. Each year, the fast-food industry spends $1 billion on advertising and promotion.

Jay Darling, president of Burger King, "I compete against anyone who sells food. I compete for the share of stomach." This remark is typical of the realistic attitude held by the leaders of the fast-food business. Although it is a far smaller chain than McDonald's, Burger King is now Number 2 in the industry and spent $109 million on advertising in 1985. In comparison, McDonald's, the industry leader, spent $226 million on ads to support its nine thousand restaurants.

And where the leaders go, the industry follows. Wendy's spent $63 million on advertising, followed by Kentucky Fried Chicken ($54 million), and Pizza Hut ($48 million) in 1985. It's a sign of determination that Kentucky Fried Chicken raised its ad figures from $54 to $80 million for 1986. The point to be stressed, here, is that the fast-food companies are extremely ambitious with their marketing departments.

According to Bruce Ley, vice-president of Wendy's, his company is very much interested in winning over more young consumers. "We advertise on MTV and we try to capture a youthful sense of humor for our advertisements." Even the conservative and somewhat old-fashioned Howard Johnson chain is beginning to see the importance of young people. Although its flagship Howard Johnson restaurants are foundering, its 200 Ground Round restaurants are succeeding by relying heavily on the young adult restaurantgoer.

These recent fast-food restaurant developments should certainly scare the food companies into taking the young consumer seriously. Such restaurants as McDonald's used to attract young people because they sold hamburgers and fries, but they now are turning themselves into restaurant-supermarkets by offering more food to choose from—salads, pies, fish, chicken, croissants, ice cream, and even freshly baked cookies.

While the fast-food companies have extended their line of products, somewhat, in order to include youth-appealing products, the industry's success at winning over the young consumer can be credited primarily to the large amount of money spent by the industry on youth advertising. Whereas the clothing industry carved out a place in the youth market through the industry's creativity, the food industry has done it through media dollars. They have bought their way into the minds of young people and, for this reason, each new fast-food operation is forced to spend a tremendous amount on ads targeted to the F.L.Y.E.R.S. if it wants to compete seriously.

The next industry to be discussed is much more similar to the clothing business in its attempt to use creativity in ads and promotion. The entertainment industry certainly spends a great deal on advertisements and promotional campaigns, but its approach is one that is based more on product innovation than on advertising clutter.

The Youth Market and the $35 Billion Entertainment Industry

The entertainment industry has always followed the direction and the interests of those who think young. The F.L.Y.E.R.S. market accounts for more than half of all movie ticket sales, and it has been documented that, once young people embrace a new movie, the adult generation will almost always follow. This pattern was set early on with Shirley Temple and the Judy Garland/Mickey Rooney "Andy Hardy" movies that were initially targeted at young people.

In this section, we will look at how the record and movie industries, as well as TV, radio, and cable companies, rely on youth-appealing concepts and strategies to succeed in attracting audiences. Through our conversations with many TV and film executives—including Frank Mancuso, Paramount's chairman; NBC president Brandon Tartikoff; MTV president Robert Pittman; WNET/Channel 13 chief operating officer George Miles, Jr.; Walt Disney Studios vice-president Robert Levin; and Metro-Goldwyn-Mayer vice-president Lois Sloane—as well as with record-industry specialists from CBS Records, Arista Records, *Spin* magazine, and *Rolling Stone,* we will also examine the incredible role that the entertainment business plays in promoting varied products.

Indeed, any product can share in the popularity of a well-liked song, movie, or TV program when that product's commercial or promotion utilizes the same singer, actor, song, or story line. And given the large number of celebrity endorsements and popular songs used in commercials, it is clear that marketers realize the benefits of associating their products with a well-accepted star or Top Forty hit. What is fascinating is that movie executives believe that sometimes the "rub-off" effect can work *both* ways. Says Robert Levin, vice-president of Walt Disney Studios, "We benefit from advertising on MTV or by tying in with other popular branded products. This allows our movie to benefit from the other product's loyal customers, too."

Jim Cawley, vice-president of Arista Records, would agree with Levin. In marketing such singers as Whitney Houston, Houdini, and other pop artists, Cawley says it is mutually beneficial for a popular star to tie in with a popular product. "Swatch sponsored the Thompson Twins on a tremendous tour, and the association benefited the group as well as the watch company."

Still, it's a tricky business. Earlier in this chapter, we discussed the volatility of the apparel business, which is even surpassed by that of the entertainment industry. Indeed, while a clothing style can remain popular for a whole season or year, a record album or song may only stay in the Top Forty category for three weeks. But this volatility can be a benefit in some ways: For instance, if materialism is in vogue, rock singer Madonna can write the "Material Girl," which captures the idea and quickly inform the rest of the world of the trend or prevalent attitude. When patriotism was becoming fashionable, Sylvester Stallone expanded on it with movies like *Rambo* and *Rocky IV.* The clothing industry cannot as easily incorporate these current ideas and attitudes as can the music, TV, and film business.

And because the entertainment industry picks up on ideas and turns them into trends faster than other industries, the public expects TV, movies, and music to tell them what they should be talking and thinking about.

Here we'll consider how various entertainment companies have tried to approach the youth market and why they've succeeded or failed. Since the industry's product is *entertainment,* we'll begin by discussing the subjects most likely to appeal to youth.

SUBJECTS YOUNG PEOPLE LIKE

The entertainment industry has succeeded, for the most part, in discovering the subjects that attract a broad audience. Clearly, both the film and record industries have made efforts— and some very successful ones—to find subjects with distinct youth appeal. Here are some of the major ones:

Student Life. Film-going audiences seem to have an insatiable appetite for movies featuring some aspect of school life. There have been dozens of successes, including such films as *Animal House, Back to School* (these about college life), *Sixteen Candles, Porky's, The Breakfast Club,* and *Fast Times at Ridgemont High* (about high school life), and *Private School* and *Class* (about boarding school life). And while young people came to these movies in large numbers they were by no means the only ones in the audience. Adults supported these movies as well.

Vacations. From *Where the Boys Are* and *Fraternity Vacation,* to *Spring Break* and *National Lampoon's Vacation,* it is obvious that vacation time is a subject that many young moviegoers want to see.

American Patriotism. Bruce Springsteen's "Born in the U.S.A." and John Cougar Mellencamp's "My Hometown" are two songs that have successfully tapped young America's feeling of patriotism. For all the alleged "corniness" of some patriotic songs, these Top Forty hits proved that there are periods when even young people can willingly admit to being proud.

While patriotism seems to be on its way out (as a result of increased government corruption), during the past few years, patriotism has been an effective subject in the movie industry. *Top Gun, Rambo,* and the *Rocky IV* were all tremendous successes.

Music and Dance. *Flashdance* was a youth-oriented, music and dance movie that told the story of a nightclub dancer/welder who wanted to become a ballet dancer. *Footloose* was a youth-oriented, music and dance movie that told the story of how a young boy brought dancing to a conservative town. *Saturday Night Fever* was a youth-oriented, music and dance movie that showed how a city boy had fun on the dance floor each weekend. *Krush Groove, Breakin',* and *Beat Street* were movies that paid tribute to new forms of music and dance; rap music was the heart of Warner Brothers' *Krush Groove.* Cannon Films' *Breakin'* and Harry Belafonte's *Beat Street* featured break dancing.

Considering the incredible success of MTV, as well as other song and dance video programming, it is no surprise that films would draw in the youth audience with stories about music and dancing. Apart from film- and record-industry efforts, how is the rest of the entertainment business reaching out to youth? Next we'll look at the major media.

TELEVISION

Commercial Programming. Unfortunately, commercial television lags behind the film and record industry in approaching young viewers. Of the three major networks, NBC is considered the most interested in the youth market and CBS the least. Still, Gerald Jaffe, vice-president of NBC research projects, admits that the network has taken on a challenge in going after young people. Jaffe noted, "it is much easier to please older audiences since they don't tire of a subject so quickly."

Public Programming. Public television, too, has begun to realize the importance of the youth market. Program directors are trying to soften the old "educational TV" image by using such popular celebrity hosts as Walter Matthau to introduce special shows, in this case the Shakespeare series. (While not popular among young people, he is at least recognizable.) It is obvious that changes like these will allow public broadcasting to attract youth as well as other adults who aren't quite ready to assume the slow, sophisticated tone of a conservative, pipe-smoking host.

"We would like to capture a greater percentage of the youth audience," says George Miles, Jr., chief operating officer of New York's prestigious PBS station WNET/Channel 13. "While public broadcasting has been successful at capturing the very young with such programs as *Sesame Street* and *Reading Rainbow,* we have been experimenting with a music-oriented program that was designed to capture both the teen audience and the older viewers who are intrigued by youthful rock music." Called *RockSchool,* the program is designed to teach viewers how to play guitar and percussion instruments. Viewers, as well as classes in high schools and colleges, are encouraged to send away for teaching materials that supplement the *RockSchool* programs.

MTV and Cable Programming. Although cable television accounts for only about $725 million in sales each year, it has become a major influence within the entertainment industry as a whole. With such brilliant successes as MTV and other channels that focus on such topics as sports, health, news, and family, cable is challenging radio as the best medium for targeting young people. According to Robert Pittman, president of MTV Networks, "Broadcast television does not focus on groups the way cable can. MTV, for instance has 85 percent of its audience in the twelve to thirty-four age-group. You can't find numbers like that elsewhere."

Barry Loughrane, chairman of Doyle Dane Bernbach Advertising believes that MTV has been a great medium for aiming directly at the young consumer. He adds, "Now network TV is following the example of cable. Many shows on network television are becoming segmented for specific age groups."

Entertainment Clubs and Magazines. From our conversations with executives at CBS Records' Columbia House record club, *Spin* magazine, *Moviegoer,* and *Rolling Stone,* it is clear that a major function of these organizations is to help consumers decide which records, movies, and videos they should spend their money on. Patricia Norman, marketing manager at Columbia House told us that since the record club offers selections from many different record companies, their main contribution is "offering a choice of the most popular records and providing convenience so that consumers don't have to hunt through the stores for the albums and singles that they want."

The entertainment magazines also serve to help consumers choose the right movie. Instead of hunting around and taking the chance of spending money on a bad film or concert, reviews in magazines like *Rolling Stone* and *Spin* advise readers on what to expect. Bob Guccione, Jr., publisher of *Spin* magazine, told us, "We didn't perform market research when creating this magazine. We knew that there were many people who needed guidance in the area of entertainment. We used logic and instinct to create something that people needed when following a complicated industry."

Once again, we find an industry which not only tries to capitalize on the trends of young people, but which also attempts to create trends that young people and others will accept as their own. In their attempt to capture this group, the entertainment industry has relied on both scientific surveys and gut instinct to decide what young audiences are ready for.

We have looked at three industries that have been highly successful at marketing to the F.L.Y.E.R.S. generation. What distinguishes these businesses from others is not just the flexibility of their products (particularly for the clothing and entertainment industries), but it is primarily their confidence. They are willing to gamble by offering unique products and shocking campaigns. They are willing to puzzle, excite or annoy consumers because these industries are confident that consumers will buy. For them, there is no traditional way to promote—so they constantly incorporate new trends and fads. And because young consumers are always seeking new items and trends, it is this very characteristic which makes the clothing, fast-food and entertainment industry marketers so successful.

In the following chapter we will look at some of the mistakes that are commonly made by companies that are creating youth advertising and promotion campaigns.

7

THE TEN MOST COMMON MISTAKES IN YOUTH ADVERTISING AND PROMOTION

There is a high awareness of the importance of the youth market in all industries. The skill is learning to communicate to young people in their own language.

—Bill Weed,
Director of the Ogilvy Group
and of Ogilvy & Mather Worldwide

*B*efore we get into the actual mechanics of crafting a YouthTrends campaign, here is a final word of caution: Today's young people cannot be judged by the yardsticks of previous generations. This first section of the book has focused on the elements that make products appealing to youth, and now we'll detail some of the most common and serious mistakes marketers make in advertising and promoting to young people.

> **1.** Portraying stereotypes of how young people act and look.
>
> **2.** Misusing the language of young people.
>
> **3.** Being insensitive to diversity of race, sex, and ethnicity.

4. Receiving negative publicity about the corporation or its product.

5. Linking a product to an inappropriate spokesperson.

6. Placing standard ads in youth-oriented mediums.

7. Staying away from the high school or college campus.

8. Sponsoring a contest or event that is not connected with the product.

9. Changing advertisements too rapidly.

10. Failing to maintain a continuing, youth-appealing impression in all advertisements and promotions.

Mistake Number 1: Portraying stereotypes of how young people act and look. As we mentioned in Chapter 3, presenting stereotypical images of young people is a very common error, and one that can do real damage to a product. Marketing campaigns should strive for realism—precision—in capturing the ways that young people actually act toward their peers, their siblings, their parents, and other authority figures. The fact that young people do not view themselves in the same way that adults see them further complicates the job of creating ads that speak to the youth market. For example, Panasonic's "Take the Music With You" advertisement portrays young people as hyperactive, devil-may-care, silly, and weird. But even less obvious diversions from reality can make an ad seem insulting to youth.

The stereotyping problem often begins with the selection of models. Unless a company is in the fashion industry or an ad's scenario requires extremes in dress, it is not advisable to feature

models in wild, outlandish outfits—even if young people sometimes do wear such styles of clothing. An example is Maxell
Tapes' ad that has its models dressed in bizarre clothing with
severe haircuts, characteristic of the punk style. The reason for
avoiding these unusual fashions is that you can easily turn off
a large segment of the intended market by linking a product to
the style of dress of a particular, nonmainstream group of
young people.

But by using the most current clothing items that are popular
with the average young person, marketers can help connect a
product to what is contemporary, exciting, and trendy. Of
course, a company may choose to sidestep problems by not
portraying young people in lifestyle or slice-of-life ads. After all,
as we will explain in Chapter 8, there are many other ways to
reach youth, including the use of certain celebrities, humor, sex,
and music.

Mistake Number 2: Misusing the language of young people.
This mistake is related to the first one, but youth language is
so frequently misused in ads that it deserves special emphasis.
First of all, many companies "talk down" to young people in
ads. Certain terms describing young people, such as *teens, children,* and *kids,* will clearly appear condescending. Some ads
address their young audience in the same way that parents talk
to children.

Secondly, an ad can ironically seem patronizing if it attempts
to employ the most current youth expressions. One problem is
that young people's language changes constantly. If an ad in-
corporates terms from the late 1970s and early 1980s, or even
from last year, it will seem dated. The obsolete slang will prove
to young people that the company really does not know how
to talk to them, and its product will appear out of fashion.
Therefore, in general, it is safer and more effective to avoid the
latest slang, and instead use appropriate youth phrasings,
pauses, inflections, emphases, and so on.

Both of these problems are evident in R. J. Reynolds' public service advertisement, "How to Handle Peer Pressure," which encourages young people *not* to smoke. This print ad gives specific suggestions on how to respond to a friend who encourages a young person to try cigarettes. Although the intention of the ad is good, it fails miserably at imitating how youth actually speak, using both inappropriate expressions and sentence structure. The phrasings are just what teenagers imagine that their parents would tell them to say.

Mistake Number 3: Being insensitive to diversity of race, sex, and ethnicity. If several young people are to appear in a nationally run ad, a reasonable percentage must be of each sex and of various racial/ethnic backgrounds. Today's young person typically does not live in a single-sex apartment or dormitory and does not attend a single-sex school. Almost always, he or she will have acquaintances of different races and be accustomed to going out with these varied groups of friends. Hence, for an ad to seem true to life, it must reflect this new reality.

Furthermore, failure to acknowledge ethnic diversity may damage a company's reputation among the growing population of minorities, who are developing increasing spending power. Given the continuing success of advertising agencies that target minority markets, such as Byron Lewis's Uniworld Advertising, ethnic advertising clearly is an important area of interest to companies of all consumer goods. Ethnic and gender balances in ads are easily achieved, will not alienate young white people, and will be of significant interest to members of minority groups. Thus, increased sensitivity to the diversity of American life should be of concern to any advertiser trying to target American youth.

Mistake Number 4: Receiving negative publicity about the corporation or its product. Their swing toward conservatism does not mean that young people are unconcerned about a corporation's image. For example, youth perceptions of Nestlé (and thus all Nestlé chocolate products) were damaged by the company's dispute with international-aid groups about its baby formula's link to infant deaths in the Third World. Dow's image continues to suffer from its involvement in Vietnam and the ensuing Agent Orange lawsuits. The same is true of companies that continue their support of the South African economy.

But even beyond such major public-relations problems, young people take press criticisms of corporations quite seriously. When Coca-Cola changed its formula, many young people were angered by the company's lack of concern for its devoted customers. Such negative impressions have real consequences on the purchasing patterns of youth, since young people are especially conscious of products' popularity and acceptability.

Mistake Number 5: Linking a product to an inappropriate spokesperson. The popularity of celebrities quickly rises and falls among young people. For example, one of the best-loved musical groups in the early 1980s was the J. Geils Band, but by 1984, the group had faded from the pop music charts. As well, polls indicated that football quarterback Joe Montana was greatly admired by young men in 1984 and 1985. However, by the time he was featured in Hershey's "All-Time Greats" commercials, his poor performance had caused his popularity to fade. Clearly, the timing of advertisements is critical to the success of celebrity endorsement.

Still, even a celebrity with continuing high popularity might be inappropriate to endorse a product. For example, Ford Motors sponsored the rock concerts of soap-opera-star-turned-singer Rick Springfield. Unfortunately, the performer's concerts were principally attended by pre-teenage girls, an audience of extremely limited interest to this automobile company. Choice of a celebrity spokesperson can dramatically effect the image of a product among young people, but the potential for incredible success is as great as it is for dismal failure. See Chapter 8 for a further discussion of spokespeople.

Mistake Number 6: Placing standard ads in youth-oriented mediums. As was discussed in Chapter 6 on the six Youth-

Trends Approaches, unless the "Pepsi Approach" or the "MTV Approach" are being utilized, it is inadvisable to use general advertisements to reach the youth market. Young people often will not respond to standard advertisements, even ones shown on television shows or in magazines aimed primarily at youth. If the ad is not appealing to youth or if young people are not sure to believe that the product is for them, being in the right place will not solve the problem of product image.

In fact, using a standard ad for the youth market can do more harm than good. For example, as we have mentioned, a Volkswagen ad featuring a middle-aged couple and their two young children often appears in *Rolling Stone* and other youth-oriented magazines. This ad, seemingly created for the general consumer market, certainly has reached the young adult consumer—but has given them the impression that this product is not meant for them.

Mistake Number 7: Staying away from the high school or college campus. Certainly, a marketer can effectively reach the youth market through a nationwide advertising campaign or a significant promotional event, such as a $1 million giveaway. However, nothing can substitute for being in the same place as most young people are throughout the day—in school.

A company can reach high schools or college campuses through event sponsorships, educational programs, advertisements in specialized magazines, or any of the other methods reviewed in Chapter 13. But whichever approach is chosen, this type of personal attention to the needs and interests of youth will most often be well remembered.

Mistake Number 8: Sponsoring a contest or event that is not connected with the product. Developing a contest and sponsoring an event are two important ways to reach the youth market. However, young people already are bombarded with these corporate sponsorships. As a result, the only ones distinctly remembered are unique and especially creative ones, those that clearly link the product to the promotion. If a product is just one of a large group of prizes awarded in a contest or, worse, only tangentially related to the sponsored event, the effectiveness of these promotional efforts will be quite limited. For example, Honda sponsored rock concerts by the musician Sting but received little, if any, notice for its efforts because, unlike Pontiac's sponsorship of Hall and Oates, the company neither promoted itself at the concerts nor linked the sponsorship to advertisements or contests.

Many companies, eager to capture the young consumer, agree to sponsor any popular rock concert or sporting event; they provide free products for any contest advertised in youth-focused magazines. However, by spending a little more time but not much more money, companies can link their products to contests or events that more effectively reach the most likely young consumers. Specific methods for developing such promotions are discussed in Chapters 10 and 11.

Mistake Number 9: Changing advertisements too rapidly. In our interviews with scores of individuals in advertising firms and corporate marketing departments, we kept hearing the same remark repeatedly: The first group to get tired of an advertisement is the agency that developed it and the client itself. If a company is successful in creating an entertaining ad, young people will be pleased to see it on television or in magazines. Young people get a kick out of watching their favorite ads, almost as much as they enjoy watching their favorite television programs; they talk about such ads and sometimes even incorporate their lines into conversations.

Unfortunately, some of the most memorable and effective advertisements are no longer on the air. For example, when asked about their favorite commercials, young people often name Wendy's humorous "Where's the Beef?" ads, despite the fact that these commercials have not be played for several years. Many complained about how quickly those ads were changed. Of course, young people do get tired of ads, but there is no reason that the most popular ones cannot return to television or magazines after several months of absence.

Mistake Number 10: Failing to maintain a continuing, youth-appealing impression in all advertisements and promotions. As Keith Reinhard, chairman and chief executive officer of Needham Harper Worldwide Advertising, explains, "The essence of salesmanship is to create a series of positive impressions. Memory recall of a particular advertisement or promotional campaign may be good among youth, but if the image is negative they will not buy your product." Given the continuing success of such annoying commercials as Wisk detergent's "Ring Around the Collar," memorability may be enough to sell a product when marketing to adults. But this is rarely the case in selling to youth. For example, the coffee industry's commercial "Coffee for the Young Achiever" was memorable to many young people—but it only reinforced the negative views that they have about coffee drinkers. It did little to encourage consumption and a lot to encourage snide remarks about so-called "coffee achievers."

To reach the youth market, a company must be concerned about how young people perceive its product. Youth are sensitive even to modest changes in positioning. Thus, to be successful, each ad must support a company's principal marketing strategy and not undercut its impact with conflicting images that raise doubts in the minds of young consumers about whether the product is right for them.

Clearly, knowing what *not* to do when creating advertisements and promotions for youth is just the first step in creating a successful YouthTrends campaign—but it is an essential step. The following chapters will provide guidance on what affirmative steps companies have taken to create youth-appealing campaigns. But avoiding these ten mistakes form the crucial foundation on which any highly successful program must be based.

8

ESSENTIAL ELEMENTS OF YOUTH APPEAL: HUMOR, SEX, MUSIC, AND CELEBRITIES

There are three things that are criminal in youth advertising: If the product does not measure up, if you lie in your ads, or if you bore people to death.

—Roger Enrico,
president of Pepsi-Cola U.S.A.

*I*n this chapter, we'll discuss the most important elements that make ads entertaining or appealing to young consumers—humor, sex, and music—when conveyed by the right spokespeople. One of these three features is almost always part of a successful YouthTrends advertisement.

The Dos and Don'ts of Humor

While the use of humor in advertising can score very well with young people and with youth-conscious adults, it requires exactness and care in execution. Today's young people prefer humor that is offbeat, mildly irreverent, somewhat absurd, cheeky, witty but not overly intellectual, sometimes slapstick, occasionally self-deprecating, even pushy and slightly obnoxious, but never too obvious. These humor styles are often different from those that appeal to many adults. According to Brandon Tartikoff, president of NBC, such television programs as *Late Night with David Letterman* and *Saturday Night Live* perfectly reflect this type of comedy, and their cult followings illustrate how devoted young people are to their kind of humor.

Of course, the comedic style used on these television programs is much more extreme than could be used in most advertising. For example, although young people enjoy presentations of bizarre situations or parodies of familiar personality types on comedy shows, they could easily find the same humor condescending and demeaning in advertising.

Humor in advertising is especially successful with youth, as John Eighmey, senior vice-president of Young & Rubicam, explains because they remember it and love to repeat it. If the humor works, youth will tell the joke over and over; this is not usually true for adults. Not only does this make people more aware of an advertisement and more interested to see it in the future, but it makes a product "in" among young people.

The following list of dos and don'ts presents guidelines for using humor in ads, based on the research of our consulting firm, of advertising companies, and of major corporations. We'll also offer case studies of some of the most successful and unsuccessful humorous advertisements.

DO use humor to rejuvenate a product's image among youth and youth-oriented adults. Humor can revive consumer perception of a brand that is considered dull, old-fashioned, and undifferentiated from its competitors. One success story, according to Peter Barnet, vice-president of Ogilvy & Mather and supervisor of the General Foods account, is the humorous campaign for Maxwell House Coffee, titled "Young Comedians," which has been shown in test markets around the country.

The commercials are targeted at fifteen- to twenty-three-year-olds with a particular emphasis on the fifteen- to nineteen-year-old age group. As mentioned earlier, each of the several commercials features a different young stand-up comic, some of whom are already popular among youth. Each comedian tells jokes and humorous stories pointing out that drinking coffee is a rite of passage into adulthood, a badge of maturity. Not only are most of the jokes funny, but they have the same central goal: to convince young people that coffee is a significant beverage option for adults. They reassure youth that coffee, like soft drinks, fits into the lifestyle of a contemporary individual.

DON'T use off-target humor. Adults might excuse a bad joke; youth are not so forgiving, and off-base humor can seriously damage a product's image. Unfortunately, major corporations frequently run humorous ads that simply miss their marks. For example, a 1986 Burger King campaign centered on a character called "Herb," who was supposed to be the only person who had never tasted the Whopper. The concept forced people to go too far in suspending their disbelief. The nerdy Herb, complete with horn-rimmed glasses and high-water pants seemed lost and pathetic and, thus, failed to strike a humorous chord among young consumers. Moreover, young people considered the gimmick dated and far-fetched. The Herb campaign obviously cost Burger King a great deal in advertising expenses, but returned little in the form of improved consumer perception.

DO use humor which is built around a brand, emphasizing important product attributes. Since humor is the most memorable part of the ad, it should be used to make the central points. Three excellent commercial campaigns from the beer, automotive, and snack-food industries illustrate this point.

William Howell, president of the Miller Brewing Company, spoke about the two types of Miller Lite commercials: One features sports celebrities who have encountered some humorous situation while coming to a bar to have a Miller Lite; the other portrays an exaggerated argument over why they drink Miller Lite. Both versions make the same points about the product—that it tastes great and that it is less filling—the two most important reasons that men will give for drinking a light beer. The quality of being "less filling" is underscored, since most beer-drinking males prefer not to admit that they are dieting. The ads have made their claims so attractively and persuasively that Miller Lite now outsells the regular Miller beer.

In the automotive industry, Subaru has used humor especially effectively. The company's 1986 campaign showed some of the most outrageous, but believable trials people put their cars through. People were shown cramming too much luggage into their cars, kicking and slamming the doors shut, and running over trashcans, to the tune of "You Always Hurt the One You Love." Since most auto commercials show a car being driven on a winding country road or on a racetrack, Subaru's ads were visually distinctive. Moreover, they clearly presented the idea that Subaru is an all-accepting vehicle that can withstand the toughest everyday wear and tear.

In the snack foods industry, Eric Weber, executive vice president and executive creative director of Dancer Fitzgerald Sample Advertising, explained how the campaign for Bonkers, a chewy fruit candy, used dramatic visual humor to highlight the candy's fruity taste. Giant pieces of fruit were shown falling from the sky onto a tired middle-aged mother, her husband, and her son. Young people found this commercial, like the two previously mentioned, easy to remember and enjoyable to watch. The humor worked because it related to the product's principal claim: that Bonkers has a big fruit taste.

DON'T use humor to advertise unconventional brands. This can make young people uncomfortable about how their peers might view them if they use such a product. For example, given the predominance of Pepsi and Coca-Cola in the soft drink industry, RC Cola has suffered from the perception that it is not a "mainstream" soft drink, and its humorous commercials contribute to that unfortunate characterization. Using the line, "Some people like Coke. Some people like Pepsi. But some people go out of their way for the taste of RC," the ads present some bizarre examples of RC drinkers. One shows Russian peasants, somewhere out in frozen Siberia, hiding with their RC from evil government authorities who demand uniformity in the choice of soft drinks. Many young people already had reservations about trying RC Cola. The ad, with its Russian peasants and weird situation, only confirmed what they had felt: They would probably neither like the product nor be comfortable trying it.

DO use humor in slice-of-life commercials. Young people consider humor a natural part of any interaction, and its use can give slice-of-life ads a current, more realistic quality. In Shake-N-Bake's "What's for Dinner?" commercial, a "typical" family sits down to a dinner of new-recipe Shake-N-Bake. The parents and children, make quips and sarcastic comments regarding the product's new recipe. For example, when the mother explains that they are having a new recipe for dinner, the son asks, "Does that like make us guinea pigs?" The mother responds in a deadpan tone, "No, your table manners do that." The commercial concludes with neither of the teenage children willing to answer a ringing telephone so as not to give up the last piece of chicken. This humorous repartee between parent and child in a mundane setting over a common product makes Shake-N-Bake seem a part of real family life. The humor adds a sense of realism to what otherwise would be a slice of life with which few could identify.

DON'T try to imitate or spoof popular television sitcoms or movie comedies. When an ad is based on a popular comedy, it raises the expectations of the young viewer. As a result, unless the ad is nearly as good as its model—which is usually impossible—young people will be disappointed. For example, young people believed that a Coors beer campaign, titled "Silver Bullet," was trying to simulate the style of the popular NBC comedy "Cheers." Although both the commercials and the program took place in a bar, the resemblance stopped there.

Not surprisingly, the ad could not rise to the same level of witty humor as the sitcom and so it came off looking like a poor imitation.

DO poke fun at competitors in ads. In talking with one another, young people often use sarcasm and friendly raillery. Thus, youth can appreciate well-delivered gibes between competing companies. In fact, humor is probably the best way to present product challenges to youth; simply stating the results of a consumer test is, in most cases, neither interesting nor convincing.

Some of the most effective humorous attacks have been used in the soft-drink industry. For example, in 1985, Coke changed its formula, releasing its New Coke, and then was forced to reintroduce the original old or Classic Coke. Pepsi responded with television and radio ads satirizing the many new names of Coke, showing a consumer, confused over which Coke was which, instead deciding to have a Pepsi. Coke responded in kind with a commercial showing a man on a desert island emptying a bottle of Pepsi and then using the bottle to send an SOS for a six-pack of Coke. Using this style of biting humor against competitors can make a brand seem fun and confident.

DON'T use the same humorous situation too long. Overexposure can destroy the positive impression that an ad originally engendered. Humor in advertising wears out much more quickly as a device than, for example, sex or music.

For example, Bud Light beer held on to its clever "Give Me a Light" campaign so long that the idea went stale. These ads used visual humor to remind consumers to ask for Bud Light, not just any light beer. They showed a person coming up to a bar, saying, "Give me a light." The bartender responded by giving the patron the wrong sort of light—a lamp, flashlight, torch, and so on.

Initially the ads were funny, quite memorable, and extremely effective at making their point. However in order to show some variation, the "light" the bartender offered got so extreme that some young people, who were not familiar with the campaign from its outset did not understand why the bar patron was being given an x-ray or a flaming hoop. For those who did follow the campaign after about a year, the gag lost its effect; it was predictable, overly slapstick, and unimaginative.

DO use humor to distinguish a brand from the competition. Gary Susnjara, chairman of Dancer Fitzgerald Sample Advertising, examined one of the most celebrated uses of advertising humor that his agency produced for Wendy's, featuring such classic ads as "Where's the Beef?" and the "Russian Fashion Show." To differentiate the Number 3 hamburger chain from its larger competitors, McDonald's and Burger King, the agency developed commercials with a humorous and feisty style. In "Where's the Beef?" the outrageous senior citizen Clara Peller complained about the size of the hamburger patty at the other fast-food restaurants. Her line became part of everyday speech; even Walter Mondale used the line to criticize opponents in his campaign for the presidency. Next, Dancer Fitzgerald took on the competition's inability to satisfy the particular taste requirements of customers with the "Russian Fashion Show." In this ad, a fat, matronly Soviet woman modeled the same drab blue dress as eveningwear, beachwear, and so on. These and the other ads in the campaign pointed to the product superiority of Wendy's—and they worked. According to Video Storyboard Tests/ Campaign Monitor, although McDonald's was outspending Wendy's by 3 to 1 during the period of this campaign, the Wendy's ads were remembered by more individuals. Furthermore, the ads were an important contributor to the 27 percent increase in Wendy's sales during the period and fully established a unique identity for the chain.

Once it is determined that humor is the appropriate way to convey a particular message to youth, the only way to assure that this message is on target is simply to test it with young people. In the next section, we see that, unlike with humor, a major conflict exists on the appropriate way to utilize sex in youth advertising.

Youth and Sex: Conflicting Views

What do such diverse products as Nestlé's chocolate, Calvin Klein fashion wear, Noxzema shave cream, Pepsi-Cola, Coty perfume, Salem and Lucky Strike cigarettes, Sheer Elegance panty hose, and Ultrabrite toothpaste all have in common? These are just some of the many products that use sex to reach youth and the youth-conscious adult. The research of our consulting firm and major advertising agencies reveal two conflicting views on the use of sex in advertising aimed at the fifteen- to twenty-five-year-old market.

Penelope Queen, executive vice-president of research of Dancer Fitzgerald Sample Advertising/New York summarizes the first view: "Young people have been exposed to a great deal of sexual imagery on television and in movies. As a result, they are more comfortable with sex than their parents are." Moreover, since young people like to think of themselves as mature, contemporary, and liberated, they are less likely to be shocked by the use of sex to sell a product.

The most important benefits of using sex in advertising are quite apparent. First, sexual images are eye-catching and memorable for both young men and young women. Young people look for entertainment value in advertisements, and often sexual images can provide such enjoyment. For example, according to Dave Vadehra, president of Video Storyboard Tests, Calvin Klein's provocative underwear ad, featuring a well-built young man wearing only white briefs, edged out the long-running Marlboro man ad, a sex symbol for two decades, as the most noticed print advertisement in 1985. Women, who actually make most men's underwear purchases, obviously liked to look at the print ad of this attractive male model.

Second, using sex in advertising often gives a product an attractive, exclusive, "in" image. As Burt Manning, chairman and chief executive officer of J. Walter Thompson Advertising/ USA puts it, "Young people are trying to express their own sexuality and to get esteem from their peers and members of the opposite sex." Products that are perceived to be "sexy" usually reflect favorably upon the people that use them. Young people especially enjoy owning a brand that makes them seem more alluring to members of the opposite sex.

On the other hand, several important problems arise in using sex in advertising, especially in targeting the F.L.Y.E.R.S. market. For one thing, while young people are comfortable with sex and not easily shocked, they are growing more conservative in their views on sexual images in all mediums, from television to movies to print. Young people want to see more romantic, sensual representations instead of pictures of partially naked bodies.

Young people are also offended by ads that seem to show the sexual exploitation of either sex. Young women are especially sensitive to this problem.

Moreover, the potential for backlash against the overuse of sex in advertising, particularly in television commercials, is growing among young people. It is unlikely that the industries that commonly use sex in ads, such as fashion clothing or perfumes and colognes, will be affected by this new conservatism. But when sex is unrelated to a product or rarely used to advertise it, young people often find sexual images offensive or insulting to their intelligence. As Larry Light, executive vice-president of Ted Bates Advertising, explains, "Using sex, just for the sake of catching attention, usually will not be effective."

For example, Nestlé's chocolate's 1985 television campaign "Sweet Dreams You Can't Resist" featured a woman gently cradling a man's neck and a chocolate bar, beside a deep pool of melted chocolate, backed by a sensual musical theme. This use of sensuality to sell chocolate bars was considered by some young people to be overly manipulative, while others found it ridiculous.

Sexual images typically appear in lifestyle ads—ads that present a kind of life that young people can fantasize about leading. But when an ad features exceptionally attractive models with impossibly perfect bodies, young consumers may have trouble imagining themselves living out the ad's scenario or using the product promoted. Young people, especially, have a lot of self-doubts and insecurities; instead of dreaming about being so popular or looking so good, they might decide that a product is not for them. This failure to identify with the advertised "lifestyle" occurs most often when the model used is the same sex as the primary purchaser.

As well, overt sexuality or displays of bare skin, can be distracting to the young consumer, who may remember the model or the scene, but not the product or the claims made. It is essential to remember that the star of any ad must *be* the product, not its good-looking spokesperson. The problem of selecting appropriate models for youth-targeted ads will be discussed later in this chapter.

With these cautions in mind, we will examine the two major trends in sex-oriented advertising today, analyzing some successful and off-the-mark campaigns.

EXPLICITNESS VERSUS ROMANCE

In recent years, ads have grown far more sexually explicit, displaying considerably more skin, frequently showing men as sex objects, presenting women as the aggressors in sexual encounters, and suggesting previously taboo subjects including group sex and sadomasochism. Some of these approaches have been very effective. For example, Jordache Jeans has created some very sexy television commercials, featuring a young man who is naked above the waist, wearing tight blue jeans; in the background plays the now-familiar theme "You've Got the Look—the Jordache Look." In one ad the model lies at the ocean shore, in another he slowly rises from a pool of water, while in yet another he seductively plays a saxophone on a steamy, hot afternoon.

Noxzema Shave Cream, using the slogan "For Him—For Her" in a 1985 campaign, showed a young man and women together in the bathroom; she was showering while he was shaving, wearing only a towel around his waist—a scene that hints strongly at the sexual relationship between them.

While these ads present obvious sexual images, there is a growing trend among advertisers toward more sensual and romantic depictions that are much less explicit and revealing. Yet, as the following examples illustrate, such ads can be just as eye-catching and pulse-quickening as those discussed above. The commercial for Coty Musk Patchouli perfume presents sexual activity as it might have been shown in an 1940s movie: Clothes are strewn on the floor, throughout a darkened apartment, leading to a closed bedroom door. The intimation is clear but more subtle than, say, the Noxzema shower scene. Sheer Elegance panty hose has taken a similar approach in its commercial titled "Helicopter." The ad shows an Asian woman in a black dress preparing to meet her date—who finally arrives in a helicopter that lands on the roof of her apartment building. Without any obvious display of sex, both commercials effectively appeal to the fantasies of young women. They create the illusion that these products are part of the lifestyle of enticing, desirable women.

Of course, an obvious implication that using a particular product will help attract the opposite sex can backfire. Especially for young people, such ads often seem heavy-handed and unbelievable, and the product's image can suffer the consequences of this negative perception. For example, Ultrabrite toothpaste has used slice-of-life commercials featuring a person who is ignored by an attractive member of the opposite sex. But after using Ultrabrite (represented visually by a blonde model in blue spandex tights who zaps the person with her Ultrabrite gun) the unrequited lover finds romance. Unfortunately, young people did not find this ad humorous and instead felt that it insulted their intelligence.

Nevertheless, our polls of youth find that romantic sensuality can be an effective device for an advertiser who finds the blatant use of sexuality inappropriate.

Many major companies have used one or both of these sexual approaches in their campaigns aimed at the youth market, with varying degrees of success. Some of the most notable advertisers who use sexual images are Calvin Klein and the makers of diet soft drinks.

Calvin Klein's Obsession. The ads for Calvin Klein's perfume, Obsession, illustrate that explicit sexual imagery may or may not involve obvious nudity. The print ads for this perfume are a shocking display of bare skin, one of them showing three men and one woman, discernibly nude, intimately entangled. The television commercials, by contrast, are minidramas suggesting sexual violence, obsessive desire, and lust between a pubescent boy and a much older woman. In these commercials, all the models are clothed; the viewer sees nothing more then a brief kiss or slap on the face.

While the print ads actually show raw sex and passion, the television commercials suggest them. In fact, some may feel that the implications made in these commercials are more scandalous than what actually is seen in print. Nevertheless, young people have been fascinated by both advertisements.

Calvin Klein's Obsession ads clearly demonstrate that bare skin is not necessarily more interesting or erotic than situations that just suggest sexuality. To use sex effectively, ads must draw the viewers' eyes to all that there is to see; then, by sparking the viewers' imaginations and fantasies about the scene depicted, they can deliver a high-voltage message.

Diet Coke, Diet Pepsi, and Diet Sprite. Over the last three years, advertisements for diet soft drinks have progressed from using blatant sex to creating lifestyle images that emphasize youth, vitality, life choices, even humor. The 1984 television commercials for Diet Sprite and Diet Pepsi illustrate this former sexual emphasis. For example, in the Diet Sprite ad, a beautiful blonde in a white bikini is shown carrying a can of soda. The voices of two unseen young women are heard, obviously envious of the blonde's fantastic figure. The Diet Pepsi commercial, which uses the line, "Now you see it, now you don't," presents numerous quick-cut views of svelte young women and a few men, usually in revealing bathing suits. Both ads clearly are targeted at the diet-conscious female.

However, Diet Coke took a very different tack, to position itself as a soft drink for the active young person of either sex. To do so it developed a series of fun-loving, vibrant lifestyle ads using quick cuts of good-looking models and celebrities, both male and female, almost always clothed, minimizing the emphasis on dieting. The bare skin displays of the other diet soft drinks may have caught the attention of young men, but the feminine-focused ads did not get them to buy the product. Moreover, the ads' body emphasis positioned the product too narrowly. Coke wanted to reach out not just to part of the diet beverage market but to the *entire* beverage market.

In response, in 1985, Diet Pepsi produced several soft-sell commercials including one featuring Democratic vice-presidential candidate Geraldine Ferraro. Using unusual camera angles and closeups, the commercials simply placed the product in appealing situations, while preserving a feminine touch. The product was displayed throughout the ad, but its name was only mentioned by an announcer at the conclusion. In 1986, Pepsi-Cola upped the ante again with an even more unisex approach: a humorous ad featuring comedian Billy Crystal and another called "Library," using an upbeat theme, "No Other Taste Attracts So Much Attention," which showed college students starting an impromptu party with Diet Pepsi in front of the library.

This progression in soft-drink ads has not been spurred by changing social mores. It has developed because, in some cases, the obvious use of sex has the drawback of pigeon-holing a product in too narrow a market. The emphasis on naked skin made many soft drink ads seems too feminine and too diet-conscious; for other products, sexy ads may seem too male-oriented, too frivolous, or too promiscuous. It's important to consider that an overtly sexy image may not be broad enough to capture all potential consumers.

However, unlike sex, music almost always is appropriate for use in youth advertising. In the following section, we analyze what kind of music is best and how to effectively incorporate it into a campaign.

Music: Image-Building Sounds

In advertising, music always has been used as "emotional short-hand" to evoke a desired mood. Like humor and sex, music can make an ad more interesting and even more memorable, by linking sounds with words (such as the product's name and its slogan). Moreover, young people have always been conscious—and adults are becoming more so—of the style of music used in commercials. In fact, according to Jane Maas, president of Muller Jordan Weiss Advertising, a recent study shows that upbeat, current music can effectively reach people of all ages. Music that is considered either too traditional or too juvenile can have a negative effect on how a product is perceived by consumers.

But, specifically, what kind of music is best? Clearly rock music is central to the youth culture; it creates a common language among all young people. Furthermore, an awareness

of the importance of rock music has grown throughout the
entire society. Even such traditional news magazines as *Time*
and *Newsweek* have devoted cover stories to rock personalities.
Not surprisingly, pop/rock music has had and will continue to
have an impact on advertising, not only to the F.L.Y.E.R.S.
market but also to the wider adult market.

The success of MTV has also influenced how music is
adapted for commercials. Certainly, many of the advertisers on
that music video channel have developed special commercial
executions to fit in with the programming format. But even
beyond this, as Robert Pittman, president of MTV Networks,
explains, MTV has placed a heavier burden on all musical
advertisements aimed at youth and the youth-oriented adult.
Through its rock videos, MTV has demonstrated to marketers
how powerful and attractive the combination of stirring visuals
and popular music can be. In addition, MTV and shows like
Miami Vice, have raised the expectations of youth as to what
can be done with the television medium regarding the use of
music. As Burt Manning, chairman and chief executive officer
of J. Walter Thompson Advertising/USA, notes, "There has
been a dramatic change in what is desirable in music in advertising." These changes are examined below with particular emphasis placed on the adaptation of popular songs and the
creation of original musical themes.

ADAPTING POPULAR SONGS

Using the music or both the music and lyrics from a popular
song seems to be the perfect way to give a product more contemporary positioning and to catch the interest of young people.

The song—the mood it creates, its beat, its musical style,
even its performer—must project the proper image for the
product. One of the most successful connections between a
product and songs/performers was Pepsi-Cola's link with two

of rock music's most important stars: Michael Jackson and Lionel Richie. In the commercials, each of these individuals performed one of his hit songs with new lyrics based on Pepsi's slogan, "The Choice of a New Generation." Richard Blossom, vice-president of marketing at Pepsi-Cola USA, notes, "What is really 'hot' can be hot among everyone." Pepsi chose two of 1984's hottest singing stars, musicians who had great popularity both among youth and with the entire population. Moreover, the use of contemporary music demonstrated to consumers that the product was on the cutting edge, that it had youthful appeal. This image was communicated through the advertisements themselves, as well as through the media coverage of these events. These ads firmly entrenched Pepsi as the soft drink of choice among youth and the youth-oriented adult. But whether a company can afford the year's hottest rock star or not, the following cautions must be observed.

Firstly, even a major hit record may no longer be popular by the time an ad is aired. In fact, some exceptionally popular songs get almost immediate overexposure on the radio. Overfamiliarity will certainly diminish the effectiveness of such a song, especially when used in a radio commercial, even if its lyrics are altered. Furthermore, musical styles change from year to year—the popularity of many rock stars falls as quickly as it rises. Connecting a product with a performer or a sound that has already come and gone will only emphasize how out of touch the advertiser is with young people's interests.

Interestingly, it has become common to use popular songs, not just from last year's Top Forty but also from the 1950s and 1960s. Sunkist Orange soda has successfully used the Beach Boys' "Good Vibrations," a hit from 1966. Why has the strategy worked? Because the song is upbeat; it is still popular, often played on the radio during the summer months; because the Beach Boys made a comeback in the early 1980s, giving major performances at the Fourth of July celebrations in Washington, D.C.; because the commercial is set at the beach, making the group particularly appropriate; and because the lyrics are slightly modified to repeat the product's name. Thus, how recently or long ago the song was recorded is not as important as how the song and its performers are perceived at the time that the advertisement is actually aired.

Secondly, without appropriate visuals to go along with the song, a commercial may still fail. Young people will immediately compare an advertisement's audiovisual combination to the images of MTV. If a record has already hit its peak, the commercial's visuals must give the song new life to make it worth watching. The Pepsi commercials, for example, were filmed as if Michael Jackson and Lionel Richie actually were performing in concert. Del Monte vegetables, too, revived an old song, Donna Summer's "She Works Hard for the Money," for its ad titled "You Work Hard For Your Body." The ad presented muscularly trim male swimmers and elegantly lithe female dancers moving to the song's new lyrics, and so linked the product itself to eye-catching youthful vigor and fitness.

Third, an advertiser must ensure that its product's attributes, not the popular song or its performer, are the stars of the commercial. The lyrics, whether as originally written or as modified for the ad, must reflect back on the product. One fine illustration of this point, using original song lyrics, is the television commercial for Hershey's New Trail granola bars. As Bill Weed, director of international accounts for Ogilvy & Mather, describes it, an unseen announcer asks teenagers questions about the granola bars, and they respond by lip-synching the words to popular songs from the 1950s. For example, the announcer asks, "What would you do if your mom ran out of New Trail bars?" and the teenager sings back, "Nothing can stop the Duke of Earl"—in the voice of the original 1950s artist. These commercials have produced a phenomenal response in sales. Here, the songs are not the focal point of the advertisement; they are used to attract the interest of the listener and to make positive comments about the product.

As the above examples show, it can be hard—but very effective—to use a popular song to help target a product to the youth market. Yet, some advertisers try to escape these problems by commissioning original themes, as we'll discuss in the next section.

CREATING AN ORIGINAL MUSICAL THEME

Developing original music for an ad offers certain advantages over using a popular song. For one thing, an original theme can give a product a unique, more perfectly targeted image. Although a product does not gain the benefits of being linked with a popular song, it also does not suffer from any negative impressions that young consumers might have of a certain piece of music. Unlike a popular song, original music will not distract the listener from the product's attributes. In addition, an ad presentation using original music will not be limited by having to fit into a form created for artistic purposes rather than for selling the product. Campbell's Soup, for example, created an original theme for a two-minute music video that runs on MTV. The message of the soft-sell ad is an extension of Campbell's overall corporate campaign to promote consumer well-being. The theme focuses on exercise, nutrition, stress reduction, and safety precautions, such as avoiding drunk driving. Lee Jeans, too, developed original music to promote its image of fashionability and sex appeal in its campaign "Lee Sensation." In two similar commercials, one featuring a young man and the other a young woman, the song suggestively inquires, "Is it what s/he's got going or what s/he's got on?—Lee Sensation!" It would be difficult to find popular songs in which such ideas could be easily expressed in catchy lines.

Still, creating an original theme does present problems similar to those of adapting popular songs for commercials:

- It is difficult to compose music and write lyrics at the same creative level as top popular musicians; young people and youth-conscious adults might find the theme unappealing;

- It may not be easy to develop a theme that offers an appropriate image for the brand;

- The song itself must remain subordinate to the product and its characteristics;

- The visuals must successfully supplement and complement the song.

To receive a positive reaction from young people, an original theme might imitate the sound of popular music. Some of Levi's "501 Blues" jeans commercials, for example, feature the popular "rap" style, in which the performer sing/speaks words to the beat of the music. Farah's Generra clothing ad, "I Love You, 'Cause You're My Style" uses a Top Forty easy listening sound. Other themes are more energetic, kicky, and even danceable, such as Cheerios' "The Unsinkable Taste of Cheerios."

Other original songs try to go beyond just creating a mood. They work to connect a product with a particular kind of lifestyle. As already noted, Michelob's "Where You're Going You've Always Known It—Where You're Going It's Michelob" linked the beer with the yuppie lifestyle. However, the term *yuppie* now has entirely negative connotations, describing people who are self-centered and driven. Not surprisingly, after trying to capitalize on the yuppie concept, Michelob registered a 5 percent annual volume decline between 1980 and 1985. By contrast, Thomas W. Evans, deputy director of advertising and sales promotion for the U.S. Army Recruiting Command, explained how the Army's "Be All That You Can Be" campaign emphasizes the most positive career and lifestyle characteristics of young people, their peers, and their parents: pride, duty, service, hard work, challenge, and achievement. The appeal of the ideals expressed in this campaign certainly has been an important reason for the Army's recruiting success over the years.

Recently, some original songs have tried to create an all-American image for products—an image that is very well-received by young people at this time. Budweiser's theme "You Make America Work—And This Bud's for You" is combined with scenes of working life to accentuate feelings of pride about work and about the country. This commercial, in praising the American worker, has a particular appeal to the noncollege-educated young adult. For similar reasons, Chrysler's Plymouth division uses the line "The Pride Is Back—Born in America," in its ads. Unfortunately, unlike the Budweiser theme, this song does not mention the Plymouth brand name. Tests have shown that young people could recall the song and even the product category, but had a hard time remembering the brand being advertised.

Another major question in developing original music is selecting appropriate accompanying visuals, as well as a group to perform it. Naturally, the advantage of using an established popular song is having a major musical celebrity to add excitement to the ad. Yet, when an original song is created, an advertisement can combine the best possible musical presentation of product attributes with the implied celebrity endorsement of a top singer. In some of its commercials, Diet Coke's theme "Just for the Taste of It—Diet Coke" is sung by Grammy-award winner Whitney Houston, one of 1986's most popular performers. If a company cannot afford such stars, it might follow the example of Cherokee sportswear's "An American Original," an ad that simply imitates the style of a rock video, using a new rock group.

Established popular songs and original musical themes can both be used effectively by marketers in targeting youth. With a popular song, the product gains an association with a popular contemporary symbol, and young people will be attracted to the ad's pitch since it is linked to the music they enjoy. With an original theme song, the advertiser gains creative flexibility and greater ability to fashion an image for the product. Whichever approach is selected, music, like sex and humor, can make commercials more exciting and entertaining—the kinds of ads F.L.Y.E.R.S. will be likely to remember.

Celebrities and Models: Who Speaks to Youth?

Whether it is Michael Jackson for Pepsi-Cola or model Christie Brinkley for Noxell's Cover Girl makeup, the appropriate celebrity or spokesmodel is a crucial question in creating any advertisement for the youth market. Even minor mistakes in casting can dramatically alter an ad's effectiveness—and, with it, the product's image. Here we'll review some essential guidelines on choosing celebrities and models for youth-appealing campaigns.

CELEBRITIES

As was noted above, there seems to be a growing use of celebrities, especially those from the music world, in ads aimed at youth and the youth-conscious adult. For example, singing star Whitney Houston appears in a rock video–style commercial for Diet Coke, and the New Edition does the same for New Coke; Hall and Oates have done print ads for Pontiac Fiero, as has John Parr for Chams; Grace Jones, Devo, Lou Reed, and Adam Ant have appeared in television and print advertisements for Honda Scooters; and, as we have discussed, Michael Jackson, Lionel Richie, and Glenn Frey have performed in spectacular commercials for Pepsi.

But actors, sports heroes, and media personalities still receive their share of ad work: Bill Cosby for General Foods' Jell-O; Margot Kidder for Tab; Mary Lou Retton and Pete Rose for Wheaties; the Radio City Rockettes for Hanes' L'Eggs panty hose; Dr. Ruth Westheimer for Dr. Pepper; and Don Johnson, Michael J. Fox, Billy Crystal, and Geraldine Ferraro for Pepsi. Today, even cartoon characters get in on the act: Rocky the flying squirrel and Bullwinkle the moose have promoted Hershey's Kisses; while the lovesick skunk, Pepe Le Peu, sold McDonald's McDLT.

But two questions remain: Are celebrities effective at reaching consumers, particularly young consumers? And how does an advertiser best choose celebrities for these ads?

As Larry Light, executive vice-president at Ted Bates Advertising, notes "Young people do care about celebrities in advertising. They look for someone to emulate." Back in the 1960s and 1970s, when youth rebelled against the Establishment young people had few heroes and those heroes would not have appeared in commercials. But now, in the 1980s, a large majority of young people do have heroes, most of whom are in the fields of entertainment and sports. In an advertisement, these celebrities can help assure self-doubting young people that a brand is indeed popular and in fashion.

Indeed, celebrities can do wonders to enhance a product's image among youth. John Eighmey, senior vice-president at Young & Rubicam Advertising, explains, "The celebrity's personality can be used for the benefit of the product." For example, Honda used rock singers to boost youth awareness and interest in its Scooters. Although Grace Jones, Devo, Lou Reed, and Adam Ant do not have the following of a Lionel Richie or a Whitney Houston, these contemporary rock performers are excellent at establishing a youth-appealing mood in an ad. In fact, rock singers' connections to current music and the popular culture seem to allow them to make an even more dramatic impact on youth ads than can movie/television stars.

As unique personalities, these performers can make an ad appear trendy and chic, a perception that is easily transferred to the brand.

Of course, the expense of hiring a celebrity must be carefully considered, especially since the cost can range from tens of thousands to hundreds of thousands to even millions of dollars. But our research suggests that, for youth, a recognizable celebrity registers the product brand better than an unknown spokesperson. But since celebrity ads emphasize the stars themselves, they may not necessarily communicate the copy points better; but, if product awareness is an advertiser's goal, a celebrity can easily achieve it. Moreover, even if young people do not see such ads personally they will hear about them from their friends. Naturally an inappropriate celebrity will get the same kind of attention, but with the result that young people will want to avoid the product.

Choosing "appropriate" celebrities does not mean selecting stars who are relevant to the products; the crucial issue is whether they are popular among youth. Of course, a distinction must be made between celebrities used in lifestyle advertisements and those who give testimonials or product endorsements.

Most of the previously mentioned ads, including all of those featuring rock singers, were lifestyle advertisements. These ads sought to portray the product as being on the cutting edge and simply used current stars to help create that image. Beyond this link, there were no connections made between the personalities and the advertised products—not even intimations that the stars actually used the brands or preferred them to competing ones. In fact, the press reported that Michael Jackson, featured in Pepsi's campaign, does not drink soda at all. This revelation had no apparent impact on the success of the Pepsi commercials.

The Michael Jackson advertisements, like any effective celebrity ads, were transformed into *events*. For young people, seeing these commercials became as important as watching a favorite television program. Enthusiasm for these celebrity ads firmly entrenched Pepsi as the drink of choice among youth and youth-conscious adults. Thus, in lifestyle ads, the level of the star's popularity seems to be the critical factor in attracting young people to the brands being promoted.

For endorsements, however, the relationship of the celebrity to the product is much more significant. Beyond the problems posed by truth-in-advertising laws, young people typically are suspicious of testimonials. For an ad to be convincing, a star must either be something of an expert on the product's area or command a high level of respect from youth. For example, since Pete Rose commands such respect from his fans and is surely a consumer of Wheaties, he has been a persuasive spokesperson. Testimonials can also backfire. Young people still remember Bill Cosby's pitch for the great taste of "not too sweet" Coke, just before the formula was changed to make the product sweeter. This action by Coke recklessly damaged the credibility of a celebrity who has great youth appeal and who could have helped the company during the New Coke introduction.

It is difficult to determine what makes a certain celebrity right for a particular ad, but certain guidelines may be helpful. To begin with, celebrities, especially rock stars, rise and fall quite quickly in popularity with young fans. Hence, unless an advertiser can ensure that its commercials will air while the celebrity is at a peak of popularity, it is best to select stars (1) with long track records of media attention, (2) with a popular, weekly television series, or (3) who are enjoying or who have just completed a successful sports season. Wheaties, for example, used Mary Lou Retton just after her Olympic gold-medal performance and Pete Rose during his record-breaking batting season for its "What the Big Boys Eat" campaign. The ads helped boost sagging sales by capitalizing on these individuals' amazing (and current) athletic achievements.

Furthermore, simply putting young stars into advertisements is not a safe strategy. It is essential to research the range of perceptions youth has about any given celebrity. For example, although a poll of youth would likely find Brooke Shields as one of the best-known young stars, our research suggests that many older teenagers and most college students have a strong negative reaction toward her while younger teenagers have a more positive image. Thus, a campaign using Brooke Shields would have a narrower appeal than one using a different celebrity. Interestingly enough, in a 1985 survey run by *U.S. News & World Report* on the Top Twenty Heroes of young people, only one—Eddie Murphy—was under twenty-five years old.

A celebrity can become an effective centerpiece in a youth-appealing ad, but only if such factors as the star's talents, popularity, and personality are carefully assessed. Good research is essential for developing an advertisement that is both cost-efficient and effective at reaching youth. Some advertisers, whether to avoid the risks at using celebrities or to keep costs down, will prefer to use models in their campaigns. We'll examine this strategy and the ways to make it work in the next section.

MODELS

It may seem easier to select models for youth-oriented ads than to choose a celebrity endorser. In fact, however, the decision is just as critical, for a mistake in casting a spokesmodel can be equally as damaging to a product. The three major problems in choosing models are: (1) finding ones that represent young people realistically but effectively; (2) avoiding youth stereotypes; and (3) making sure models affirm the self-image of youth.

As Gary Susnjara, chairman of Dancer Fitzgerald Sample/ New York, explains, "People say that they want to see themselves in advertisements. But it is not true. They don't want to see people exactly like themselves because they want products to produce immediate good looks or popularity." Companies in the fashion business have always recognized this contradiction. Cover Girl makeup uses stunning models and Jordache jeans ads feature sexy men and women, with nearly "perfect" looks, to sell their products. Even Dove soap, according to Jane Maas, president of Muller Jordan Weiss Advertising, uses twentyish-looking models to appeal to the beauty concerns of middle-aged women. Today many products including soft drinks, cigarettes, automobiles, and canned goods have begun to recognize the value of impressive models, especially in lifestyle ads.

However, a clever advertiser can make even "ordinary" people appear desirable and interesting. For example, Esprit print advertisements feature brief profiles of customers and employees shown modeling its clothing. These ads make the typical consumer seem special, even glamorous, and allow other consumers to imagine themselves in the ads. The strategy is very effective—to generate excitement by placing the average purchaser on a pedestal to show that the ordinary become extraordinary when wearing Esprit.

In attempting to present effective images at youth, advertisers risk simply perpetuating stereotypes. It is probably impossible to escape stereotypes totally. After all, stereotypes would not exist unless there were some real groups in society to inspire them. Moreover, since no one can create a true, three-dimensional character in a thirty-second commercial or in a print ad, an advertiser must cast certain looks or types: the all-American boy or girl, the preppy, and so on. But even if stereotypical images are unavoidable, it is possible to sidestep some of the worst pitfalls.

One common advertisers' mistake is the failure to recognize that today's youth differ from those of the recent past. Images of teenagers and college students from the 1960s and the 1970s seem ridiculous to young people of the 1980s. Another error is over-stereotyping—using situations or characters so extreme that an ad seems to be spoofing young people. Some advertisers portray certain young people as freaks, especially those whom adults consider outside the mainstream. For example, the "It's Worth It" print ad for Maxell Tapes showed several young models dressed in punk styles, but went too far—one girl wore an earring in her nose and Boy George-style outrageous clothes. Young consumers could not identify with such extreme types or else perceived that the manufacturer was mocking the new styles of youth.

Benetton sportswear's "United Colors of Benetton" campaign also featured exceptionally wild styles of dress, but with a difference—the models were presented as trendsetters, who were clearly enjoying themselves. Consequently, even if young viewers would never dress like the models in the ad, they could respond favorably and appreciate the fashionability of Benetton clothing. Unfortunately, some advertisers have trouble discerning whether young models are being presented in a positive light or in a condescending, insulting manner.

One ad agency that has considered this problem seriously is Dancer Fitzgerald Sample/New York. As Penelope Queen, executive vice-president and director of research explains, studies on young people's self-image helped the agency select a diverse range of model types for its client Pioneer stereo. Her research found that there was no single style common among youth. Today, young people think of themselves in many different ways—as punks, as buttoned-down, as preppies, and so on. The one connecting thread was that all young people prided themselves on their individuality. The different styles are reflections of their attempts to "find themselves."

For the Pioneer campaign, models were selected in light of these findings. The commercials typically feature two young people or two groups of youth, one person (or group) appearing punky or funky, with the other dressed preppy or pin-striped. The ad script has the different types meeting and relating to each other—since, after all, musical styles (and the interest in quality equipment to play that music) cut across all groups of young people. Why do these different types get along? Because they are "pioneers" (not coincidentally the brand name of the stereo); that is, both types want to be ahead of the crowd and are willing to take advantage of opportunities.

The models Pioneer used represent styles recognizable as popular among young people, and their diversity allowed a broad audience of young consumers to identify with the ads and their sponsor. Most importantly, the models were presented as people who were proud both of their styles and of the statements that they were making—whether they are teenagers who like heavy metal or recent Ivy League graduates who prefer jazz. The Pioneer ads were effective because they showed tolerance of diverse lifestyles, a concept with widespread support among young people, and because they demonstrated that the product could satisfy even those with disparate tastes.

Clearly, celebrities and models play a critical role in helping a product reach the youth market. But in choosing an appropriate spokesperson for a product, it is essential to consider young people's perceptions of themselves. By realizing that they view themselves differently than adults see them, an advertiser will be better able to communicate a positive, appealing message.

9

THE DEVELOPMENT OF A YOUTHTRENDS ADVERTISING CAMPAIGN

The youth market must be the Holy Grail to most advertisers either because it is a critical market today or because it is critical to have young people predisposed to purchasing the product in the future.

—Burt Manning,
chairman & CEO of J. Walter Thompson
Advertising/USA

*I*n the previous section, we outlined the special elements that make campaigns appealing to youth. Now we will focus on constructing an actual ad campaign—everything from creating a compelling slogan or jingle to planning print, radio, and television ads to, finally, devising special promotions that target young people directly.

Creating a Youth-Appealing Slogan or Jingle

Naturally, a slogan or a jingle is the cornerstone of an ad campaign, encapsulating the product's identity. Effective slogans are especially important in targeting young consumers. After all, what young person of the 1960s and early 1970s didn't memorize and sing the Wrigley's Doublemint chewing gum jingle, "Doublemint adds to your fun . . . double pleasure all in one . . ." or the Salem cigarette tune, "You can take Salem out of the country but . . . You can't take the country out of Salem"?

Young people enjoy the humor of slogans and jingles, and often recite them on a school bus, in a dining hall, or at a party. If a slogan is appealing enough, it can end up on a TV show such as "Saturday Night Live" or even in a presidential candidate's speech, as did the Wendy's hamburger's slogan, "Where's the Beef?" More than any other group of consumers, young people are able to popularize a product simply because they sing the slogans or jingles and adopt them as a part of the youth culture.

Rules for Creating Slogans

There are seven basic rules for creating a catchy slogan, which differ slightly from the five guidelines for devising jingles.

1. ALWAYS INCLUDE THE NAME OF THE COMPANY OR YOUR PRODUCT

As simple as it sounds, this first rule is ignored by many experienced marketers. But to assure that young people remem-

ber your brand and your image observing this rule is essential.
For example, neither Levi-Strauss or Lee use their name in their
jeans advertisements. As a result, few young people remember
who manufactures "The Brand That Fits" or who holds that
"Quality Never Goes Out of Style." (The first is Lee, the second
Levi's.) Neither slogan mentions the brand name or even type
of product.

In contrast, two other jeans manufacturers, Jordache and
Sasson, have managed to create very appealing slogans incorporating their brand names. "The Jordache Look" and "Ooh
La La Sasson" are two simple slogans that say nothing while
saying everything. They speak to young people, who are extremely conscious of brands and who want to feel that a name
brand really matters.

2. KEEP THE SLOGAN TO EIGHT WORDS OR LESS

Slogans should be short and to the point. Since a slogan is
designed to summarize the image of a product, it must use as
few words as possible, while also setting the appropriate tone.
When a slogan exceeds eight words, it often becomes unwieldy
and forgettable. Long slogans with complicated metaphors and
unusual phrases will never be remembered or understood by
young people. As condescending as it sounds, a slogan should
not challenge a consumer's intelligence or logic.

Such slogans as "Dodge Boys Have More Fun" or the old
"I'd Walk a Mile for a Camel" became successful because they
were easy to remember and easy to understand. They succeeded
because they did not force consumers to think. "One of the best
examples of a short, effective slogan," according to Frank
Mingo, chairman of Mingo-Jones Advertising, "was our slogan
for Kentucky Fried Chicken." There were many ways to say it,
but Mingo said it the easiest way, "We Do Chicken Right."
There was a great slogan in just four words.

3. WHEN USING POPULAR YOUTH SLANG, MAKE SURE THE TERMS ARE CONTEMPORARY AND UNDERSTOOD IN EVERY REGION OF THE COUNTRY

It is easy to alienate or to confuse young people even when trying to make them feel comfortable with a product. Young consumers may be put off by slogans that incorporate popular slang terms in the hopes of making products seem youthful and hip. For one thing, slang dates quickly, and passé terms will certainly diminish the effectiveness of a campaign. Second, a certain term (or terms) may not be recognized by young people in all areas of the country.

For example, consider some of the different groups of young people in the United States. Would a Valley Girl, who spends her weekends at the Sherman Oaks Galleria, really use the same slang terms as an East Coast preppie, who belongs to the junior league? Of course not. Furthermore, one group hardly realizes that the other one even exists. Unless a company has done its research, it should avoid slang when trying to establish a slogan that will universally appeal to young people.

4. TEST THE SLOGAN TO MAKE SURE IT CARRIES NO NEGATIVE CONNOTATIONS

Beyond simply avoiding slang, it is important to make sure that a slogan's language will not alienate young people. Word usage and attitudes change each generation and even from one year to the next, so it is worth a marketer's time and expense to test any new slogans with focus groups of young people. Why risk losing potential young buyers with an insensitive concept or offensive wording, even if a product's audience is divided between adults and the youth population?

For example, one slogan that offended many college-aged women (and men as well) was St. Pauli Girl beer's slogan: "You Never Forget Your First Girl." The campaign, which must have been aimed at young men, had overwhelming sexual connotations. Furthermore, it used the word *girl* to refer to women. A decade or so ago, it may have been acceptable to refer to a woman as a *girl,* but this generation finds it insulting.

Although St. Pauli Girl would have lost the chance to play on its product's name, it would have been wiser to avoid a slogan that carried such negative connotations and offended so many consumers.

Izod Lacoste, the clothing company which made the alligator famous, was another company which created a problematic slogan. And perhaps, by sheer coincidence, we had pointed out the problem with their slogan during one of our nationally broadcasted speeches just months before Izod's owner, General Mills, announced that it wanted to sell the unpopular clothing brand. At the time, Izod was losing its young consumers to another pull-over shirt manufacturer, Polo by Ralph Lauren. Izod's new slogan was "Izod. Now more than ever." We discovered from interviews that many college students sneered at the slogan and its inevitable association with Richard Nixon's campaign slogan. It was an unfortunate coincidence, but one that could have been avoided had the marketers paid attention to current attitudes or responses of young consumers.

5. TRY TO HIGHLIGHT AN UNUSUAL FEATURE OR ASPECT OF YOUR COMPANY'S PRODUCT

"United Colors of Benetton." "Pepperidge Farm Remembers." These are just two slogans that successfully highlight their companies' uniqueness. More than anything else, the Benetton clothing company is known for its almost limitless variety of colors, and with this wonderful slogan, the company can remind the consumer of that fact. The cookie and dessert company, Pepperidge Farm, is distinguished from other bakery products by the fact that it follows old-fashioned recipes. And what better way to remind consumers that it is the choice for those who prefer old-fashioned goodness than to brag about it in a slogan?

Not only should a slogan use the product's name but it should also note the product's most unusual feature, to encapsulate the product's image as completely (and succinctly) as possible. Sears used this formula in developing its new slogan, "There's More for Your Life at Sears." A store that was trying to rid itself of a tired image, Sears no longer wanted consumers (especially young ones) to think that it only sold hardware, paints, and car batteries. With its new slogan, Sears told America that it carries more personal products as well.

6. WHEN CREATING A SLOGAN, KEEP THE COMPETITION IN MIND

In a similar vein, when creating a slogan, a company must make sure that the message applies *to it alone*—and not to its competitors as well. For example, Burger King developed the slogan "Have It Your Way" to show that it was the only hamburger chain that offered customers meals cooked to order. There was no way that McDonald's could have encroached on Burger King's territory with a similar slogan or concept. Because Burger King thought about what distinguished it from its competitors, it was able to come up with a winning slogan.

It also pays to think about using a slogan that publicly challenges competitors. The third largest burger chain, Wendy's, did this with its slogan, "Where's the Beef?" While Wendy's vice-president, Bruce Ley, does not acknowledge that the campaign was an assault on his competitors' hamburgers, when the question, "Where's the Beef?" was asked, consumers were forced to think about the smaller hamburgers that were served at other establishments. Thus, phrases or mini-slogans can be very effective, at least in part because they assail their competitors' weaknesses.

Pepsi-Cola issued a much more subtle slap with its slogan

"The Choice of a New Generation." With it, Pepsi admitted consumers are free to choose among the many colas on the market. But they needled Coca-Cola and every other competitor by implying that Pepsi is for the current generation and every other choice was for a previous, outdated generation.

7. AFTER TRADEMARKING A SLOGAN, USE IT WHENEVER POSSIBLE

Young people like to wear T-shirts, caps, and other articles of clothing that carry brand-name advertisements. They find nothing tacky about a T-shirt that reads, "This Bud's for You" or a painter's cap with a picture of a favorite suntan lotion. Who would have thought that one day Coca-Cola would be introducing its own successful line of designer clothing?

Clearly, whether a product is related to leisure clothing items or not, it can gain extra mileage from a slogan or logo placed on banners, sweatshirts, and so on. Such placements are constant free advertising, not only generating interest in a product but also making it part of young people's lifestyle.

Rules for Creating Jingles

While many companies have stopped creating the singable advertising messages that were popular during the 1950s, 1960s, and 1970s, the jingle is still alive. It can be an important marketing tool in reaching today's young people. Some of the rules of slogan writing also apply to jingles, but there are a few factors to keep in mind as well. Here are the five major rules for creating jingles:

1. Always include the name of the company or the product.

2. It doesn't hurt to be a little corny when writing the words for a jingle.

3. Don't expect young people to recall old songs—even if they were Top Forty hits.

4. Don't change a jingle too often, or consumers will forget the product.

5. Keep the music fun and simple so that young people will sing it, hum it, and popularize it.

1. ALWAYS INCLUDE THE NAME OF THE COMPANY OR THE PRODUCT

This rule is so important that it bears repeating. For the same reason a product's name should be included in a slogan, it should also appear in the lyrics of any jingle. The whole point of using a jingle is to promote a product when your commercials aren't screaming at the consumer. A jingle that can be sung by young people can offer constant free advertising—as long as it mentions the brand name.

Some of the most effective jingles are the simplest, such as the Miller Brewing Company's song, "Miller's Made the American Way," and Coca-Cola's "Coke Is It." Both are light, short phrases, set to catchy melodies that feature the names of their products.

2. IT DOESN'T HURT TO BE A LITTLE CORNY WHEN WRITING THE WORDS FOR A JINGLE

A creative genius, Eric Weber, executive vice-president of Dancer Fitzgerald Sample, says he often works by sheer instinct in creating campaigns and jingles. For his Dr. Pepper ads, he developed a jingle that was "so zany and fun that the TV show, *Saturday Night Live* did a skit on it during the late 1970s." The lyrics were undeniably silly—"I'm a Pepper, She's a Pepper. . . ."—but irrestible. A little bit of corniness can go a long way with young people because jingles are most appealing when they aren't too serious.

Corniness can also help to make a jingle memorable. As *Business Week* magazine pointed out recently, many young people still remember the "Choo Choo Charlie" jingle developed by Good 'n' Plenty candy—although they hadn't heard it for more than ten years. Writing a good jingle is serious business, but that does not mean that the song can't be fun and frivolous.

3. DON'T EXPECT YOUNG PEOPLE TO RECALL OLD SONGS—EVEN IF THEY WERE TOP FORTY HITS

In many of its current commercials, Ford's Mercury division uses songs from the 1950s to promote its cars. Although many of the tunes (now set with new lyrics) were wildly popular Motown songs, they sound like mediocre jingles to the twenty-year-old who wasn't around and doesn't recall them. As a result, young people will fail to recognize the significance of the jingle. Don't expect young people to wax nostalgic over something they can't remember or never heard. To appeal to young consumers, a tune must sound fresh and contemporary.

4. DON'T CHANGE A JINGLE TOO OFTEN, OR CONSUMERS WILL FORGET THE PRODUCT

According to Alan McDonald, president of Nestlé Foods, a new version of the old jingle, "N-E-S-T-L-E-S, Nestlé's makes the very best." was being revived because of its former popularity. In general, this is a smart move for other companies to consider. All too often, the manufacturer and its agencies get so tired of a jingle that they think the public is ready for a change as well. Usually, however, by the time the company is bored with its jingle, consumers have just begun to identify the song with the product. Rather than confuse consumers with new campaigns, it is better to preserve successful ones.

5. KEEP THE MUSIC FUN AND SIMPLE SO THAT YOUNG PEOPLE WILL SING IT, HUM IT, AND POPULARIZE IT

Unfortunately, most of the songs used in today's commercials are just impossible to sing. Souped up with sophisticated synthesizers and percussion, the *melodies* are too complicated for the average person to remember, never mind the words. More successful jingles use simple, upbeat tunes, with lyrics that are fun to repeat. A perfect example is Burger King's late 1970s jingle, "Hold the pickles, Hold the Lettuce. Special Orders Don't Upset Us. . . ." Every young person knew this song.

Valerie Graves of the Uniworld Advertising agency cites one of Burger King's more recent commercial jingles, "Who Beat the Stuffin' " as the kind young people repeat. "We were promoting Burger King's new Croissandwich, and we showed young people on a school bus who were singing, "Who beat the stuffin' out of Egg McMuffin." The jingle was memorable as a light-hearted assault on one of McDonald's primary products. And in creating a singable jingle, Burger King reaped the free-advertising benefits of having its message enter the youth vernacular.

Once a company has developed a slogan or a jingle reflecting the image it wants to express to young people, it can begin to disseminate its message—usually through the mass media: print, radio, and television. Ideally, efforts in each medium will be closely coordinated, to form a cohesive marketing strategy and campaign. But each medium offers different benefits to the advertiser, and also holds its own special perils. Here we'll discuss some of the guidelines for developing youth-targeted ads in each medium.

The Thirteen Steps Toward Designing Successful Print Ads

It should come as no surprise that marketers use special rules in designing youth-oriented ads for magazines, newspapers, posters, and billboards. In reaching young consumers, these media are as important as television and radio; print ads can be more potent than electronic commercial messages because they are read, saved, and then reread. Still, when selling youth-oriented products, marketers have to be careful about *how* they spend their print-ad dollars and, just as important, about *where*.

One problem is that, since young people (especially teenagers) read much less than their parents, print ads must be especially appealing. Secondly, young people often bypass traditional publications and so can be reached best through their own high school newspapers, college publications, and young-adult fashion and entertainment magazines, as well as through poster and billboard displays in youth-populated areas. The following are thirteen rules that savvy marketers keep in mind when creating or targeting a print ad to youth or youth-oriented consumers.

1. SHOCK READERS WITH THE HEADLINE

According to John Eighmey, senior vice-president of Young & Rubicam Advertising, "Advertisements should be interruptive." Many others in the advertising industry agree that ads should reach out and grab the reader's attention, becoming as important or *more* important than the editorial pages that frame them.

Assume that readers are not going to read everything. Assume that they will thumb through a publication, waiting for something to catch their attention. Because magazines intersperse so many ads with their editorial pages, the only way to catch readers' attention is to shock them with provocative head-lines. Although the body of an ad can be a softer sell, the first line should make an outrageous statement or offer.

2. TRY TO TELL A MEMORABLE STORY

Young readers enjoy and remember ads that tell stories, whether they are simple testimonials ("Before I used Brand X . . . and now that I use Brand X, I . . .") or longer narratives that unfold in episodes each month. Stories might be told in comic-strip fashion, with dialogue in separate boxes. Naturally, readers are drawn to these ads, curious about the new develop-ments.

3. MINIMIZE TALK AND TYPE

There are several reasons why it's not a good idea to use a lot of explanation and type in a print ad. For one thing, an ad becomes graphically unattractive when it has too many words. Secondly, readers won't analyze sentence upon sentence to glean an advertiser's message. Young people, especially, are reluctant to spend time on an ad that reminds them of a reading assignment. Finally, ads that overexplain can seem didactic. No young person wants to be lectured about a product or to feel he was talked into buying it.

4. INVOLVE READERS IN THE AD

Young people are easily distracted, and if an ad doesn't rouse their curiosity, they will simply turn the page. For this reason, it is important to pull readers into an ad, by asking them a question, making them fill in a blank space—do anything to get them involved with the ad's copy or its graphics. Just as in-volvement brings excitement to a promotional event, it can direct interest to an ad that would otherwise be easily ignored.

5. GIVE PRICES IN PRINT ADS

It is no longer considered taboo to talk about money or to give prices in an advertisement. For many young people, especially, the cost of a product is a critical concern in purchase decisions.

For example, many students were drawn to Budget Gourmet frozen dinners because the ads announced the product's low price. Naturally, the manufacturer could not list prices for every store in the United States, but the ads offered its suggested retail cost of $1.69.

Obviously, it is to no advantage to list a price that is higher than the competition's, but giving a reasonable cost can help dispel consumers' fears that advertised items will be too expensive.

6. BE DARING AND DIFFERENT

In developing a campaign for the hairstyling gel Dippity-Do, Jerry Siano, president of NW Ayer Advertising, created daring and lively ads to match the product. "The product has a weird, funky name, and we were determined to popularize it again," he says. The brightly colored ad features the words, "Do it!" actually spelled out in the pink- or green-colored gel. The only other line in the ad reads, "For all the crazy looks inside of you," which emphasizes the sense of humor of the product and the advertisement.

Ads that use humor, sarcasm, sex, and color effectively are sure to stand out because they require effort and creativity. A more detailed discussion of these elements appears in Chapter 8.

7. SET A MOOD THAT FITS THE PRODUCT

A print ad can set a mood just as powerfully as any television commercial can. Strong visuals are essential, for lighting, shadows, and colors, form an environment for the product. Nike, for example, has used photography well to create a quiet, mysterious look for its models and athleticwear. This same type of mood works well with perfumes and expensive imported products. Snack foods and soft drinks, for example, may need a more upbeat treatment, with brighter colors and clear lighting. It is important to define a distinct image for the product, and then create an appropriate mood for its advertisements.

8. STRIVE FOR ACTION VISUALS

Rhonda Gainer, advertising director of Daniel Hechter Clothing, says that her company aims for print ads as action-filled as its television fashion videos. In advertising the Hechter dress suits, Gainer clothes her models and has them jump off cliffs into waterfalls or hang glide two hundred feet in the air. "Because our ads are active," Gainer explains, "there is a greater retention factor on the part of readers. We have shown people dressed in our suits in the most amazing situations. We will show them climbing glaciers, skiing on sand—and these activities tell the consumer that we have a sense of humor."

9. DISPLAY THE PRODUCT PROMINENTLY OR SHOW IT IN USE

Some creative marketers like to tease consumers by burying or withholding the products name until the end of the pitch. While they believe that this technique will pique the consumers' interest, such an approach rarely works for young people. Generally, young people are too busy and active to wade through a full-page ad just to find out the product's name. If the ad is selling typewriters, it should feature at least one typewriter, prominently displayed.

Better yet, says Max Imgruth, president of Swatch Watch, products in ads should be worn, eaten, or used. Imgruth holds that consumers want to imagine themselves using the products they see in ads. For this reason, he has specific rules for print ads featuring Swatch products: "All Swatch products must be shown *on* people. Each model must wear five to six Swatch Watches with at least three Swatch Guards per model. Three New Shields [sunglasses] must be on each model with Chums [neck strap for sunglasses]. . . ."

By showing people using the product, an ad can bring the concept to life.

10. BE SENSITIVE TO THE AUDIENCE

While youth-oriented magazines are always eager to attract advertisements, they must be especially careful to avoid products and ads that can offend or negatively influence young people and their parents. For magazines that cater to an especially young group, negative influences might include references to alcohol, sex, or cigarettes. As a matter of fact, even the R. J. Reynolds Company's antismoking ads have generated controversy. These ads, claiming to discourage teenagers from smoking, talk about peer pressure and other youth-oriented concerns. While some teen magazines accept the ad, *Scholastic* magazine does not. Ed Chenetz, its associate publisher, says, "We pulled that ad because it was creating a discussion that did not need to be discussed at all."

Sex is an even more sensitive area for youth. Jim Rainsford, advertising director of *Seventeen* described an eight-page Swatch ad that offended parents. "Many parents were annoyed . . . because the sixth page showed a scantily clad woman being held in a sexually suggestive manner."

11. INCLUDE WOMEN AND MINORITIES

People look at ads to decide if products are for them. If a print ad features five white males wearing a watch, the rest of the world will see the watch as peculiar to white men. Nowadays, women and members of minority groups expect to be represented in ads, and especially in those featuring more than two people. According to Frank Mingo, chairman of Mingo-Jones Advertising, "Through research, we have found that black consumers remember which products use blacks in their ads and commercials." Mingo and many others agree that consumers will turn against a product when they feel that their group is not being addressed in an advertisement.

As Grey Advertising chairman, Edward Meyer, says, "Advertising should be a mirror of society"—and that means including blacks, Hispanics, women, and others who realistically represent the consumer population.

12. TURN AN AD INTO SOMETHING CONSUMERS WILL KEEP

When an ad is attractive enough to become a poster in a dorm room or offers useful tips and references, a reader will tear it out of the magazine and hold on to it. One such ad is Ford Mustang's list of the twenty hottest places to go during spring break." Because every student is looking for a spring break resort, he or she is sure to keep it in a notebook or over a desk. Many of the beer brands including Budweiser have gone so far as to turn their more attractive print ads into large posters that young people can mail away for or even purchase. These posters provide constant advertising for their products, making them part of the young consumer's daily life.

13. CONSIDER UNUSUAL VENUES AND SPECIAL PUBLICATIONS

Because young people often ignore the traditional print media, marketers should consider reaching out to them by less conventional means. According to Michael Moore, director of media planning at D'Arcy Masius Benton Bowles, "Marketers should never overlook outdoor and indoor signage when trying to catch the attention of young people. Because they are constantly on buses and in train stations, they will see ads in those places. Because they go to concerts and sporting events, it is wise to advertise on billboards in those areas."

Billboard ads, like those created by the 13–30 Corporation, can catch attention in student dining halls, dormitory hallways, laundromats, discos, and bars. Companies, including Kodak and M&M's/Mars candy, frequently use this method to capture the young, mobile consumer.

There are also many special youth-targeted publications, from education-related magazines issued in high schools and colleges to young-adult fashion and entertainment periodicals. The most important thing to consider when looking at circulation figures, is how a publication describes its own readership. Does the magazine target teenagers? Is it aimed at both college and high school students? Does it attract mostly teenagers, yet also advertise to adults? Are its readers mostly female or does its audience encompass young men *and* young women?

Ed Chenetz, associate publisher of Scholastic magazines, showed us a recent list of magazines ranked according to the number of teenage readers they attracted. The top six publications were *TV Guide, Scholastic* magazines, *Seventeen, People, Reader's Digest,* and *National Enquirer.* At first glance, many would be surprised to find *TV Guide, Reader's Digest,* and *National Enquirer* on this list, but careful marketers know its compiler, Simmons Research, doesn't attempt to account for these magazines' non-teenage readers.

If a company wants to reach *only* a large teenage market, it will have to look beyond this list to find magazines with a more concentrated young readership. Better venues for ads targeted *solely* to teenagers would be such magazines as *Scholastic, Seventeen, Young Miss, Tiger Beat, Teen,* etc. See Chapter 13 for a more detailed discussion of the specific publications aimed at each segment of the youth market—teenagers, college students, and young adults.

In the next section, we'll look at the medium many advertisers consider the best for reaching young people—radio.

The Five Rules for Radio Commercials

Gary Susnjara, chairman of Dancer Fitzgerald Sample Advertising/New York, says, "Radio is a good medium to find people with little waste. But it is much harder to get your message heard on radio." Indeed, as effective as radio can be at reaching young consumers, it has one built-in liability—it is impossible to ensure that the radio audience will truly listen to the ads. Here we'll examine some ways to overcome this problem by developing ads with strong youth-appeal.

Young people listen to approximately three hours of radio daily, slightly less time than adults. But in the 7:00 P.M. to midnight time slot, there are many more teenage listeners than adults, and on weekends their rate compares to adults' as well. Of course, as for television, youth radio listening rates rise during the summer when students are out of school.

Even if adults spend more time listening to the radio, advertisers can reach young people more directly, thanks to well-targeted youth radio programming. Unlike television, radio offers formats specially tailored to young people. According to the Simmons Market Research Bureau, young people aged twelve to seventeen favor stations that play "progressive music" followed by "dance music"; while those age eighteen to twenty-four favor "soft rock" and then "progressive music." These formats are popular among youth-oriented consumers as well.

On radio, an advertiser can use the "American Express,"

"Snickers," or "Newsweek" approaches discussed in Chapter 5—creating separate campaigns or special ads aimed directly at the F.L.Y.E.R.S. market—and capitalize on the fact that young people are especially responsive when singled out for attention. In addition, radio allows advertisers to target young male and female listeners separately. For example, rock programs are skewed female, although more males listen to non–Top Forty rock. As with television, broadcasts of sporting events usually skew male.

Unfortunately, coupled with this targeting advantage is a significant drawback: radio advertisements have a much harder time getting and keeping the young listener's attention. One problem is the competition among advertisers: There are more radio commercials per hour and more commercials per break than on television, and increasing numbers of radio stations run periods of programming without commercial interruptions, further distancing program content (which the listener wants to hear) from somewhat longer advertising blocks (during which the listener can mentally tune out or switch stations). Then, too, many young people use the radio even more than television, simply as background for other activities, including studying or talking to friends. And because most radios have poorer reception than television sets, advertising messages may lack clarity and impact.

To counter these problems, radio ads must be lively, dramatic, and creative. Some general guidelines for formulating ads that will hold young listeners' attention are:

1. HAVE A UNIQUE SOUND

There is so much conpetition on the airwaves—and so many distractions on the listeners' environment—that it is critical for an advertiser to establish a unique sound for its message. Whether the ad is distinguished by its music, its jingle, or its announcer's voice, is should be compelling enough to make the audience stop and listen, just as they would stop to listen to a favorite song. As an example, Eric Weber, executive vice-president and executive creative director of Dancer Fitzgerald Sample, cites his firm's radio ads for its client Molson Golden. Since 1981, the beer's radio campaign has revolved around a man (Garrett Brown) and a woman (Ann Wynn), both possessing quite unusual voices, engaged in a mildly humorous conversation. A soft musical theme plays under their discussion. Although the ads change frequently, since they all have the same audio quality, they are immediately identifiable as Molson's. Moreover, since young people know that the conversation will be interesting and funny, they stop to listen to the ads to catch up on new developments.

Achieving a unique style is the single most important step toward creating a successful radio commercial, one that the audience will not only hear but heed.

2. KEEP IT SIMPLE

Young people, especially, play the radio for background music while doing other things. Consequently, they may only half listen to ads and, distracted, will be unlikely to glean more than a single idea from advertising copy. For this reason, it pays to keep radio ads simple, limited to one, strong point. If the copy gets complicated, less time will be allotted for each point to be made, making it less likely that young listeners will remember any of the message.

Naturally, radio ads must present the brand name and product's characteristics more forcefully than television ads. One way to highlight this information is simply to repeat the central line of the ad. Commercials often play so quickly and so much else is happening that the listener misses information the first time it is presented.

Another method is to make an ad interruptive—that is, one dramatically distinct from the program format. For example, if the product or service being offered is serious, then the ad should sound serious. Jane Maas, president of Muller Jordan Weiss Advertising and a trustee of Hofstra University, described a successful, fact-filled recruitment ad the university ran on rock radio stations. Its no-nonsense tone was shockingly different both from the programming and from other advertisements; as a result, it caught the interest of its intended targets, high school students and noncollege young adults.

3. USE THE DISK JOCKEY

It can be very effective to have a well-liked disk jockey read the text of an ad, rather than an unknown announcer. First of all, an ad can take advantage of the disk jockey's popularity, receiving a kind of implied editorial endorsement; and secondly, an ad read by the disk jockey will be closely linked with the music programming, and so will be more likely to be heard by listeners. However, the advertiser will often have to give up some control over how the disk jockey delivers the copy, running the risk that he or she might criticize the ad or the product. But even a less than traditional copy delivery or some criticism can get a lot of positive listener attention; young people usually look more favorably on a brand when an advertiser shows a good sense of humor about its own product.

4. RUN PROMOTIONS ON LOCAL RADIO

Radio giveaways create an interaction between manufacturer and listener that can be extremely appealing to youth. Young people, especially noncollege young adults, appreciate the immediacy of such promotions (typically listeners phone in to win), the connection of a product to a favorite local station, and the fact that the winner is someone living in their own area. Moreover, a contest can call more attention to a product than numerous repetitions of an advertisement. Although record, movie, and beverage companies very often use contests to promote their products, manufacturers of medium-priced consumer goods would do well to consider them, too.

In addition, radio is an appropriate medium to let consumers know about other promotions or sponsorships done either in their community or around the country. Our polls indicate that young people are favorably impressed when a company is involved in projects that they are interested in. Strategies for creating effective contests and promotions for youth will be discussed in Chapter 10.

5. DON'T JUST USE THE AUDIO FROM TV ADS

Many companies simply use the audio track or some adaptation of the sound from their television commercials for their radio ads. Of course, there are significant benefits to this method. Once a television ad is created, there are only minimal costs involved in modifying it for use on radio. In addition, the radio ad directly reinforces the message presented on television.

But all too often, an audio track is less forceful and interesting. Because a television commercial usually uses visuals to make its pitch, it may be difficult to get the ad's points across using only the audio. Further, since it was not originally developed for radio, the audio will probably not take full advantage of the medium's power to stir the imagination, to create a mood or situation in the listener's mind. Finally, since most television ads are targeted to a broader audience, the audio portion will typically not be aimed specifically at young people through the use of the "American Express," Snickers," or "Newsweek" approaches; hence, it may not make the best use of radio's targeting benefits.

Of course, using the audio portion of a television commercial is better than not using radio at all to reach youth. But if a company intends to use its audios on radio, it should take care to ensure that television ads are designed with radio play in mind. Clearly, certain types of TV ads will be much harder to translate—ones that feature animation and special technical effects as well as those based on demonstrations of the product attributes. Obviously, ads using animation and special effects will lose the all important dimension on radio. And since viewers won't be able to see a product being used, demonstration ads will disintegrate into simple presentations.

Slice-of-life ads, too, may be very hard to translate to radio. Since the listener cannot see the situation or the individuals, it becomes more difficult for him to identify with the ad. And though lifestyle ads may also suffer from losing their visuals, many young people do find this format appealing on radio, especially if an ad has a compelling, current-sounding musical theme.

Whatever medium they appear on, celebrity testimonials are viewed quite cynically by young people. However, since radio is more intimate with messages delivered by an unseen person direct to listeners, testimonials do seem somewhat more believable on radio than on television. Still, unless a testimonial ad features a major celebrity, the ad will be easy to tune out mentally. Generally speaking, testimonial ads as a form are rather uninspired and uninspiring, and the slight edge they gain on radio is not enough to make them interesting to young people.

The most common type of radio ad is the Brand-Focused-Through-Presenters format: an announcer reading copy, sometimes with music playing in the background. Simply because these ads are so common, it is particularly difficult to get young people to listen to them. However, by implementing some of the guidelines in this section the audiotrack from this type of ad can become much more attractive and engaging.

While radio offers special benefits to advertisers targeting youth, television is truly the medium of the 1980s. In the next section we'll look at the special challenges it presents and the most effective methods to surmount them, using the Youth-Trends model.

The Six Basic Types of Television Commercials

"Advertisers must finally realize that, for young people, watching television is not like reading a book with pictures," says Robert Pittman, president of MTV Networks. Indeed, young people have grown up watching television and consider it the primary medium of entertainment and information. They see it as entirely distinct from radio or print and thus expect more from it, especially more visual stimulation, than most adults do. Most young people are very visually sophisticated, more aware of and susceptible to imagery. They are much more responsive to the "quick hit" of television information than most adults, and their minds and eyes can absorb such information at a much faster rate.

As a result, television networks have been making slow but steady progress toward realizing the visual potential of the medium. The highly visual MTV, which is very popular among F.L.Y.E.R.S., is on the cutting edge of these experiments. And since the members of the young "television generation" will be the adults of the future, these trends will have a continuing influence on television for decades to come.

Still some advertisers make the blanket statement that young people do not watch much television. According to the A. C. Nielsen Company, young people watch television approximately twenty-three hours per week—on average, approximately seven hours less each week than the older general public, but still substantial. During the summer months, youth television viewing is comparable to that of adults. In addition, Saturday morning is better for reaching teens than adults, and teenage television viewership during the early fringe (4:30 P.M. to 7:30 P.M.) and prime time is not significantly lower than the general population's. In fact, young people spend more time watching television than listening to the radio or reading magazines and newspapers. In any given week, television reaches over 90 percent of all teenagers.

The Nielsen ratings also omit several million college students from its surveys of television viewers—those living in dorm rooms or watching television in groups in student activity centers or fraternity/sorority houses are not measured. This underestimates the share of the youth audience for all programs, making it difficult for some advertisers to see that certain shows such as late-night programs, daytime soap operas, game shows, and even cartoons (both afternoon and Saturday morning) are very popular among F.L.Y.E.R.S.

Of course, it may well be inefficient to run commercials for products that are narrowly aimed at the youth market during prime time. But commercials using the "Pepsi," "MTV," or "Swatch" approaches, will appeal to youth as well as the wider population and thus are appropriate for this time slot. Commercials using the "American Express," "Snickers," or "Newsweek" approaches, which are more specifically targeted at the needs and interests of young people, can be effectively placed on non-prime-time network television programs, such as *Friday Night Videos, Late Night with David Letterman, Saturday Night Live, American Bandstand,* certain sporting events, and Saturday morning shows.

Certain cable television channels draw even higher proportions of young viewers. For example, MTV is able to translate the selectivity of radio programming into a visually compelling medium. Two-thirds of its viewers in the 30 million households it reaches are between twelve and twenty-four years old.

Beyond targeting, there are problems in attracting young consumers with television ads, some of which apply to the adult population as well. For example, a 1985 survey by *Advertising Age* magazine found that half of all television viewers could not recall a single commercial. One reason for this finding is that television is growing increasingly cluttered with ads, station identifications, public service messages, program promotions, and so on. Not only is it difficult for viewers to retain all they see, they are annoyed by the number of commercials shown during breaks. In addition, young people, especially, use television simply as a background for other activities.

Another 1985 study, done by the advertising firm of Ogilvy & Mather found that 44 percent of television viewers thought ads were either boring or irritating. They found that ads were unrepresentative of their own lifestyles, some even condescending. As Barbara Coffey, managing editor of *Glamour* magazine, explains, "Television commercials lag well behind print ads in portraying people, especially young women, in situations which are relevant and true to life." As well, people complain that some ads are too obvious in their sales pitches or rely so much on emotional exploitation as to make them offensive. Our own studies indicate that many young people believe that companies place subliminal messages in their ads. Although, of course, this fear is unfounded, it illustrates how cynical many are becoming about television advertising.

Then, too, with 45 percent of households receiving cable television and 25 percent able to rent movies for their VCRs, viewers are losing interest in network television programs. This lack of interest means that not only are fewer people reached through television but that those who are watching may be paying less attention to the programs and commercials. These concerns have resulted in both "zapping," using television remote controls to switch channels quickly to avoid having to watch commercials, and "zipping," taping a program on a VCR and fast-forwarding through commercials.

Clearly, part of the solution to these problems is developing commercials viewers will enjoy and even want to watch. The

YouthTrends Approaches can help advertisers develop commercials that entertain and therefore hold the young audience. There are six basic types of television commercials: demonstrations, testimonials, brand focused through presentations, animation and special technical effects, slice of life, and lifestyle. Of course, there are areas of overlap among these six styles, but in analyzing commercials, it is useful to make these distinctions. Studies and polls of young people done by our own consulting firm, as well as by national advertising agencies, have indicated how how young people respond to each type of presentation. Below we'll offer guidelines on the most effective use of each type, with brief case studies of well-known commercials.

1. DEMONSTRATIONS

Demonstration ads establish certain attributes of a product and sometimes compare them to those of the competition's. Although demonstrations are usually used for detergents and household cleaners, one of the most famous youth-oriented demonstrations was run in the early 1980s by a soft-drink company—the "Pepsi Challenge." PepsiCo ran millions of taste tests across the country in order to show that more people preferred the taste of Pepsi over Coke's and then, on television, showed ordinary people choosing Pepsi over Coke in blind taste tests. During the "Challenge" commercial campaign, Pepsi began to outsell Coke in food stores for the first time, proving that people were indeed making a choice.

Although this campaign worked for a while, its effectiveness soon began to fade. Why? The reasons for its demise can be applied to most demonstration ads. First of all, young people are skeptical about demonstrations; they strongly suspect that the presentations are rigged or do not show the whole truth about a product. As a result, they are naturally resistant to this form of advertising.

Secondly, the "Pepsi Challenge" succeeded in part because it was one of the first demonstrations that actually *named* the competing product; it was no longer "our brand versus Brand X," but a real competition between known products. But Pepsi's success caused companies in its own and in other industries to imitate this method. Consequently, through overuse, this ad style began to lose its effectiveness with consumers. People soon tuned out to demonstration ads, failing even to note who won these challenges.

Third, many consumers, especially F.L.Y.E.R.S., find the hard-sell aspects of demonstrations unappealing. They do not like to be told in a heavy-handed manner that one brand is more effective or superior to another brand.

Fourth, certain product features that are of paramount importance to young consumers, such as its image, cannot be shown through demonstration ads. That is not to say that ads should never try to assail the product's competitors. Indeed, challenging other brands, especially larger ones, can be a clever, effective strategy if done with wit and style, as we discussed in Chapter 8.

2. TESTIMONIALS

Testimonial ads, which feature celebrity or an ordinary consumer explaining why he or she prefers a particular brand, are not usually targeted toward the youth market. The most serious problem with testimonials is that they are even less credible than demonstrations, despite truth-in-advertising laws that have limited abuses in both formats. Young people know that the celebrity, the expert, or the "man on the street" has been paid to endorse the advertised product and so are extremely cynical about taking testimonials at face value. Then, too, testimonials are hard-selling ads, too heavy-handed to be attractive to young consumers.

3. BRAND FOCUSED THROUGH PRESENTERS

These ads use celebrities, created personalities, or spokespeople (who may or may not be seen) to focus attention on and present information about a product. An excellent example of this type of advertising is Mars, Inc.'s commercials for its Snickers bar.

As we discussed in Chapter 5, the Snickers campaign has several versions featuring a mother, a workman, or a student explaining that Snickers is great for satisfying hunger. Each presenter is chosen to appeal to a different group of potential consumers. These ads are more believable because they focus on significant qualities of the product, not on the reliability of the endorser.

Of course, this advertising approach does present certain problems: for one thing, a presenter may emphasize product features that do not interest the specific consumer targeted, as when celebrity Mark Harmon described growing barley in an ad for Coors beer. Secondly, style can easily seem dated since it usually involves no more than the presenter reading copy points about the product. Finally, the presenter may not appeal to all consumers or even to the targeted segment of consumers (see Chapter 8 for a discussion of choosing spokespeople young people like).

For young people, the most unappealing presenters are found in so-called "gatekeeper" ads; here, a spokesmodel parent explains how good a product is for the children and how much "the kids" enjoy it. Commercials for the snack food Combos ("Cheese Filled Combos—Combos Really Cheeses Young Hunger Away") follow this pattern exactly. These ads make teenagers, who want to be seen as adults, feel like children. Even if gatekeeper ads convince a parent to buy a product once, by alienating young people, they will ensure that the product is not purchased again.

Another problem with presenter ads—as well as with other types of television commercials—is that they often fail to grab the viewer's attention in the first frame. Since nowadays viewers often zap commercials or mentally tune them out, it is essential to make ads interesting right from the outset. MTV has opened many advertisers' eyes by proving that it is possible to present a persuasive message in an unconventional way. The following three types of ads, which offer greater flexibility, can surmount this problem and help advertisers capture their young target audience more readily.

4. ANIMATION AND SPECIAL TECHNICAL EFFECTS

These techniques, borrowed from major motion pictures as well as music videos, can provide a new twist to youth-oriented ads. Of course, these methods can make an ad seem either like it is a "rip-off" of the movie or like it is aimed at much younger children. For example, the commercial announcing the return of the chocolate candy Chunky had 1950s-style cartoon characters singing "Chunky's Back" to the tune of "My Boyfriend's Back." But instead of appearing fun and trendy to young people, the stiff cartoon characters and the old-fashioned tune made the commercial seem juvenile and silly; young people felt the ad was not aimed at them and were unsure whether it was targeted at their parents or at their preteen siblings.

By contrast, 1985 ads for the tortilla chip Tostitos interspersed footage from old episodes of "Leave It to Beaver," "Mr. Ed," and "Dragnet" to make it seem as if the shows' characters were involved in a discussion about the product. These distinctive, humorous ads, using current filmmaking techniques, were well-received by F.L.Y.E.R.S., especially young adults, who knew and enjoyed these television programs from their childhoods or from recent, syndicated repeats.

5. SLICE OF LIFE

Slice-of-life commercials are particularly effective at reaching youth because young people can often feel alienated from the larger adult and corporate worlds. It is easy for young people to identify with the individuals and situations these ads portray, and thus with the product used. Of course, to allow such identification, slice-of-life ads must represent current youth experiences accurately. As Burt Manning, chairman of J. Walter Thompson/USA, notes, "Young people will not respond to messages couched in old, meretricious slices of a life that never existed."

Two effective examples of slice-of-life commercials are Lipton Cup-a-Soup's "After the Game" and the soft drink Sprite's "High School Announcements." The Lipton ad revolves around two teenage brothers, the older one trying to cheer up the younger, who has just lost a football game, by making Lipton Cup-a-Soup for lunch. The ad accurately reflects the fact that most mothers of teenagers have jobs and so are not at home to prepare lunch. The boys talk and joke with each other; the older boy comments that it is too bad his brother did not "attack" the game the way he did the soup.

The Sprite commercials show high school students talking, joking, and even flirting as they get books out of their lockers. The morning announcements come over the public-address system and the students are pleased to hear that since more people prefer the taste of Sprite to Seven–Up, Sprite will be replacing Seven–Up in the lunchroom.

These two ads encompass some of the most important features of slice-of-life commercials. First, both ads, particularly Lipton's, have an youth-appealing soft-sell quality that could not be achieved easily by using the former four advertising styles. Second, to better allow youth to identify with the ad—in the best commercials the young people act, speak, look, and dress like average youth. Third, both ads deal with believable situations, unlike the 1986 "Mr. Right" commercial for the Gillette antiperspirant Right Guard. In Gillette's ad, a beautiful girl in a bar is confronted with "Mr. Wrongs"—aliens from outer space—who magically turn into "Mr. Rights" after using Right Guard. Finally, the best commercials relate the product to genuine concerns of young people—unlike an ad for Canoe cologne that shows product users able to paddle a canoe, floating in midair, past a long line at a nightclub or up to their girlfriends' doors.

Even accurate slice-of-life ads may still fail if they are insensitive to the problems of young people. For example, Oxy-10 acne medication commercials feature an unfortunate teenage boy, who is called various denigrating names, including "Zitzo," by an unseen announcer with a deep, bellowing voice. Later in the ad, the boy puts a bag over his head because of his acne problem. Although these feelings may be realistic, it is callous for a company to humiliate potential customers by preying on their embarrassment or making them feel freakish.

Another problem in creating youth-aimed slice-of-life commercials is representing young people's dealings with parents and adults. For example, one ad for a major fast-food chain showed teenagers on a school trip stopping in the restaurant. The commercial failed miserably in testing because the teachers were too polite to the students and the students were too obedient during the bus ride. The ad never aired.

A far more effective ad, described by Bill O'Neill, director of public relations at Pontiac, was the 1985–86 commercial for the Pontiac Sunbird titled "Still Young." This ad presents a realistic relationship between a high school-age boy and his mother, who may be a single parent. The son suggests that his mother buy a red Sunbird, but she feels it may be too sporty. The son reassures her that she is "still young." Later, he is pleased when she picks him up at school in her new red Sunbird. He tells her, "I think it's *you*, mom." When she persists in her doubts— "You really think so?"—he answers, smiling, "Well . . . actually—it's more *me.*" Young people like to see this type of comfortable and playful relationship between teenage children and parents. Moreover, the commercial is also effective at reaching adults.

Certainly, slice-of-life ads present many pitfalls, but when one is on target it can be extremely effective in convincing youth to try a product.

6. LIFESTYLE ADVERTISING

The lifestyle ad is the type most commonly used to target youth. And indeed, the style is very effective because it "soft-sells" young people by making them feel that a product is appropriate for their lifestyle. However, an ad's success depends on how much young people identify or hope to aspire to the lifestyle being presented.

Sometimes the effort to link a product to an extremely desirable lifestyle can go too far. William Howell, president of Miller Brewing Company, notes that one Löwenbräu beer campaign— "Here's to Good Friends—Tonight Let It Be Löwenbräu"— failed because it made the product seem inaccessible to the average beer drinker, a beer that was only for special occasions. The company's more recent campaign, "This World Calls for Löwenbräu," corrected this image problem by linking the beer with everyday, social drinking around the world, wherever great beer is loved.

Some of the best lifestyle ads, specifically aimed at teenagers, have been done by Mountain Dew. This soft drink is specially formulated to appeal to teenagers. It is very sweet, low in carbonation, high in caffeine, and citrus-based. Each year, at least one of its commercials focuses on a current or coming trend of young people. For example, in 1984, Mountain Dew ads featured break dancing; in 1985, they showed bike dancing (aerial tricks done on a bicycle); and in 1986, skate boarding and mountain surfing (surfing against the tide on a stream).

Similarly, the American Home Sewing Association's campaign "Be an American Original" featured the trend toward unique, unusual fashions in developing a music-video-style commercial encouraging teenagers to begin sewing their own clothes.

Moreover, as Richard Blossom, vice-president of marketing for Pepsi-Cola USA, explains, "Youth can be a communication tool to help show what is hot, in tune, current. Parents can relate to these best qualities of youth." This is the basis for the "Pepsi Approach" lifestyle advertising. For example, young athletes illustrating the qualities of health, vigor, and fitness are the focus of Del Monte canned vegetable's "You Work Hard for Your Body" commercial. Of course, commercials for fashion products such as Levi 501 Jeans' "501 Blues" and Jordache Jeans' "You've Got the Look" predominantly feature young people, since youth is often viewed as setting fashion trends.

Another important consideration in creating effective lifestyle ads is setting a mood unique to the product. Bill Weed, director of Ogilvy Group and of Ogilvy & Mather Worldwide, produced the highly stylistic "Sports Illustrated—Get the Feeling" commercial for his client *Sports Illustrated.* The commercials focused on the feelings of a single athlete in the midst of competition, creating an atmosphere of tense drama, excitement, and explosive emotions of success or failure. Sometimes a good strategy is to repeat a key visual or audio image, closely linked to the product or its attributes, throughout the commercial. For example, Edward Meyer, chairman and president of Grey Advertising, described a clever 1985 ad developed for one of his firm's clients, the roast beef restaurant chain, Arby's. The campaign, titled "Be Lean," highlighted the fact that Arby's roast beef was lean. The key visual showed young people engaged in various activities literally "leaning" to one side, interspersed with shots of lean, appetizing roast beef.

For young people, this advertising style probably has the greatest ability to establish a youthful image for a product. This youthful image can make the product the most popular brand in its category, but it can work just as powerfully against the product.

In the previous chapters, we advised on the selection of a YouthTrends Approach that would provide the strategic framework for any campaign. We provided advice on how to effectively use humor, music, sex, and celebrities, and how to evaluate those ads against the competitions. We also noted the most common mistakes to avoid in developing an ad. In this chapter, we reviewed the final tools that marketers must use to create youth-appealing ads. We examined the particular advantages and disadvantages, opportunities and pitfalls, of incorporating any combination of these factors along with a slogan or a jingle into mass-media advertisements. In the next two chapters, we analyze how promotions can supplement any YouthTrends advertising campaign.

10

THE DEVELOPMENT OF A YOUTHTRENDS PROMOTIONAL CAMPAIGNS

Many of our clients are interested in creating events
and sponsorships to capture the youth market. We
have created youth-oriented or youth educational
programs for companies as varied as Aetna Life
Insurance, Milton-Bradley, Miller Brewing, and
Hershey Foods.

—Paul Alvarez,
chairman of Ketchum Public Relations

*A*ccording to Edward Meyer, chairman of Grey Advertising, "The young adult audience is the most difficult audience to reach through mass advertising." Because young people neither read or watch television as frequently as other consumer groups, many of them miss both print and TV ads. Given this reality, a critical part of any youth-targeted campaign must be promotions—activities aimed directly at young people—that can reach them in places where ads don't normally exist: at a beach or in a movie theater, on a college campus or in a mall, or even at a rock concert.

As with advertising, the primary purpose of promotion is to

sell a product or service. A promotion sells much more in-
directly than advertising, often by getting the consumer involved in some type of activity—a contest, a lecture, a coupon
redemption, or any other offering that elicits a desire to participate. Though it may require more effort on the part of the
consumer, a promotion will often seem to be less of a sales pitch
than an ad that shouts, "Buy me!"—and it can be a lot more
fun. As Paul Alvarez, chairman of Ketchum Public Relations
reminds us, "It is usually a non-biased third party, like a news
story or magazine article, which heralds the product. While it's
not as direct, it's often more believable than an ad."

Promotions can be used to introduce new products, to
change the images of existing products, or to popularize an
existing product that people have basically forgotten about.

There are many different forms of promotion, all designed to
serve different purposes. To begin with, there is the basic publicity that a company might seek from newspapers or news programs for new types of products or services to be introduced to
the market.

A more active promotional strategy is direct-mail marketing,
a misunderstood, underused but very effective method for
reaching young consumers. According to James Schaefer, president of Needham Harper's DR Group, "Direct marketing is a
highly sophisticated way of segmenting the market and deciding which groups of people would most likely buy a particular
product. Frequently, this method will be aimed at receiving a
direct response and can single out the customers who will most
likely respond to future products made by the same company."
Schaefer points out that all those toll-free numbers in TV ads
illustrate the popularity of direct marketing, as does the new
interest that young people are showing in mail-order catalog
shopping.

Other forms of promotion include contests and special events
that companies sponsor to attract potential buyers. Although
these programs might seem easy to implement, they often re-

quire as much publicity and advertising support as the company's product itself. Still, they offer significant benefits by involving young consumers, who are often beyond the reach of traditional media, creating excitement about a product and establishing a personal connection between the product and its potential purchaser. In the following pages, we will discuss the promotional experiences of our own consulting firm and those of public relations executives at Burson-Marsteller, Ketchum Public Relations, Manning Selvage & Lee Public Relations, Coca-Cola, General Motors, American Express, and others.

Specifically, we'll examine three major promotional strategies—direct mail, contests, and events targeted at youth—as well as an unconventional new practice, promoting through the movies.

Using Direct Mail

Direct-mail marketing offers companies some very significant advantages. First of all, it allows them to target young consumers directly, based on a wide range of criteria including age, sex, geographic area, and interests. Mailings that come right into young people's homes focus attention on a product over a longer period of time than can be achieved through a print, radio, or television commercial. Furthermore, direct-mail pitches distinguish companies from competitors who use only traditional advertisements to reach young people.

Obviously, the effectiveness of any mail campaign depends on how well a company can follow up on the promotion. Ideally, each mailing should induce some action by the consumer—to visit a store, to return a card for more information, to enter a contest, or to receive a free sample or a discount coupon—because it is this action that reinforces the product's name in the young purchaser's memory. With such procedures, direct mail can be an effective method of presenting a product to the youth market.

WHAT TO SELL

What products are promoted by direct mail today? The range is almost unlimited. For example, Patricia Norman, marketing manager at Columbia House Records, explains that they have established a very successful direct-mail marketing program. This record club offers new members eleven albums for one cent, if they agree to buy seven more at full price over the next three years. Amazingly, 40 percent of its customers are respondents to direct-mail solicitations, including a large percentage of youth members.

Clothing companies, too, have entered the direct-mail stakes, as Rhonda Gainer, advertising director for Daniel Hechter menswear, explains. In 1985, this manufacturer of high-fashion garments for the young, athletic man sent out 500,000 direct-mail pieces to the college market and to previous purchasers of Daniel Hechter suits. The principal purpose of the mailings was to encourage the consumer to see the company's new lines in their local clothing stores. The promotion was supported by in-store displays highlighting the products shown in the mailings.

A wide variety of other products—clothing accessories, posters, calendars, and stationery—are now being sold through catalog, newspaper, and magazine mail orders. The United States Armed Forces is also joining the ranks of direct-mail marketers. According to Thomas W. Evans, its deputy director of advertising and sales promotion, the Army probably runs the largest youth-oriented direct-mail campaign in the country. Each year, it sends 20 million pieces to high school juniors and seniors, to recent high school graduates, to law and medical school students, and to members of the Army Reserve. High school juniors receive one or two mailings to acquaint them with the various Army programs and benefits, and then are contacted once again in the fall term of their senior year. Further mailings follow based on the student's response.

One thing that the Army does to encourage students to respond is to offer special premiums. For example, it may send those who request additional information free Army-logo tube socks, sweatbands, or posters. Overall, the program is a tremendous success, with a remarkable response rate of 5 to 6 percent. Certainly, if the Army can sell young people on a new profession through the mail, corporations should be able to devise direct mailings and followup procedures to encourage the purchase of their products or services.

MAILINGS TO COLLEGE STUDENTS

The Army's direct-mail program is aimed chiefly at high school students, but college students may prove even better targets for other products and services. For one thing, while still in school, these consumers are easy to find. Companies interested in college graduates, with their higher earning (spending) potential, can seek them out on campuses and begin to build brand loyalties before students disperse into the larger adult population. Sears Roebuck and Company, Montgomery Ward, Texaco, and Mobil are among the major firms now using direct mail to encourage college students to apply for their credit cards.

College students can be located through the student directories published by most universities. Although some private schools balk at providing listings to corporations, in most states, nonprivate college student directories are public documents available to all interested parties. One problem with using directories is that college populations are by their very nature transient. Each year at least one-quarter of the students will no longer reside at the addresses that appear in these directories (the result of graduation, dropouts, and transfers) and an even greater number will move to different apartments or dorm rooms. However, mailings can be directed to dorm rooms or box numbers, rather than to individual occupants. Though many college students quickly develop an aversion to junk mail and do not bother to open unpersonalized letters, this method can be effective if the materials sent are eye-catching enough to warrant notice.

Just to illustrate the magnitude of this market, there are roughly 1.5 million box numbers of college dorm rooms, assigned to some 2.5 million students at over four hundred colleges. Approximately 40 percent are freshmen, 30 percent are sophomores, and 15 percent each are juniors and seniors. Having procured the list of dorm room addresses/box numbers, a company will have to update it only when new dormitories are built.

Another way to locate college students and other young people is to rent an address list. For lists, many marketers turn to Martin Lerner, president of the American List Corporation and its subsidiary, the American Student List Company. His company is the largest student list firm in the country and the only one whose shares are traded on a stock exchange. Its lists include the names and addresses of 2.7 million high school students, as well as some 3 million college students, cross-referenced by class in school as well as field of study.

The strong growth of this company attests to the fact that companies are increasingly using direct mail to reach the youth market; the firm's 1985 revenues came to $3.5 million, up almost 30 percent from the previous year. The clients of the American Student List Company include various national youth organizations, magazine publishers such as *U.S. News & World Report,* insurance companies, and branches of the U.S. Armed Forces. As Martin Lerner explains his success, "Young people like to receive literature in the mail. Just getting their own mail for the first time in their lives is exciting."

Sponsoring Youth Events

Event Marketing is a very important aspect of any promotional campaign aimed at young consumers. While many companies would rather spend all of their promotional monies on ads because they seem less complicated, it has been shown that companies that sponsor events create a more personal identity for themselves and establish a more loyal following among their potential customers. As surprising as it may sound, concerts and other music events represent only a small fraction of the wide variety of youth-appealing events available for sponsorship.

There are eight major points to keep in mind when designing an event for young people:

1. SPONSOR PARTICIPATORY RATHER THAN OBSERVABLE EVENTS

In order to gain the enthusiasm of the youth population, an event has to invite their involvement. Young people are compelled to spend most of their time in school, sitting uncomfortably and listening to teachers lecture. As Tony Tortorici, head of public relations at Coca-Cola says, "At Coca-Cola, we like to work with or develop events that have a high participatory nature." And to get young people involved, an activity has to be fun. Jane Barr, senior vice-president of Burson-Marsteller Public Relations, says, "Young people are very hard to excite. When we want their attention, our presentations have to include a sense of humor, involvement, and, most importantly, a relevancy to their lifestyle."

One event that met all three of Jane Barr's criteria was developed by Milton Bradley and Ketchum Public Relations. Ketchum's idea was to create the world's largest Twister Game (the body game you play by stretching hands and feet onto a giant playing mat) at a Florida beach during spring break. Not only was the game fun, but the sole participants were young people. Other kinds of participatory events that companies might want to sponsor include high school or college track meets or other sports competitions—even jazz and rock concerts. Concerts can be made even more appealing if they are connected to a charity or a nonprofit group. While young people could only observe such events such as Live Aid, Farm Aid, and Drive Aid, the fact that these concerts raised funds for worthy causes gave attendees a sense of participating.

2. PLAN EVENTS UNIQUELY SUITED TO THE PRODUCT BEING PROMOTED

If a company sells typewriters, it doesn't make much sense for it to sponsor a beauty contest. If a firm sells panty hose, it shouldn't sponsor a swim meet. While these cautions may sound like simple common sense, many companies systematically fail to match their products with events that are uniquely suited to, or even appropriate for, promotion.

Young people are not as naïve as many marketers seem to believe and will certainly look cynically on silly or inappropriate sponsorships. For example, Leaf's Good & Plenty, the popular coated-licorice candy, hosted a ski chase dubbed New England's finest ski marathon. After all, why would a candy company sponsor an event designed to appeal to athletic, health-minded individuals, who would shun sugar?

Edward Stanton, president of Manning Selvage & Lee Public Relations, developed a promotion much more logically linked to a product. "Several years ago, before the drinking age was raised, I was trying to think of a way to popularize Bordeaux wines and realized the best audience would be graduate students and college students." After considering several creative ways to promote the wines, Stanton says, "I decided that we would *teach* students about wines and wine-tasting by sponsoring on-campus wine appreciation seminars. Campuses around the country found the seminars exciting. It was public relations at its best—no advertising and no heavy sales pitch."

Converse, the major athletic sneaker manufacturer, created an equally innovative event that tied in well with its products. It sponsored the Converse Test Run, personally inviting almost 200,000 active joggers in seven different American cities to try out its new models. Not only did the promotion generate publicity, it enabled thousands of potential customers to try the new product.

3. DECIDE EARLY WHETHER EVENTS WILL BE LOCAL OR NATIONAL

It is very important to determine the scale of a promotion from the outset. Will it be one large event held at a centrally located site, or will there be several events running in different parts of the country? Not only will early planning help fix a budget, it will also allow time to work out publicity plans. It may be hard to raise enough "hoopla" over any single event—no matter how lavishly designed and executed it is. If the product being promoted is distributed nationally, it may be more logical to organize several smaller events than to expect one large event to attract the national media. Even such an event as the Jackson's Victory Tour, sponsored by Pepsi, was locally structured, with Michael Jackson and his brothers garnering a new audience and new publicity at each city on the tour.

When staging a local event, it is often a good idea to enlist the help of local dealers and distributors of the product being promoted.

4. SCHEDULE EVENTS AT TIMES WHEN YOUNG PEOPLE ARE AVAILABLE

Most young people attend school throughout much of the year and have limited mobility during semester exam periods, standardized testing times, and the recruiting season. Therefore, schedule youth events over the summer—but not on weekdays, as most students hold jobs—during breaks, and on holiday weekends. Without doubt, the most popular time for youth-oriented events is, the spring break period between mid-March and mid-April.

Another vacation time that many event planners neglect is the intersession break, from late December to mid-January, that most schools allow their students. Unlike most companies, which focus solely on spring break, Busch beer has developed a range of promotions for this period, including ski competitions and ski reports on local radio stations. These sponsorships tie in well to Busch's advertising campaign and to its slogan, "Head for the Mountains." Other companies might well consider planning events for this winter vacation slot, rather than to compete in the overbooked spring break period.

5. DECIDE WHETHER TO SPONSOR A SERIOUS EVENT, A FUN EVENT, OR A GIMMICKY EVENT

As much as the type of event, the mood of the promotion must be suitable for the product. While fun or gimmicky promotions may attract more attention than serious events, they may not always be appropriate. The ideal event is probably one that can deliver a serious marketing message, if need be, while allowing participants to have fun. Examples of serious events might be workshops on improving study skills or on surviving a job interview. ArtCarved Class Rings has promoted such academically oriented events.

Undoubtedly, some of the most successful youth-oriented events are those that focus on entertaining or fun activities. Such promotions might include music concerts or sports events such as the Cracker Jack Old-Timers Baseball Game or the Hi-C Frisbee Throw. Miller Lite beer sponsors comedy showcases on college campuses that not only feature professional comics but also allow young student comedians to perform. Miller is also the exclusive sponsor of the National Intercollegiate Rodeo Association, which stages many rodeo events around the country.

Another clever event that fell under the "fun" category was Wendy's "Where's the Beef?" Monday Night Football Game. According to Bruce Ley, Wendy's marketing vice-president, "We tried to create a fun concept by bringing together two upbeat concepts: the popularity of Clara Peller, the hamburger chain's comical spokesperson, and ABC-TV's fun-filled weekly football games."

The gimmicky event category would include a project sponsored by Johnson Wax's new Raid Flea Spray for dogs. Called the Raid Flea for All, this event was a dog-washing contest that took place in high schools. According to Susan Harris of Manning Selvage & Lee Public Relations, "We organized this event as a fundraiser for high schools and their proms. For each dog that was sprayed and cleaned at this event, Raid donated a dollar toward the school prom." This outrageous gimmick attracted many young people, as well as a lot of notice to the fact that Raid was now selling something other than garden spray.

6. DETERMINE WHEN TO INVOLVE A COSPONSOR AND CHOOSE ONE WITH A COMPLEMENTARY PRODUCT

When staging an event that is too costly and complex for one sponsor, a company should evaluate its copromoters carefully. Young people are too easily distracted to sift out one firm from a long list of sponsors. Even a single second sponsor who will help save money, can dilute the attention that a solo promoter can garner.

When it is absolutely necessary to have a co-sponsor, choose a company that is not, in any way, a competitor. And no matter how reputable the company is within the business community, make sure that it enjoys a positive image among young people.

It makes no sense to undercut the benefits sponsorship offers by hooking up with a product that young people consider old-fashioned. Ideally, a cosponsor will naturally complement a company's product and image, or even help to enhance them. Best of all is a cosponsor who does not have an identifiable product to sell—such as a sports team, a shopping mall company, a radio station, and so on.

7. CHOOSE AN EVENT SITE WITH NATURAL YOUTH APPEAL

Where an event takes place is as important as the event itself. Not only must the site be accessible to a group that sometimes lacks the mobility of their car-owning parents, but it also has to have an atmosphere that appeals to young people. Some ideal sites for events include dance clubs, shopping malls, stadiums, department stores, college campuses, and amusement parks. *Spin* magazine has used dance clubs for some of its events. Says Diana Holtzberg, vice-president and marketing manager for the music/entertainment magazine, "Our event locations can help us draw a lot of publicity. At a recent party we gave in a New York dance club, we were visited by the *Entertainment Tonight* TV show."

Another company that chooses creative promotions sites is Anheuser-Busch, the makers of Budweiser beer. Instead of competing with all the other firms who ran spring-break promotions in Fort Lauderdale and Daytona Beach, Budweiser developed an image-enhancing public service. Jack Mac-Donough, vice-president of Anheuser-Busch, explains, "Since many people drive to their vacation spots, we sponsored coffee and doughnut pitstops along the three major highways that led to the Florida beach areas." The company was thus able to promote safe driving, a positive image for its brand name.

8. INVITE YOUNG PEOPLE TO HELP PLAN AND PUBLICIZE AN EVENT

No matter how elaborate an event becomes, don't forget about the target audience. It is a very good idea to check all of the plans with some of the young people who will actually attend the event. These insiders can advise on the nuances of campus life—and advise whether the student lounge is more comfortable than the dining hall—and warn of major conflicts, such as a big football game scheduled for the very same afternoon.

These young people can also help publicize the project, especially if they are campus leaders. Good word-of-mouth advertising from such people as the student body president or fraternity and sorority officers will give more strength to a company's ads, posters, and press releases.

Specific types of events to target each segment of the youth market are discussed in Chapter 13. Another special kind of promotion that will both attract young consumers and enhance a company's image is a contest, which we'll cover in the next section.

Creating Youth-Appealing Contests

Contests, in a way, are the quintessential youth event. They offer young people the chance not only to participate but also the anticipation and thrill of winning a prize. And for companies, they offer significant benefits as well, from short-term media attention to good will and brand loyalty. If designed properly, contests can launch new products and make old ones appear more popular, as well as alter the image of an established product and its company.

After working with many clients and interviewing several others who have conducted successful contests, we have compiled ten rules for running a contest, from its planning stages, through to its selection of winners and the awarding of appropriate prizes.

1. USE CONTESTS TO INTRODUCE PRODUCTS OR TO REVITALIZE OLDER ONES

A contest can be used to popularize a product and make it seem up to date. There are many product categories and brand names that could benefit from the trendiness a well-publicized contest can impart. McCall Patterns and General Foods are just two of the major companies that have used contests to make their products more popular among young people.

It was no secret to McCall's that sewing was no longer considered a popular activity for young people. So, both to improve the activity's image and to encourage young people to consider it as a hobby, McCall's developed its clever Sew 'n Show contest. The company's president, Earle Angstadt, reports that the eight-year-old contest has revitalized the hobby's image, and thus, slowed down the projected decline in pattern purchases among young people.

Faced with a similar problem, General Foods joined *Seventeen* magazine in sponsoring a contest to encourage young people to cook. This highly promoted cooking contest required the use of many General Foods products that wouldn't normally catch the attention of young people (for example, Minute Rice, and Stove Top Stuffing). Not only does the contest introduce a new generation to these products, the contest's popularity also can make cooking seem trendy and attractive to young people.

2. CHOOSE A CONTEST FORMAT THAT IS RELATED TO THE PRODUCT

Just like events, contests should clearly reflect the images of sponsoring companies. Both the prizes and the rules should be logically connected to the product being promoted. For example, the Danish Tourist Board created an extremely successful contest by keeping it closely tied to its product—Denmark. Called the Hans Christian Andersen Essay Contest, it required contestants to write a 100 to 300 word essay about Hans Christian Andersen's fairytales. Only fourteen-year-olds were eligible to enter—young people the same age as Hans Christian Andersen when he traveled around Denmark. Prize winners received free tours of Denmark.

3. GIVE CREATIVE, APPROPRIATE PRIZES

Most young people don't consider cost in determining what they like. A contest's prizes may cost a fortune, but if they aren't appropriate, young people won't bother to enter. For instance, few young people would want to win a trip to Mexico for one person. They will be just as reluctant to compete for a chance to win such prizes as rare hand-made guitars, attaché cases, or artwork.

Cash is always a welcome prize, but it's not original enough to make a contest really exciting to young people. The best prizes are creative ones, things that a young person could never buy in a store. For example, Canada Dry offered winners of a contest the choice of $1 million or a dinner with Joan Collins. While the choice was outrageous, many young people were excited by the prospect of winning a dinner date with a favorite TV actress.

Cosmetic companies can offer free makeovers in department stores to their winning contestants. Many companies, like Noxell, promise contest winners the chance to appear in an upcoming ad—certainly a prize that no young person could buy. Food and snack companies can reward their winners with an all-expense-paid party at a club or restaurant in their home city—and tickets to sold-out concerts are always attractive prizes. When Pontiac sponsored its Hall & Oates concert promoting

Fiero, it ran a contest giving away free passes to the performance.

Donna Alda, who has designed some of MTV's most creative contests, described some of her company's unusual prizes: "We had a contest related to an album by John Cougar Mellencamp, and we decided to buy a house in his hometown of Bloomington, Indiana. The winner received the house (a risky, yet successful choice for a prize) as well as a housewarming party. We have given away trips to London to see popular music performers, as well as the stretch limousine that appeared in Dan Akroyd's movie *Doctor Detroit*. Young people like our prizes because they are exciting fantasy prizes that relate to the MTV product." Alda's ability to choose appropriate awards attracts as many as 500,000 entrants to her contests.

As noted above, McCall Patterns runs an annual sewing contest, requiring entrants to make a piece of clothing using one of the company's products. General Foods asks participants to try out its products for a cooking contest it sponsors with *Seventeen* magazine. Makers of more expensive items have contestants visit dealers in order to be eligible to win. For example, an auto company might say, "Test drive our car and get the chance to win $50,000 in our contest." A typewriter company might advertise, "Visit one of our dealers. And if you test type our new model, you'll have a chance to win a European Vacation." There is always a way to bring the contestants closer to a product.

4. TRY TO BUILD IN EARLY INSTANT-WIN INCENTIVES

Because young people are skeptical, as a rule, and because there are so many competing contests, a sponsor can gain more enthusiastic participants by providing some easy-win situations. No matter how complex the rest of a contest is, young people are more likely to enter it if there is a preliminary stage that lets them win money or a prize instantly. Ogilvy's Michael Vaughn mentioned that his agency used such a tactic in the Hershey contest. "We said that if the purchasers of the candy bar found a picture of Groucho Marx on the inside of the wrapper, we would instantly award them five dollars."

As Jane Maas, president of Muller Jordan Weiss Advertising, remarked, "When young people receive instant gratification from a contest, they have a better feeling about your product."

5. CREATE RULES THAT REQUIRE ENTRANTS EITHER TO SAMPLE OR TO PURCHASE THE PRODUCT

A sample brings consumers more in touch with the product and with its company's image. A "sample" might be a taste, a makeover, a try-on session, a free test drive, a purchase, or a personal examination of the product. After all, a sponsor needs more than just a one-time sale to warrant the costs of promotion. Ideally, a contest will introduce groups of young people to a product and will encourage them to think about the brand name. If no sampling or purchase is required to drive the message home, the product will soon be forgotten.

A purchase should be required for inexpensive items such as candy bars or soap. This can be achieved by requiring proof-of-purchase seals or by placing the rules inside the products package. As Michael Vaughn, senior vice-president of Ogilvy & Mather, explains, "We organized a contest for Hershey's chocolate called the '400,000 All-Star Greats Game,' and we put the instructions on the inside wrapper, along with an announcement on the outside of the candy bar wrapper."

6. WHEN POSSIBLE, BUILD IN REAL CONTESTANT PARTICIPATION

To establish a company's image or make a product memorable, it is absolutely necessary to have active involvement by contestants. No company will benefit by simply giving away money without making any demands on the entrants.

For example, to promote the movie, *Down and Out in Beverly*

Hills, Walt Disney's Touchstone Films division ran a unique contest. As Disney's senior vice-president Robert Levin says, "We sponsored a contest that got our audiences involved. All that people had to do was complete the sentence, 'I'd rather be down and out in Beverly Hills than —————.' We received more than twenty thousand entries." Levin also created a contest to promote the Judge Reinhold comedy *Off Beat.* "Since young people were the primary audience, we developed a fun contest for students who were vacationing in Florida during spring break. To compete in the contest, each person had to perform the 'Off Beat Jump,' which is displayed in the film."

Simple as these strategies were, they were critical to ensure that viewers remembered the names of the movies, as well as to reinforce Disney's positive image among young people.

7. DON'T CREATE RULES THAT IMMEDIATELY ELIMINATE MANY ENTRANTS

If a product or service is aimed at a large audience, the contest should be similarly targeted. Don't create rules that unnecessarily cut down the number of potential entrants. Nothing is more frustrating to a young person than seeing his or her favorite brands create contests with rules requiring, for example, a driver's license in order to enter.

Remember, too, that poorly phrased rules can unintentionally discourage potential contestants. This problem often arises in contests promoting products that are frequently, but not necessarily, associated with a certain sex. When running a cooking contest or a batting contest, be sure to work against sex stereotypes by emphasizing that both men and women are encouraged to enter.

Other rules that may discourage entrants are those that ask for the participation of the young person's parents or other family members. Requiring family involvement will immediately turn off a group that wants to feel independent of parents.

8. CHOOSE CONTEST COSPONSORS CAREFULLY

Again, like an event, a contest can lose its promotional value if there are too many cosponsors involved. Cluttering a contest with lots of brand names will leave young people confused as to the companies actually responsible and, consequently, feeling loyal to none. Worse, a cosponsor with a poor image among young people can make the contest unappealing, destroying any potential promotional benefits for its primary underwriter.

Other cosponsorship arrangements can be made with media companies, such as radio stations and magazines. As Richard Robinson, chairman of Scholastic, Inc., says, "We have been involved with our own Scholastic contests as well as ones sponsored by other companies. Since we are distributed in the schools, the *Scholastic* magazines are a favorite for those companies who are trying to reach the junior high and high school population." Many other magazines, such as *Seventeen, GQ, Glamour, Young Miss, Teen,* and *Mademoiselle* have also supported contests.

9. PUBLICIZE A CONTEST ON HIGH SCHOOL AND COLLEGE CAMPUSES

As Ed Chenetz, vice-president of Scholastic, says, "The best place to find students is in their own environment. Since our magazines are distributed in junior high and high school buildings, many companies come to us for assistance in the publicity stages." When Columbia Pictures ran a contest to promote the movie *Close Encounters of the Third Kind* to high school students, it went to *Scholastic,* exclusively, and advertised in the magazine.

When trying to reach college students, a company should advertise in campus publications and on college radio stations. It is also helpful to send information to the financial-aid office, the career-counseling center, and the student affairs department. These offices will help publicize a contest by hanging up posters and speading the word to students who are looking for ways to earn or win money.

10. USE CONTEST WINNERS TO HELP PROMOTE THE PRODUCT

Since young people like to get involved, it pays to use them in product promotions once a contest is over. Such contests as Miss Teenage America have winners appear in magazines for interviews (with a mention of the contest sponsors, of course), as well as on talk shows.

Direct mail marketing and event or contest sponsorships are time-honored ways for companies to approach the elusive youth market. In the next section, we'll look at a less conventional strategy, promoting through the movies, and the companies who use it successfully.

Promoting Through the Movies

During the past few years, one new form of promotion has emerged, particularly for products aimed at youthful, trendsetting consumers—promotion through feature films.

It's a simple, clever strategy: All a company has to do is display its product prominently in a movie, where young potential purchasers will see it. These onscreen promotions are totally different from the commercials or trailers—that is, frank advertisements—that run before or after a film. A name-brand item that actually appears in a movie is likely to influence the audience subconsciously (or consciously) when they are next in the store or supermarket. Placements may be as blatant as Hershey Reese's Pieces candy, which appeared several times in *E.T.: The Extra Terrestrial,* or as casual as the Polaroid camera that Madonna used in *Desperately Seeking Susan.*

Such major companies as Lever Brothers, Guinness beer, MasterCard, and Hershey Foods have placed their products in feature films, either as background pieces or as important props used by the actors. Some of the products that have recently made specially placed "appearances" include General Mills' Wheaties cereal in *Rocky III,* Pepsi in *Flashdance,* All Detergent in Teri Garr's *First Born,* Mumm's champagne in *Jewel of the Nile,* AT&T Computers in Richard Gere's *Power,* Master-Card in Danny DeVito's *Wise Guys,* Campbell Soup in *The Cotton Club,* and Coca-Cola in Margot Kidder's *Little Treasure.*

Many placements are arranged by Frank Zazza, president of Advertising in Movies. "My job," he says, "is to function as a movie agent for any of my client products, like Polaroid Camera or Maxwell House Coffee, in the same way that the William Morris Agency functions for its client actors and actresses." Other agencies include Associated Film Productions, Unique Product Placement, Ensorcell, and others, many of which are on the West Coast; in addition, some companies, such as Pepsi–Cola, have established their own special departments to meet with movie producers and place products.

Generally, a placement agency charges a client company an annual retainer in exchange for ensuring a set number of product appearances. "But first," notes Zazza, "my client explains his advertising approach to me so that I can understand both the product's image and its intended audience." Once the agency understands how a manufacturer wants a product pitched, it offers some appropriate film scripts. At this point, Ford Motors, for example, might suggest that an MGM film character should drive its Mustang, or Smith-Corona might ask that the character playing an investigative reporter in a Universal movie use one of Smith-Corona's typewriters. The agent then elicits an agreement from the movie company that the film will capture the brand name or the product's likeness in reasonable detail.

Which brings us to the question, Who benefits from this promotional method?

Many marketers and movie people agree that both the products *and* the films gain from this new form of promotional association. According to Michael Moore, director of media planning at D'Arcy Masius Benton & Bowles Advertising, "Reese's Pieces candy was put on the map when it was placed in a movie as popular as Steven Spielberg's *E.T.*" But, in general, placement agents say that the products that gain the most are ones that people have already seen or purchased. If the featured product is too new, it may seem just like another prop in the movie.

And what about the movie company itself? How does it benefit from the placement of products in its films? Zazza, for one, feels a film is more realistic when a character opens a refrigerator and pulls out a loaf of Wonder Bread, as opposed to an unlabeled bag. He adds, "It breaks the continuity of a film for a character to drink from a can that says *soda* on the side. It no longer seems real to the audience."

But in addition to finding suitable vehicles for products, major placement agencies all organize the complex programs that the industry refers to as "front-end" and "back-end" promotions. When a company pays Frank Zazza a $50,000 retainer, he not only places its products in films but he also works with it to coordinate promotions that will help boost the movie's popularity. For instance, in-store, point-of-purchase displays may advertise the film or the maker might offer a discount coupon to shoppers. "My agency," adds Zazza, "is able to offset advertising costs on the part of the movie company as well as on the part of my clients' products."

Do film promotions really reach consumers?

According to Burt Manning, chairman of J. Walter Thompson Advertising, "Young people are especially influenced by the ideas and messages conveyed in the TV shows and movies they watch." Given this fact, as well as the incredible life cycle of the average popular film—from theater to video cassette to pay–TV to network television—a product's appearance in a single movie can have great impact. And because so many young people, especially, look to celebrities who endorse the "right" products, promotion in the movies seems to be a logical method for attracting F.L.Y.E.R.S., as well as other groups that want to keep up with the hottest trends.

Although the returns might not add up as quickly as those from print ads, the benefits of creating a youthful image through popular movies are incredible—so much so, in fact, that agencies are beginning to place client products on television programs as well. Recently *Dynasty, Dallas,* the *Love Boat,* and *Family Ties* have featured such products, respectively, as IBM personal computers, Visine eyedrops, and Sunlight detergent.

To those who know how badly Clark Gable hurt the T-shirt industry when he appeared barechested in *It Happened One Night,* it will come as no surprise that audiences respond to what they see on film. Just as that 1934 movie scene caused thousands of men to stop wearing undershirts, a single movie scene today can cause millions to begin buying a product that their favorite star is using on the screen.

So, as we see here, effective promotional campaigns can include not only direct-mail marketing, contests and special events, but they can also include a less traditional method of promoting a brand name—the placement of brand name products in popular, youth-oriented feature films and on popular TV programs. Whichever method is used, the result is the same: The young consumer is forced to think about the product one more time.

Just as essential as the advertising campaign, a company's promotional campaign can have a far-reaching effect on young consumers in that it can be designed to increase the excitement over a product (via contests and events), as well as eliminate the problem of waste (via direct mail), which many major advertising campaigns are simply unable to avoid.

11
FOUR SPECIAL PROMOTIONAL STRATEGIES

Most of the trends in our culture are begun by young
people. They set the styles for each other, as well as
for adults who want to look and feel youthful.

—Midge Turk Richardson,
editor-in-chief, *Seventeen* magazine

- Attracting Young People by Making a Product News-
  worthy
- Supporting Charitable Causes
- Making a Product a Status Symbol
- Turning a Product into a Trend or Fad

In Chapter 10, we discussed the basics of creating a widescale
promotional campaign using direct mail, special events, and
contests. But every marketer would like to give a product that
extra push, to ensure that the message reaches targeted consumers, or even to start a fad. Clearly, there is no formula for
making a product a trend, especially among cynical young
consumers. But advertisers can develop images for their products that go beyond mere positioning, to give them special
cachet through campaigns that are newsworthy (to earn special
attention), that glamorize them (to make products status symbols), or that capitalize on their trendiness (to maximize their

attractiveness to youth). Here we'll examine how companies have tried to tap—successfully or not—the image-conscious youth market.

Attracting Young People by Making a Product Newsworthy

"Pepsi's Slice is the first national juice-added soft drink. . . ." "Colgate-Palmolive has the first liquid dishwasher detergent. . . ." These are the kinds of news headlines—free product promotions—that every manufacturer would like to see when introducing or improving a product. While there has long been liquid detergent for use in the sink, the invention of a liquid for electric dishwashers in 1986 was remarkable enough to merit notice in newspapers around the country. What might seem a mundane development became a media event, thanks to intelligent marketing and public relations.

One of the primary reasons for a public relations firm's existence is its ability to make a product worthy of the media's attention. Paul Alvarez, chairman of Ketchum Public Relations and author of *What Happens in Public Relations,* explained "In my profession, we ultimately want to reach the consumer, but we have to do that by using a third party. This third party can consist of newspapers, magazines, and television news or interview programs. They repeat our message to the public."

But what does it take to make a product newsworthy? What does an advertiser have to do to attract the attention of a popular magazine, a newspaper, or the six o'clock news camera crew? This chapter will focus on companies who have succeeded, through various methods, in reaching youth's attention.

GIMMICKS

Very often, marketers court the press with gimmicks, such as creating a five-hundred pound salad for salad dressing (as Alvarez did at Ketchum Public Relations) or hanging a hundred-foot-long watch from a Japanese office building (as Swatch did). Perhaps the simplest gimmicks are the ad-carrying blimps that fly over cities and beaches. In 1985 McDonald's launched its own "McBlimp," named the *Big Mac I,* making sure to inform the media that its blimp is the world's largest airship.

Other gimmicks include sending a product into outer space! "Of course this was important to the media," said Pepsi-Cola president, Roger Enrico. "But sending Pepsi up in a space shuttle was most important for our employees, bottlers, and those people over at Coke."

SOCIAL SERVICE

Obviously, creating a gimmick is just one of the many ways in which a marketer can make a product or service noteworthy. The McDonald's hamburger chain deserves special credit for its newsworthy programs, sponsorships, and events that create positive publicity while also contributing to the public good. As the most popular restaurant among the F.L.Y.E.R.S. age group, McDonald's sponsors the Ronald McDonald House, a nationwide system providing housing near hospitals for parents of young, critically ill patients. Begun in 1974, the program is funded by local McDonald's restaurants, along with voluntary contributions. It now boasts fifty Ronald McDonald houses around the country. More than 200,000 family members are able to reside in the houses each year.

Another McDonald's program that attracted wide media coverage was its contribution to the new holiday in honor of Nobel Prize-winning Dr. Martin Luther King, Jr. McDonald's sponsored a twenty-city traveling exhibit that paid tribute to

King's achievements and recounted the history of the U.S. civil rights movement. Along with the exhibit, McDonald's commissioned a sculpture of King, as well as a movie. At the end of the tour, it donated the exhibit to King's Center for Non-Violent Social Change in Atlanta for permanent display.

Among other activities that maintain McDonald's national presence, the company sponsors the McDonald's All-American Basketball Team, the McDonald's Gymnastics Classic, and the Lorraine Hansberry Award for playwrights (the winning play was staged at Washington's Kennedy Center in 1983). All these programs ensure McDonald's at least periodic coverage in just about every major or hometown paper in the country involved with issues of concern to young people. From a sponsorship standpoint, McDonald's has cleverly created newsworthiness through its generosity.

Supporting Charitable Causes

Apart from direct social programs, companies also gain public relations benefits by contributing to causes young people support. Hands Across America, Live Aid, Farm Aid, and Drive Aid were all efforts to advance worthy causes through music and youth events. As Tony Tortorici, director of public affairs for Coca-Cola said, "We sponsored Hands Across America, the fundraiser to help disadvantaged Americans, because it was needed and because it reinforces our own product's positive image."

Referred to as "cause marketing," these events are ideal vehicles for reaching young people as they often involve celebrities, rock music, special videos, and tremendous participation on the part of local citizens. They are a news reporter's—and a marketer's—dream come true.

NEWSWORTHY PROCLAMATIONS AND ENDORSEMENTS

When Nabisco's Oreo cookie—the most popular cookie among young consumers—celebrated its seventy-fifth anniversary, it was a major topic in the news media. And why shouldn't it be? Why shouldn't Nabisco invite reporters to local cookie plants to get an on-the-spot story? Why shouldn't a local mayor proclaim an "Oreo Cookie Day"? Not enough companies announce or openly celebrate their anniversaries and thus miss out on invaluable publicity for their products.

Equally important are announcements of major shifts in company policies. For example, according to its vice-president James Klein, Avon Products was anxious to let the media know about its noteworthy trade with the Soviet Union. Although far more serious than hanging giant Swatch watches from Japanese office buildings, the move brought the company considerable publicity beyond the business community. Since cosmetics were not a very popular item among Soviet women, Avon garnered publicity in this country and elsewhere as they told newspapers about their cosmetics' introduction to a new culture that wanted to try something that was truly American.

Another way that companies attract media attention is through endorsements by major public figures. For example, when vice presidential candidate Geraldine Ferraro appeared in a Diet Pepsi commercial, hundreds of papers, magazines, and news programs talked about it.

VIDEO NEWS RELEASES

So once a company has done something, how does it let the media know about it? Of course, there is the written press release. But recently, the public relations world has been using something even better—the video news release that can actually be aired by TV stations. These videos feature company spokespersons, as well as quick cuts of the product or a press gathering. While some people question whether video releases undermine the honesty of broadcast reporting, they certainly make it much easier for a TV station to cover a company's events or announcements.

Making products newsworthy can certainly enhance its appeal to young consumers. Media coverage shows young people that companies share their concerns, in social service and cause marketing. Most important of all, products appearing in the news gain a measure of glamour in the eyes of young people, merely by association with the powerful communications industry. To image-conscious young consumers, a product that is important enough to warrant media coverage is important enough—and accepted as popular enough—to merit their own attention. Media coverage confirms or justifies the brand choices of insecure, uncertain youth.

In the next section, we'll examine the question of status more closely, analyzing how and why certain products become status symbols.

Making a Product a Status Symbol

In talking about the popularity of his products, William Howell, president of the Miller Brewing Company, claims that, for many, Lite Beer is a status symbol. "Beer is a badge product that creates a certain image for the person who drinks it. All consumers care about the image of the products they buy."

Indeed, in every product category, there is at least one brand that outranks its competitors in prestige. Many companies reason that their own brands can and *should* assume that elite role. For one thing, status symbols are much easier to sell than products commonly perceived as mediocre in quality, cost, or prestige. Once it reaches status-symbol level, a particular product is usually promoted not only by its manufacturer but also inadvertently by its competitors. For instance, competing Product X will constantly compare itself to status Product Y in its ads, claiming, "We are just as good as Product Y," or "We cost even less than Product Y." When a product becomes a status symbol, it is constantly used as the gold standard, further solidifying its Number 1 position in consumers' minds.

Everyone likes status. It makes people feel secure and confident. And young people, especially, are constantly looking for security in their world governed by peer pressure and the need for peer approval. More than any other group, young people want to own the right brand name in every product category— the right stereo, tennis racket, jeans, or even knapsack. Any high school student can tell you that every sneaker brand has had its day—from Keds to Pro Keds to Converse to Puma to Pony to Adidas to Nike to New Balance to Reebok. While they all sell at comparable prices, there are always certain labels that are in vogue. Today, an eighteen-year-old with Nike or Reebok basketball shoes has more status than does a Keds-wearing teenager.

Max Imgruth, president of Swatch Watch, agrees that young people are status conscious. "Our watches have become an important status symbol among teenagers and other young consumers." Just as adults enjoy choosing status-symbol cars, vacation spots, and clothing, young people choose items with the same thoughts in mind—although their criteria for status might be different.

HOW YOUNG PEOPLE JUDGE STATUS

When young people consider purchasing a product, they ask themselves a number of questions: Will it impress my friends? Will it catch attention? Will people laugh at me? Will it make people respect me more? Will it help me fit in? Is this what everyone is talking about? Will it make me seem more popular?

Does it seem better than the other products that I could buy? Is it unique?

While these seem like superficial concerns, they are very real to any young purchaser. The marketer who wants to push a product as a status symbol *must* address these concerns in the campaign. They are far more important to young people than some of the yardsticks that many adults use to judge status—more crucial, for example, than price.

At the present time, wearing a $30 Swatch watch will bring more status to a young person than would a $200 Tourneau. Among certain social groups, it is a status symbol to have a subscription to *Sports Illustrated* or to *Mademoiselle.* And while these magazines sell for less than $2.50, they allow their readers to enjoy respect from onlookers.

Indeed virtually any product can be turned into a status symbol—a snack food, a soft drink, a typewriter, a brand of perfume—anything that a young person can talk about, recommend, or brag about. Products become status symbols among young people chiefly because they carry with them easily recognizable images. When Boy Number 1 walks down the street eating ice cream from a cup that says "Haagen Dazs," he is making a stronger statement than Boy Number 2, who eats ice cream from an unlabeled cup. When people see Boy Number 1, they will think, "He is eating that new ice cream that everybody is talking about." They will conclude that Boy Number 1 has more status (money, taste, or whatever) than Boy Number 2.

Even "nonproduct" products such as movies and TV shows can become status symbols for young people. Even though the electricity costs the same for thirty minutes of the *The Cosby Show* and for thirty minutes of *Let's Make a Deal,* status-seekers know that *The Cosby Show* offers greater payoffs in prestige in conversations among friends.

WHEN IT PAYS TO EMPHASIZE PRICE

Many years ago, L'Oreal Cosmetics achieved great status by declaring that its products cost more than other haircare and beauty aids. At the end of each commercial, L'Oreal models would say, "But I'm worth it." This clever gimmick comforted even the wealthiest or most frivolous consumers who could then feel justified in spending more for L'Oreal hair coloring or shampoos.

By the same token, in selling to young people, it rarely pays to announce blatantly, "We cost more," without any special qualifiers or explanations. But, as for L'Oreal, it may help to raise the issue of price if the product can be shown to warrant its higher cost. Young people are more likely to link higher price with status if: a product is imported, a product has been proved to last longer than any other, or a well-known product has been fully redesigned and repackaged.

STATUS BY ASSOCIATION

Because there is no foolproof scale—not even price—for measuring status, young consumers generally assess products by comparing them to others on the market. Which brand is the newest? Which brand are magazines and stores advertising as the popular style? Which brand is worn by celebrities and famous athletes? Which brand is worn by their own group of friends?

There are certain social groups that can popularize a product and turn it into a widely accepted status symbol. Fashion designers, for example, have learned to launch their clothing lines at the most popular dance clubs. They know that if the "beautiful people" adopt their styles, the rest of the public will follow.

Still, a pitch to the top of the social hierarchy, with very sophisticated, materialistic advertising, may backfire among young people. As Janet Pines, manager of the Graduating Student program at American Express, explains, "Many college students are turned off when we attempt to tell them that the American Express card is a status symbol. Instead, we show them that it will help improve their lives by making purchasing more convenient." Even the term *status* has negative connotations among young people who live outside of such large urban areas as New York, Los Angeles, and Chicago.

HOW COMPANIES TRY TO CREATE STATUS SYMBOLS

Unfortunately, there is no surefire way to turn a product into a permanent status symbol. There are, however, methods that companies use to gain temporary prestige for their products. Many try offering celebrity endorsements. For example, actress Cybill Shepherd brought status to Reebok sneakers when she wore an orange pair to a formal awards ceremony.

Others repackage their products to give them a new image. Michael Vaughn, senior vice-president of Ogilvy & Mather Advertising and director on its Hershey Chocolate account, says that products like candy rely on product personality. Many would agree that Hershey's successfully created a status symbol when it introduced their Golden Almond candy bar in a very expensive-looking metallic gold wrapper.

Still other firms try advertising average-priced items in the same manner as higher-priced ones. For instance, according to Eric Weber of Dancer Fitzgerald Sample Advertising, "We created an ad for Nabisco's Bubble Yum bubblegum that used a formally dressed woman with a black gown, black hat, and long rhinestone earrings. She turns slowly toward the camera and then suddenly blows a big bubble with Bubble Yum." Associating a sophisticated, wealthy-looking person with Bubble Yum makes the product seem like a special kind of status symbol—a bubblegum for sophisticated people who want to have fun.

Perhaps the ultimate status symbol is the product that esta-

blishes a fad or a trend. In the next section, we'll look at some
of the ways companies have tried to push their products into
this league and why they have succeeded or failed.

Turning a Product into a Trend or Fad

Some executives say that it's impossible to create a trend,
though others would disagree—especially those who have succeeded. Whether a trendy or a faddish product can take on a
life of its own and survive once the public's excitement has
passed is still an open question.

For example, in 1984, when General Mills was having diffi-
culty with its Izod Lacoste clothing division, an executive tried
to explain the problem by saying that the "alligator shirt" had
simply been a fad that was now coming to an end. While he may
have been right, it hardly seems plausible that a fad would
simply die after going strong for two generations.

When most people are asked about fad products, they generally don't think about clothing or other everyday items. They
usually recall youthful, gimmicks like the Hula-Hoop, which
was popularized in the 1950s by the Wham-O manufacturing
company. And they mention the Pet Rock, which had its hey-
day in the 1970s. But do people ever consider such equally
popular items as the Swatch watch or the disposable cameras
made in Japan? Why aren't these considered fads? Is it because
they are perceived as practical, everyday products?

According to Robert Pittman, president of MTV Networks,
many thought that videos were going to become a short-lived
fad. "It took advertisers a long time to accept us as a new form
of media and entertainment that was here to stay." MTV has
become wildly successful and very influential. At some point it

ceased to be considered a fad and became what many marketers call an "existing trend."

Jane Maas, president of Muller Jordan Weiss Advertising, says a fad usually lasts for six months or less. "A trend suggests that there is interest which can last a longer time," Maas explained. "And it *is* possible for a trend to develop from a fad. A perfect example of this was the wearing of jeans. At first, jeans were a new fad for young people. But when they became accepted by adults, it became a widely accepted trend."

It is generally accepted that the media has the ability to turn an attitude or concept into a trend, as it did with the preppies, then the yuppies, and now the F.L.Y.E.R.S. *Seventeen* magazine's editor-in-chief, Midge Turk Richardson, and other media executives admit that their publications have the ability to start trends.

But what about nonmedia companies? Can they start trends and fads? "I've heard people in this business say things like, 'We are going to turn this product into the latest fad,' " remarked Burt Manning, chairman of J. Walter Thompson Advertising. "This is the wrong approach. I believe it is death for an advertiser to try to create a trend. The culture creates a trend and the marketer takes advantage of it."

Celia Visconti, senior account executive at Bozell & Jacobs Advertising, may disagree to some extent with those who don't believe in the creation of trends. In working on the Andrea Cosmetics account, which is aimed at the fifteen- to twenty-five-year-old age group, Visconti makes each Andrea product seem like a separate trend. Of course she has help from the manufacturer, which produce some spectacular items, such as fake eyelashes that are designed to look like black knitted lace.

"We keep up with current trends among young people and incorporate them into the marketing of our cosmetics," explained Visconti. "We have a lip color called 'Miami Ice' because of the obvious popularity of *Miami Vice*. When Madonna was just becoming popular, we dressed our models in Madonna garb."

Then, too, like Swatch, Andrea Cosmetics uses product names and ad lines that are truly outrageous, and which almost beg young people to buy them. Its makeup remover pads are called Eye Q's. One print ad, titled, "Rock Glitterati," shows a model with multicolored fingernails, and another ad shows black lace eyelashes advertised with the slogan, "Ooh la la lace!" The outlandish creativity that goes into the products and the ads is so overwrought that Andrea's line seems too trendy for a young person to pass up.

Another company that turned its product into a trend or fad was Dr. Pepper. Perhaps, again, it was outrageousness that gave the soft drink its trendy image. Through its "I'm a Pepper, You're a Pepper" theme period, the soft drink's name began to take on a new meaning—almost attempting to define a whole generation and its attitudes. As Robert Gleckler, senior vice-president of Young & Rubicam Advertising, tells it, "When the 'Be a Pepper' campaign was launched in 1978, we did it because we wanted to be talked about." Dr. Pepper became such a fad that the "I'm a Pepper" slogan was worn on T-shirts, shorts, and other products. This development made Dr. Pepper the third largest selling soft drink, just behind Coca-Cola and Pepsi-Cola.

Another executive who believes that companies can make their products trends is Edward Stanton, president of Manning Selvage & Lee Public Relations. He claims to have created a trend among college students during the 1960s. "By holding wine appreciation classes on college campuses," explains Stanton, who represented the California Wine Institute, "we *taught* them how to select and appreciate the product." More recently, Stanton is working on a project with *Seventeen* magazine and the fur industry. "We are trying to get more young women to wear furs. We sponsored a promotional contest in order to encourage students at design schools to create more youthful fur styles."

These are just a few examples of the companies that have attempted and succeeded in establishing their products as trends and fads. Nearly any product can become trendy, at least for a short time, as IBM learned several years ago when Apple became the hot computer among young people.

HOW COMPANIES KEEP A PRODUCT TREND GOING

Once a company has turned its product or service into a trend, there are several methods it may employ to maintain the public's interest. Beyond simply generating continuing publicity, the common avenues to consider are brand extension and licensing.

Some food companies, for example, are creating whole new lines in order to make their brand names seem new or current among the many recently developed products. Hershey's moved from producing chocolate candy to chocolate milk, and then when the granola bar craze started, it started making them as well. Nestlé Foods, too, capitalized on the popularity of its products by creating Nestlé's Quik ice cream bars and Nestlé Crunch ice cream sticks. By keeping its name associated with trends, Nestlé has become a fashionable brand.

Other companies have stayed in the public eye by licensing their names—that is, by renting the rights to their names and logos to other manufacturers. Perhaps the earliest examples of licensing took place in the film industry, with T-shirts, posters, buttons, and games carrying the names of popular movies and movie characters. As Lois Sloane, vice-president of licensing at Metro-Goldwyn-Mayer, says, "In the beginning, the movie industry and others only saw licensing as a way to publicize a movie, with a name or logo on T-shirts. Eventually, they saw that licensing went beyond publicity and was a business that could survive on its own." By working with manufacturers of clothing, games, sleepwear, plush dolls, porcelain mugs, posters, school supplies, and other products, Sloane has increased the popularity of MGM's past and current film properties. And indeed, the licensing business itself has thrived, developing into a $45 billion industry.

In addition to representing us in the licensing of "F.L.Y.E.R.S.: Fun Loving Youth En Route to Success" and its special logo for a line of youth-oriented products (which include sportswear, posters, etc), Sloane licenses *The Pink Panther,* Sylvester Stallone's *Rocky, Gone with the Wind, James Bond* and others.

Now the film companies have been joined by Coca-Cola, Yves Saint Laurent, *National Lampoon* magazine, Jordache, and Burger King, among other companies who have licensed their brand names for the creation of other products. Bruce Ley, vice-president of Wendy's, says that when the "Where's the Beef" line caught on, the company started to license the phrase for T-shirts and other products. Murjani, the company that licensed Gloria Vanderbilt's name for jeans, turned Vanderbilt brand and swan logo into a $600 million business, eventually encompassing such items as Vanderbilt Perfume and Vanderbilt tofu frozen dessert. Coca-Cola, too, went to Murjani to launch its line of Coca-Cola sportswear, as well as Coca-Cola umbrellas, radios, watches and so on. Whether they succeed financially or not, the products will keep the primary Coca-Cola product at the center of the public's attention.

12
Youth-Appealing Product Development

*V*irtually every product or service offered today has a potential youth market, even if young people are not its primary consumers. But in addition to considering youth-targeted marketing strategies, we must look at the product, itself, at the criteria young people use in making purchase decisions. Often there are ways to make minor modifications or to improve a product's packaging to enhance its youth appeal. Here we'll offer some ideas on changing established products, extending product lines, or even developing new products to tap the youth market while attracting youth-conscious adult consumers.

Features of a Product to Emphasize

Often targeting a particular product toward youth is just a matter of emphasis—without changing the basic product, simply recognizing those features that will make it attractive to young consumers. For example, it should come as no surprise that young people are eager to buy foods and beverages that contain natural ingredients. Whether or not this eagerness is a passing fad or not, young people certainly are more conscious of natural flavors, natural colorings, and so on. In recent years, well-publicized research has linked certain artificial ingredients, such as saccharine to cancer. Furthermore, many young people remember the controversy over Red Dye Number 2, the food coloring that was discontinued a few years ago. (In fact, there's currently a persistent rumor among young people that red M&M's temporarily disappeared because they contained Red Dye Number 2.)

When Philip Morris still owned Seven-Up soft drinks, it grabbed the young consumer's attention by pointing out that the cola beverages contained caffeine. Since young people realized that caffeine could be detrimental to their health, many of the noncola soft drinks jumped on the bandwagon and openly advertised on their cans that they did not use caffeine. And of course the original "troublemaker"—Seven-Up—placed a smart slogan on its own bottles and cans: "Caffeine. Never Had It, Never Will."

The low-sugar and low-sodium craze has given rise to dozens of food products, such as Del Monte Light and Lite Salt, as well as all sorts of "Lite" or "Light" frozen meals. To take this one step further, there are many snack food purchasers who are delighted to hear that their Cheetos cheese puffs contain real cheddar cheese or that Nabisco now offers natural ingredients in its Chuckles fruit slices.

And don't think that foods and beverages are the only products that can benefit by highlighting their use of natural ingredients. Shampoos such as Faberge Organics are now labeled "Contains pure wheat germ oil and honey" or "Made with whole milk and eggs." Many hair creams advertise that they contain natural beeswax. While the consumer has no idea of the actual benefits of honey, milk, eggs, wheat germ, or beeswax on hair, the ingredients seem healthy and appealing.

Awareness of concerns important to young people can help companies identify other qualities of their products that can attract this essential consumer market. A few more of these considerations will be covered in the next section, "Product Improvements and Modifications."

Product Improvements and Modifications

Often it takes only minor modifications to make a product substantially more attractive to young people. For example, like Walt Disney Productions, you can modify your product to make it more in tune with the youth lifestyle. Young people think of Walt Disney Films as the maker of "family" films, films that they should try to avoid as soon as they are old enough to voice a choice. However, we spoke with Robert Levin, senior vice-president of motion picture marketing at Walt Disney Productions, about the company's Touchstone Films. The mission of this division is to produce high-quality movies primarily rated PG–13, although some would be PG or R rated. The division's first film was the smash hit *Splash;* the extremely successful comedy *Down and Out in Beverly Hills* was its first R–rated picture. Not the typical "teen exploitation film," these Touchstone films have been well-received by young people, who buy half of all movie tickets.

As well, product improvements can come about by improving on the best design of competing products. But companies must make modification decisions by better understanding the needs, concerns, and attitudes of young people; by knowing how they feel about brands within a product category; by hearing how they describe competing products; by looking to the criteria on which they make decisions among brands, whether it be price, quality, image, style, etc.; and by learning what they hope to see next.

For example, as Keith Reinhard, chairman and chief executive officer of Needham Harper Worldwide Advertising, explained, one of his firm's clients, W. R. Wrigley, modified its traditional stick gum to fulfill the quality demands of young consumers. In the late 1970s, Beechnut, one of Wrigley's major competitors, launched Bubble Yum, the first soft chunk bubblegum, in response to research showing that young people wanted a softer gum that could blow bigger bubbles. And, indeed, this change made Bubble Yum the nation's largest-selling gum. However, as Wrigley discovered, there was a problem with Bubble Yum: When these bigger bubbles burst, they would stick to the face and hair of the bubble blower. So Wrigley invented Hubba Bubba, a soft chunk gum like Bubble Yum, which could produce big bubbles that would not stick. Wrigley attracted young consumers by improving its quality.

Sometimes a simple change in presentation—to make a product seem special or more trendy—can make the difference. Sealtest Ice Cream, for example, increased its market share through a clever but easily implemented design modification. The company had long produced a line of two-flavor ice creams, with the flavors placed side by side in the carton. But now, to enhance the product's appeal, Sealtest places the flavors in a checkerboard pattern. Although the new plan involves only a small modification, young people have found the difference visually attractive and exciting. Clearly these experiments offer some lessons for every industry.

Generally speaking, there are three major ways that companies can modify products to attract young consumers.

1. By making a product higher quality or lower priced. Many companies do not realize that young people are very quality conscious. Wrigley's learned that, by considering the drawbacks of the competition, it could improve product quality and capture a larger share of the market—with all other considerations, including price, being equal. Young people are willing to pay *more* when product quality seems to warrant it. Whether the product is sporting equipment, entertainment, clothing, cosmetics, stereo and electronic equipment, automobiles, televisions, or any other medium—to high-priced consumer good, most young people will look for the "best"-priced item, not necessarily the lowest-priced item.

2. By making a product more convenient to use or more appro-

priate for a young person's lifestyle. For young people, convenience and easy use are important aspects of product quality. Many young people reside in apartments or dorm rooms. They have no basic household conveniences, and they are often on the run. Products that are ready to use, more accessible, smaller, more compact, or time-saving can better be made part of their lives.

3. By making a product's design or presentation more stylish. As Sealtest's experience shows, it pays to make a product attractive to young people. Whether the result of modifications in color, size, shape, texture, smell, or taste, the product will benefit from seeming refreshed and renewed.

Packaging: A Critical Factor for Young Buyers

Often, a simple change in the packaging of a product can enhance its appeal to young people. It is wise to assume that young consumers will *always* judge a product by the design of its cover, container, or wrapper—and they will favor the ones with more contemporary, innovative styles.

Who says that running shoes must be sold in a cardboard box or toothpaste in a tube or potato chips in a bag? Pringle's Potato Chips became a craze among young people several years ago simply because they were sold in a tube-shaped cannister. Not only were the chips stacked perfectly, but the package prevented them from breaking. The package was brillant, but unfortunately, Pringle's went wrong in its initial selection of ingredients. Not only did the potato chips taste artificial, they were. Now the snack has returned to the shelves, with natural ingredients and with that extremely clever cannister package.

Clearly, packaging alone cannot sustain a product that does

not deliver on quality. But as the Pringle's experience shows, innovative packaging can make an immediate impact on potential young consumers.

Companies should assume that young consumers will always judge a product by its cover. Richard McLoughlin, publisher of *Reader's Digest* told us, "While the *Digest* is edited for adults, we feel young people will enjoy it if they pick it up." So why aren't more young people picking up the *Digest?* As we have discovered through interviews with our consulting firm's network of student testers, they don't even consider the magazine because of its staid, old-fashioned reputation.

Let's disregard the *Digest*'s "reputation" and place the magazine in front of a young person who has never heard about it before. What will cause him to pick it up and examine it? The answer is its packaging. Consider the front cover of the *Digest;* it is simply a table of contents that runs down the entire page—littering the cover with small type. This is not especially inviting to a reader—young or old—to say the least. The older generations come back to the magazine because they know it contains quality stories, and are willing to overlook an unappealing jacket. But what about potential new readers who know nothing about the publication's quality? Looking at the dull cover, they aren't persuaded to pick it up, disregarding the maxim "Don't judge a book by its cover."

Even established products can benefit from new, unusual packaging that makes them seem special or better. For example, Colgate has put its toothpaste in jars, tubes, aerosol containers, and finally in freestanding pumps. According to Roger Pisani, executive vice-president of Ted Bates Advertising, "Colgate was the first company to nationally launch the popular pump as a new manner in which to dispense dental cream." And not only did sales soar exponentially, but competitors copied the pump as well.

Recognizing how quickly young people picked up on this new packaging, Colgate expanded on its success with new commercials designed specifically to capture the young consumer. As Pisani, whose ad agency has handled Colgate since 1941, explained, "young people in the U.S. have a great influence on what their parents will choose." When Colgate's pump caught the attention of young people, the company knew that parents, the primary purchasers, would follow.

At least part of the pump's appeal was the gimmick—young people love "gadgety" products—but by eliminating the need to cap the toothpaste after use or to remember to squeeze the tube from the bottom to save paste, it was also a useful improvement.

It is worthwhile to experiment with new ways of storing or dispensing products. Chesebrough-Pond's, for example, recently introduced the Aziza Polishing Pen through its Prince Matchabelli division. Traditionally, nail polish has been packaged in a bottle with a brush, but the new Aziza nail polish comes in a tube shaped like a pen. The polish is applied with a flat pen tip, rather than with a brush, that gives the user much more control. While the nail polish pen may seem like just a gimmick, it is a very practical one, a real innovation. And it has been a great success, exceeding expectations by one-third, with sales of almost $15 million in the first year alone.

When considering repackaging a product or changing its present design to make it more attractive to young buyers, companies should keep four simple rules in mind.

1. DON'T CLUTTER A PACKAGE WITH TOO MUCH WRITTEN INFORMATION

Nothing is more likely to scare off young people than a cover or package that provides too much written information. Every package—whether it holds aspirin or cupcakes—should feature an appealing artistic design that doesn't require a lot of reading. Few purchasers will take the time to study an unfamiliar label so the pitch has to be made quickly and visually. And with a

lot of jumbled text running across a package, there is no room
for white space or the kind of colorful graphics that young
purchasers like.

Diet Seven-Up, for example, came up with a very effective
package for its recent no-caffeine, no-saccharine, NutraSweet
formula—handling a lot of essential information in a minimal-
type, visually exciting way.

Instead of running all the facts together, the designer sepa-
rated them into separate units, setting each one off in a different
corner of the label, in a different color or graphic format. In the
upper left-hand corner is a red diagonal stripe for the no-caffeine announcement. In the bottom right-hand corner is a red
oval-shaped graphic to signal the exclusion of saccharin, and at
the very bottom of the label, in a red rectangle, is the Nutra-
Sweet logo to broadcast the addition of the new sweetening
agent in the fewest possible words.

2. TRY TO DESIGN A PACKAGE THAT DOESN'T HIDE OR DISGUISE THE PRODUCT

People like to see what they are getting. And in the case of
snack foods, especially, young people are attracted to the product that looks the best. For years, Hostess has wrapped its
cupcakes in clear plastic. Why? One reason is that no piece of
art can be as appetizing as the real food itself. But beyond this,
displaying a product under clear plastic attracts the new purchaser, who may have never seen or heard of it.

Young consumers are often trying products for the very first
time; no matter how long a brand has been produced, the young
shopper may know nothing about it. If Bic didn't put its disposable shavers in a clear plastic package, would an eighteen-year-
old—who is unfamiliar with Bic and who has never bought a
razor before—take a chance on them? And just what *is* a Dorito
or a Cheez Doodle? If it weren't for those clear plastic windows,
the young, first-time purchaser wouldn't recognize either as
appetizing.

See-through packaging is especially important for newly released products. It was for this reason that the always-innovative Swatch Watch company used unusual, clear plastic watch cases to show off its product. As Swatch Watch president, Max Imgruth, told us, "Our product was new, and we knew that the watches' design and color had to be fully displayed to the consumer. Clear Lucite packaging was necessary." And young consumers responded to the colorful, wildly patterned watches since they could see them through the package, making Swatch popular for both its product and its presentation.

3. KEEP UP WITH CURRENT TRENDS IN DESIGN, COLOR, AND TYPOGRAPHY

While it certainly isn't necessary to change product packaging every year, it is important to realize that a product can begin to look nondescript on a shelf when it's sitting next to products that make use of current colors and styles. Today, for example, many packages are taking on a contemporary, hi-tech look. Containers for the popular ice cream Früsen Gladje and the yogurt Yoplait are very slick and glossy, with a style that looks and *is* very plastic, alive with vibrant colors. Of course, Früsen Gladje may not actually taste better than Breyer's or Yoplait any better than Dannon, but the young consumer feels that the hi-tech package makes what's inside seem more exciting and up-to-date. Contemporary packaging is especially important for "badge products," which convey an image to friends or to people the young purchaser wants to impress.

Like packaging design, colors also go out of style. Look at the Hershey's chocolate bar wrapper, with its dull brown and gray design. That package has remained virtually the same for several generations. Hershey bars get lost on the display counter. How can they compete with the loud reds, blues, bright oranges, and metallic silvers that grace other candy bar packages?

Steve Centrillo, the Bozell & Jacobs Advertising vice-president who handles Nabisco's Baby Ruth and Butterfinger candy bars, explains that lettering is another important consideration. When Nabisco acquired these products from Standard Brands, one of its first moves was to make the lettering bolder on their labels, while maintaining the colors that had been used traditionally.

Of course, in some cases, traditional packaging ties in with a product's image. Pepperidge Farm Cookies, for example, has a terrific slogan, "Pepperidge Farm Remembers." Its commercials, with an elderly spokesman, emphasize that Pepperidge Farm uses old-fashioned methods to maintain an old-fashioned flavor. The simple design of the cookie packages helps underscore this point—a concept appealing to young and older consumers alike.

4. WHEN ALTERING AN EXISTING PACKAGE DESIGN, EASE CONSUMERS INTO THE CHANGE

As much as they are captivated by packaging innovations, young people should not be bombarded with changes, changes, changes. If they see dozens of ads screaming, "See our new package . . . We look different, bolder, rounder, flatter, . . ." cynical young people will quickly pick up on the announcement and ask a doubting "Why?"

Pepsi faced this problem when it changed the Diet Pepsi logo and typography on cans and bottles in early 1986. Consumers were accustomed to the old Pepsi design, which was still strong enough to be fashionable. But according to Richard Blossom, marketing vice-president of Pepsi-Cola, "Diet Pepsi was twenty years old and we wanted a can that looked more contemporary."

Diet Pepsi used a special TV ad to announce the change, enlisting *Saturday Night Live* comedian Billy Crystal to appear in it. As Blossom described his plan, "We wanted a humorous way to say that we look different. We wanted to charm, rather than insult the consumer. The last thing we wanted was a serious commercial which said our can is now brighter and bolder."

The result was a very clever commercial that had comedian Crystal pointing to the new can and using his famous *Saturday Night Live* line, "You look mahhvelous." Young people knew Crystal's routine from the show, so his introduction of the design made them feel comfortable.

Line Extensions and New Product Introductions

Some companies are so conscious at the impact of the youth market that they are extending their present lines or even developing new products targeted at young consumers. For example, in 1985, Pepsi–Cola extended its line of soft drinks to include juice-added (lemon-lime, mandarin orange, cherry, and apple) carbonated beverages under the Slice brand name. As well, *Business Week* magazine has created *Guide to Careers* magazine for college and professional school students. Thus, a strong youth base has enabled companies to expand into new product categories. Brands that mean "quality"—especially those associated with a particular style or image—have been extended into entire lines of youth-oriented products. For example, after we labeled the group of thirteen- to twenty-five-year-olds as F.L.Y.E.R.S. we worked with Metro-Goldwyn-Mayer to create "F.L.Y.E.R.S." brand products. Our trademarked term was incorporated into a unique logo combining the look of a college insignia and a casual, trendsetting style. Then the term and the logo were licensed in diverse product categories: sportswear, stationery products, accessories, posters, sleepwear, buttons, and games.

Swatch Watch went from making colorful, plastic watches to sunglasses to sportswear and clothing accessories. Anheuser-Busch went from beer to snack food with its new Eagle Snacks brand of salty, crunchy treats.

Certainly, there can be problems with line youth-targeted extensions outside a company's primary product area. A company may not understand how the youth market regards products in these other industries. Young people, who are just beginning to become familiar and comfortable with new products, can become unsure of what the company name or brand name stands for. Youth also can become suspicious, even feel cheated, if they believe a company is just churning out more and more products without regard for their concerns. Furthermore, if young people find one product to be of inferior quality, unpopular, or unfashionable, they may come to frown on the rest of the company's line.

One of the most questionable examples of extension to date has been undertaken by Coca-Cola. First, the company licensed its Coke brand name, which until then had only been associated with its cola and diet cola soft drinks to an entirely unrelated industry, a line of apparel and accessories. Time will only tell whether or not such expansions of a brand name into an unrelated industry will prove successful.

However, line extensions can offer companies important benefits. Diversification into new product categories does provide an opportunity for growth and for a greater share of the $200 billion youth market. Young people who support a company's other products will take an immediate interest in its new ones, or new products might encourage nonusers to try the rest of the line.

Young people are highly aware of product modifications and extensions into new product lines. Youth are just beginning to learn which brands fill their needs and are continually searching for greater satisfaction. They see the companies developing new and different products as being on the cutting edge, always improving in response to their needs—and these are the companies they'll continue to support as they grow up.

Throughout the last six chapters, we have developed advertising and promotional strategies to effectively reach the entire youth market. However, some companies may wish to develop a more comprehensive program or to target particular segments of this market. In Chapter 13, we examine teenagers, college students, and young adults in greater detail and propose additional marketing approaches for each group.

13

TARGETING THE THREE SEGMENTS OF THE YOUTH MARKET

> It is essential to communicate believably to youth
> because they are the future of all companies.

> —Leslie Zeifman,
> associate publisher, *Rolling Stone*

The $55 Billion Teenage/High School Market

Together, the 23 million teenagers in America have an annual income of $50 to $55 billion. According to the 1984 Rand Youth Poll, the sex and age distribution of that income looks like this:

- Thirteen- to fifteen-year-old boys have average weekly incomes of $22.75 (earnings of $11.40 and allowances of $11.35), or $1,183 annually;

- Thirteen- to fifteen-year-old girls have average weekly incomes of $23.60 ($11.90 earnings and $11.70 allowances), or $1,227 annually;

- Sixteen- to nineteen-year-old boys report average weekly incomes of $53.45 (earnings of $31.65 and allowances of $21.80), or $2,779 annually;

- Sixteen- to nineteen-year-old girls have average weekly incomes of $54.60 (earnings of $32.55 and allowances of $22.05), or $2,839 annually.

It is interesting to note that, on average, total income, earnings, and allowances of women exceeded those of men in each age group. Earnings also exceeded allowances for both sexes in both age ranges. In addition, although 80 percent of all teenagers indicated that they saved money, 75 percent did so simply to make more expensive purchases in the future.

Furthermore, although the number of teenagers has declined over the past five years, the Rand poll found total teenage income has increased 3 to 5 percent per year. The reasons for this dramatic rise in purchasing power is twofold: First of all, allowances are larger, with the average thirteen- to fifteen-year-old receiving over $600 a year and the average sixteen- to nineteen-year-old getting $1,250. This has occurred, in part, because of the rise of two-income families, with more money to spend. According to the U.S. Census, for households with teenage children, two-income families have increased from 39 percent to 60 percent of the total between 1970 and 1980; this number is expected to grow to 75 percent by 1990. As well, married couples are having fewer children and are having them later in life, making more money available for allowances. And, when both parents are working, there is a greater need to allow teenage children to purchase many of their own products.

Secondly, more teenagers hold part-time jobs or even full-time jobs. Specifically, according to the Census, 21 percent of fifteen- to sixteen-year-olds work, compared with 49 percent of sixteen- to seventeen-year-olds and 67 percent of eighteen- to nineteen-year-olds.

LIFESTYLE AND SPENDING PATTERNS

Since parents pay most of their housing and living expenses and since most of their income is untaxed, percentagewise, teenagers have especially large discretionary incomes. Not surprisingly, teenage women, with larger incomes, also are bigger spenders than teenage men. The Rand Youth Poll shows that young women visit stores more often; are more socially involved; have less consumer resistance, especially to sales; are more conscious of fashions and fads; and are greater impulse buyers. In fact, teenage women list shopping as one of their primary activities.

Overall, teenage girls spend over $16 billion annually on their wardrobes, $5 billion on beauty aids, and $1 billion on jewelry. One-third have at least one credit card and one-quarter have a checking account. And although they often change the brands they purchase, by their early twenties they have become as faithful to certain brands as older women. A *Glamour* magazine poll found that nearly a third of women aged twenty to thirty-five report that they are still using products that they used as a teenager.

Teenagers are also particularly important to several industries: they buy nearly half of all soft drinks and more than half of all movie tickets; and they are the largest purchasers of rock and "new music" records. According to the Rand Youth Poll, the leading spending category for thirteen- to fifteen-year old boys is "food and snacks," followed by "movies and entertainment." For thirteen- to fifteen-year-old girls, it is "clothing," followed by "food and snacks" and "cosmetics." The primary spending for sixteen- to nineteen-year-old boys is "movies, dating, and entertainment," which consumes nearly 20 percent of their income; for sixteen- to nineteen-year-old girls, it is "clothing" (25 percent of their total income), followed by "cosmetics" (20 percent), and then "cars and fuel." Furthermore, as various studies show, teenagers—not parents—nearly always choose the products and the brand names to be purchased. Given that they earn most of their income, it is not surprising that parents would give their teenage children greater latitude in making decisions about what to do with their own money.

A more complete breakdown on teen spending for the wide range of products they consume is given in Table 1, "Teen Spending Patterns, 1974–1984."

Table 1*

Teen Spending Patterns, 1974–1984

	Percentage Teenage Ownership		
Product	1974	1984	Percent Change
Car	9%	18%	+100
Securities (stocks, etc.)	5	14	+180
Motor Scooter	5	10	+100
Television	19	38	+100
Telephone	11	23	+109
Hand Calculator	9	40	+344
Tennis Racket	15	30	+100
Skis	4	10	+150
Stereo/Record Player	53	69	+30
Tape Recorder	20	39	+95
Typewriter	25	36	+44
Camera	65	89	+37
Electric Shaver	30	36	+20
Watch	76	85	+12
Radio	82	92	+12
Bicycle	77	82	+6
Food for home	61	87	+43
Restaurants	63	74	+17
Electrical Appliances	37	49	+32
Household Toiletries	19	34	+79

*SOURCE: The Rand Youth Poll

INFLUENCE AND ATTITUDES

Not only do teenagers spend billions of their own dollars, they also exert substantial influence over the purchases of their parents. Teenage girls have a particularly strong influence over their families' food budgets. According to Simmons Market Research Bureau, more than 75 percent of teenage girls do some shopping for the family. Overall, teen purchases account for more than 15 percent of the total annual family food budget. Moreover, the Simmons figures are conservative estimates; studies by *Seventeen* and *Scholastic* magazines indicate that up to 80 percent of teenage girls and 60 percent of teenage boys shop for their families, controlling 39 percent of the annual family food budget.

With regard to other products, the Rand Youth Poll of teenagers reported in 1985 that 74 percent of girls and 68 percent of boys personally urged parents to buy items for the home and for the family—an increase of 12 percent for girls and 13 percent for boys over just ten years. The number making such requests and the range of products they requested increased from 1974 to 1984, often substantially.

Clearly teenagers strongly influence family purchase decisions, even for such mundane items as appliances and toiletries.

As this examination of income, spending, and influence shows, major changes throughout society have drastically altered the roles of parents and teenage children. The family of the 1980s is far less structured. Teenagers perform duties within the household as well as holding outside jobs. Mothers are no longer only housewives but are also breadwinners. Parents are not making all the brand decisions for household products but are sharing them with their children. The actual shopping is done by all members of the family.

Moreover, young people are especially impressionable during their teenage years. Because of personal insecurities, they are greatly affected by their peers, by members of the opposite sex, and also by advertising and promotion—so marketing aimed at teenagers can be especially persuasive. Since teenagers have no preset brand loyalties, they are more willing than adults to respond to promotions, if products are targeted properly. Throughout this book we have developed more comprehensive marketing campaigns that capture the F.L.Y.E.R.S. sensibility, but here we'll offer some specific, narrower strategies for attracting teenage consumers.

Targeting the Teenage Market

Teenage students have certain interests and concerns, as well as extracurricular activities and leisure pursuits, that are distinct from those of college students or nonstudent young adults. Most notably, teenagers spend the better part of their time around high schools or involved in various kinds of education-related activities. Consequently, schools are an excellent place to begin campaigns aimed at teenage consumers, through advertising in publications or through direct involvement in events.

1. TEENAGE/HIGH SCHOOL PUBLICATIONS

"Advertising speaks loudest in the quiet of the classroom," maintains Richard Robinson, president of Scholastic, Inc. Scholastic, Inc., produces five publications for high school students, dealing with current events, science news, writing skills, reading comprehension, and life skills. Unlike other national magazines, these publications are read and discussed in class in over 80 percent of the nation's high schools. Because they're "required reading" in so many schools, the Scholastic magazines provide a unique medium of communication to the high school market for any interested advertiser. There are also

nonschool-oriented national magazines that have a strong audience among teenagers. These include *Seventeen* (with a teenage
audience of 4.1 million in 1985), *Tiger Beat* (2.9 million), *Teen*
(2.6 million), *Young Miss* (2.3 million), *Teen Beat* (1.2 million),
Boy's Life (1.2 million), and *Creem* (900,000). Any of these
might be good venues for ads or special promotions.

2. HIGH SCHOOL PROGRAMS

It is also possible for a corporation to come directly into the
high school classroom, incorporating a product into an academic program or an extracurricular activity. One of the most
successful programs of this type is sponsored by McCall's Patterns to encourage young people to sew. As Earle Angstadt,
president of McCall's explains, "If our industry is to be stimu-
lated into an upward movement again, it has to start with young
people."

Twice each year, the company sends a wall poster to forty
thousand high schools and junior high schools for their sewing/
home economics classrooms. The poster pictures about a dozen
contemporary outfits worn by teenage models, all of which can
be sewn by beginning students. The featured outfits are so
fashionable that they give students a positive feeling about sewing their own clothes. In addition, since only a limited number
of patterns are featured and since special ordering incentives are
offered, it is easy for high school teachers to incorporate them
into their curriculums. Angstadt believes that the annual high
school marketing effort has given approximately 300,000 teenage girls their first sewing experience, using McCall's patterns.

For fifty years, *Time* magazine has run an educational program in secondary schools around the country. Edward J.
Meell, education circulation director for Time, Inc., describes
the program as reaching five thousand high schools, primarily
for use in social studies classes. Each week the participating
schools receive copies of a current edition of *Time,* as well as

a two to four page "Weekly Guide" for the teacher. The "Weekly Guide" suggests topics for class discussion, includes a vocabulary exercise and current events quiz, and provides supplementary material related to the cover story. In addition, *Time* provides fifty- to hundred-page booklets on subjects of general interest such as "The Presidency," "China in the 1980s," and "The Vietnam Era." These topical summaries supplement textbooks that are frequently out-of-date. Not only does *Time*'s program demonstrate the firm's interest in keeping American students informed, it also works to generate long-term reader loyalty to the magazine, beginning in the high schools.

It is important that any high school program not be too commercial or too much of a hard sell. Even if the school does accept the program, a campaign that is more advertisement than education can easily turn students off.

Clearly, by approaching state and national teachers' groups, associations of private and parochial schools, and even local boards of education, corporations in a wide range of industries can find creative ways to link their products to academic subjects. Brand-name food product companies can work with home economics courses; personal or household products companies with health classes; automobile makers with drivers' education; computer, appliance, and other industrial companies with science classes; and financial services firms with mathematics, economics or social studies courses.

However, even if a product or service does not fit well into an established curriculum or extracurricular activity, a company can still come into the high school. One strategy might be to create a lecture or an audiovisual presentation to be shown at school assemblies, selecting a subject of interest to high school students, and that also is relevant to the product or the company.

3. NATIONAL, REGIONAL, AND STATEWIDE CONVENTIONS

There are numerous national, regional, and statewide conventions that attract thousands of high school students each year. Examples include conventions of boy scouts and girls scouts; boys' state, girls' state, and governors' honors programs, along with other academic/leadership competitions; the National High School Model United Nations Conference and other model U.N. programs for high school students sponsored by colleges across the nation; similarly sponsored Model Congress conferences; debate and public speaking competitions of the National Forensic League and the National Catholic Forensic League; National Scholastic Press Association/Columbia Scholastic Press Association conventions for high school editors of newspapers and yearbooks; and even regional athletic competitions.

Unlike corporate-sponsored programs within high schools, these conferences and competitions allow a company to appeal to high school leaders from many different secondary schools. An appeal could come in the form of free samples, a contest, sponsorship of a social event, through prizes to outstanding conference participants, and so on. To establish or maintain the predominance of a brand among youth, such exposure to student leaders from widely dispersed geographic areas can be extremely important.

4. LOCAL STUDENT SPONSORSHIPS

A company or a product that is connected to a teenager's community or high school can earn the teenager's loyalty. For example, a corporation might provide internships in the company during the summer months, give awards to recognize high achievement in certain academic or extracurricular endeavors, sponsor local or high school athletic teams, grant college scholarships at high school graduation based on criteria appropriate for the sponsoring company, or supply materials for graduation parties and proms. By connecting a product to an important event in the lives of teenagers, such as graduation, a company creates a positive awareness and memorability that can remain strong for years to come.

5. TEENAGE/HIGH SCHOOL CONTESTS

For teenagers, especially, contests help to create a real connection to a product and encourage brand loyalty. Such contests should be developed to appeal to the particular interests or avocations of high school students. For example, Procter & Gamble's Orange Crush soda runs a competition for the best high school rock bands; Love's Baby Soft body spray holds its own beauty/modeling contest; and General Foods sponsors *Seventeen* magazine's cooking contest. Interestingly, there are far more contests for teenage girls than for teenage boys. Refer to Creating Contest in Chapter 10 for more information on contests.

6. COLLEGE FAIRS

Choosing a college is an important event in the lives of nearly half of all high school students. One important way that students and their parents learn about various collegiate programs is by attending college fairs. At these events, representatives from different colleges—admissions officers, alumni, and current students—come to answer questions and to recruit prospective students.

Clearly, the high school students and parents in attendance at college fairs are a forward-looking group. Thus, if a company manufactures a product needed for college or for setting up a new household, a fair is an excellent place to reach potential consumers, who also are some of the most ambitious high school students. Barron's Publishing, for example, sets up a booth to sell its many guides on colleges.

A company could also highlight its involvement in a fair by sponsoring a speaker or a panel discussion on an appropriate topic. Another strategy, might be to distribute a leaflet of helpful information related to college preparation and admissions, which would include brief mentions of the company or product.

The approaches described above are some of the most important ways to reach the teenager/high school student population directly. Next we'll consider income, spending patterns, and special interests of college students.

The $45 Billion College Student Market

There are 12.4 million college students in America, representing 5 percent of the total population. Of these students, 7.2 million are aged eighteen to twenty-four, and 4.5 million attend four-year colleges full time. Overall they represent a $35 to $45 billion market. Unlike the youth market as a whole, the size of the college market continues to rise, at a rate of approximately 200,000 people per year. In 1963, just 26 percent of eighteen- to twenty-four-year-olds were enrolled in college; this figure rose to 36 percent by 1973 and to 42 percent by 1985.

Beyond mere demographics, college students are significant to marketers because of their high current, and expected future, income, their special lifestyle, and their influence on attitudes in the broader culture. As we said in Chapter 2, college students have high incomes, first, because they work—90 percent of college students are employed during the summer and 60 percent during the school term, according to Simmons College

Market Survey. Secondly—and importantly—46.9 percent of college students come from families earning $40,000 or more, with only 19.3 percent come from families earning less than $15,000. Thus, the upper-middle-class parents of most college students are able to ensure that, even away from home, their children maintain a high standard of living, high even when compared to the average American family. And while students benefit from improvements in the economy, they are sheltered by their parents from any downturns in economic growth.

Moreover, when college students graduate they will command relatively high salaries, especially since the number of students majoring in lucrative fields such as business and commerce is growing rapidly. For example, in 1985, the average starting salary for college graduates was $19,300, compared to $14,511 for nongraduates. This 33 percent wage disparity between college-educated and noncollege-educated workers will continue and even increase throughout their working lifetime. Thus, it can be extremely profitable for companies to capture the brand loyalties of college students; in the not-too-distant future, the preferences of these well-paid college graduates can be translated into repeat purchases as well as purchases of more expensive items.

LIFESTYLE AND SPENDING PATTERNS

The college market is unique because of the college campus and its lifestyle. There is no other time in life when so many same-aged people, with such similar interests, with so much money to spend, and with such potential for even greater incomes in the future will be found together in the same general area. After all, the enrollment of some major state universities rivals the population of some medium-sized cities.

The U.S. Census finds that of all college students aged fourteen to twenty-four, 4.4 million live on campus, either in student housing or in fraternity/sorority houses, or have their own households near the university. Hence, most of the full-time college students spend their time around the college campus both during and after class.

Each of these students must acquire the same goods that a family needs—brand name food, personal care items, and household products for a dorm room or an apartment. Even if students live with other people, they typically will not pool products as a family would; for example, each are likely to have his own tube of toothpaste, box of cereal, bar of soap, even his own stereo. In addition, they purchase a wide range of medium to high-priced items, such as furniture, appliances, and automobiles. For this reason the college market can be a superior area for growth for manufacturers of many products.

INFLUENCE AND ATTITUDES

The research of our consulting firm, F.L.Y.E.R.S. Consulting, reveals that today's college students are more self-concerned and career-oriented than previous generations. Conservative viewpoints are more vocally expressed on many college campuses, but on the whole, students are not necessarily more conservative on political and social issues. Nevertheless, they seek change by working with the system, not by trying to overthrow it. Compared to the more idealistic, far-reaching concerns of students of the 1960s, today's students place first priority on their own personal problems and their own futures.

However, students of the 1980s are more confident, optimistic, and pleasure-seeking than the students of the late 1970s, who are today's self-possessed, money-hungry yuppies. The 1980s students are not less concerned with becoming successful, but they measure that success in broader terms than just having a career. To them, success also means having the financial security and the opportunity to enjoy entertainment, travel, and socializing with family and friends.

Their lives are also more fast-paced and time-pressured than those of previous generations. Consequently, convenience, simplicity, efficiency, and speed are the qualities likely to be emphasized in the brands they purchase for their households. Their small living quarters, including dormitory rooms or studio apartments with limited cooking, sleeping, and living facilities, require durable and nondurable products different from those utilized in their parents' houses or in multiroom apartments.

With their campus-centered lifestyle, college students live in close proximity to one another and share many common experiences. Thus, they can exert a great deal of influence over one another, including influence on purchasing decisions. And like other young people, college students have not established brand loyalties. Many are getting their first taste of independence, setting up the first households of their own, and so are more likely than adults to try new brands and products.

All these factors make the college market a unique marketing challenge. If a company can establish a favorable presence on the college campus and positive word-of-mouth, it can gain a hold on these consumers, both for the present and in the future. In the next section, we'll discuss some strategies for reaching the college market through traditional media, including television, radio, print, numerous college-focused media sources, and other special means.

Targeting the College Market

In some important ways, the college lifestyle is different from those of teenagers and nonstudent young adults, as well as from that of adult consumers. Since student life centers around the campus, quite apart from the outside world, marketing strategies must be college-oriented to be effective. We'll begin by examining the problems of approaching students through the traditional media.

1. TELEVISION AND RADIO

According to Simmons College Market Study, college students do not watch as much television, listen to as much radio, or read newspapers and national magazines as often as the general population. For example, college students watch television approximately 1.3 hours per day, one-third as much as the general population. Of course, there are certain television programs to which they are extremely loyal, including certain prime-time shows, music video programs, athletic events, late-night television, soap operas, and even cartoons. Although youth-oriented advertisements are often seen in the first three kinds of programming, they are less likely to be found in the latter three types.

Despite the fact that college students watch less television than the general population, their awareness of television advertising is not measurably lower—possibly because, when they do decide to watch television, they are more enthusiastic viewers. Also, since they watch one-third the amount of television, they are only exposed to one-third the number of commercials and thus may have a greater tolerance for them.

College students do listen to the radio, with 75 percent tuning in every day and 91.2 percent listening on Monday through Friday evenings. On average, college students listen to radio two hours per day. Of course, those two hours are not necessarily spent listening to campus radio stations. The college listenership of campus stations is not easily monitored, especially in larger cities where there are many popular local stations. Also, in many cities, college radio stations feature alternative programming, playing newer artists and less mainstream styles that may or may not appeal to the students on their campuses.

2. COLLEGE PUBLICATIONS

College students read a wide variety of publications, according to Simmons College Market Study: 53 percent read a daily newspaper, 52 percent read the college newspaper, 26 percent read *Time* magazine, 20 percent read *People* and *TV Guide,* 17 percent read *Newsweek* and *Glamour,* 18 percent read *Sports Illustrated,* and 15 percent read *Rolling Stone.* To approach students, however, it may be more effective to use nontraditional, special media—publications specifically targeted at college students. These five are the most important:

Directory of Classes, an advertiser-supported listing of available course offerings, is an official school publication on its seventy-five campuses. Published by University Communications, which is owned by Ziff-Davis Publishing Co., it has a circulation of over 1.5 million.

Newsweek on Campus, a news magazine focusing on the interests of college students is published six times each year by Newsweek, Inc., with a circulation of 1.2 million.

Campus Voice, a college news/issues magazine, also has a circulation of 1.2 million and is published by the 13–30 Corporation.

Ampersand, a music, arts, and entertainment magazine, is published by Alan Weston Communications, with a 1.5 million circulation.

Business Week Guide to Careers, which like *Business Week* is published by McGraw-Hill, has a 450,000 circulation.

These magazines can be of great assistance to virtually any advertiser interested in developing a separate campaign targeted at the youth market. As Warren Guy, publisher of the 13–30 magazines, says, "The college environment is unique.

Students are like the traditional mother. While they are in school, they buy soap, detergent, food and other products. Advertising in these magazines can create brand loyalty before they graduate and before they marry."

To develop an ad for a college magazine, a company might use the visual from its general ad, replacing the headline and text with copy points relevant to college students. Or if the design of the general ad does not easily translate to the campus market, these magazines are excellent mediums for special college-oriented ads—whether to encourage present or future purchases, to create appreciation of the company or its products, or to recruit potential employees. Further, companies can go beyond placing a simple ad in these magazines. Honda sponsored an entire issue of *Business Week Guide To Careers.* American Express placed an advertising supplement, titled "The American Express Real Life Planner," in six editions of *Newsweek On Campus;* each supplement covered one issue of interest to soon-to-graduate college students such as "Office Politics," "Networking," and "Money Management." And for the last ten years, Nissan has sponsored its own semiannual student travel magazine, *America.* The magazine has helped Nissan remain the best-selling imported car on college campuses, even after it was overtaken by competitors in other markets.

3. COLLEGE PROGRAMS AND EVENTS

A direct connection between a company and the campus can demonstrate its concern about college students in a way that regular advertising cannot. As popular speakers on the college lecture circuit, we have been sponsored by numerous companies to give speeches on college campuses. Based on the particular sponsor, we determine an appropriate topic for the speech and often create a product promotion around the event.

But there are many types of college programs. Pepsi-Cola, is the sole sponsor of the College Satellite Network, a unique programming event held several times a year and simulcast to three hundred college campuses. These events can include concerts, panel discussions with major national/international figures, and special conventions of college students.

Two other successful on-campus programs were run by *Rolling Stone* and American Express. In fall 1985, *Rolling Stone* presented a Music Showcase and Expo on ten college campuses, featuring the popular rock band Lone Justice. The event was cosponsored by various companies, including Daniel Hechter menswear, who held a fashion show as part of the program. And each spring, American Express runs its own college lecture program on credit; the topic and timing of the speech ties in perfectly with a pitch to graduating seniors to apply for the American Express Card.

4. NATIONAL, REGIONAL, OR STATEWIDE EVENTS

By sponsoring an intercollegiate sporting event or convention, a company can reach students from many different schools at an important and memorable moment in their college careers. Many companies are involved in promoting collegiate sports, especially football. For example, Sunkist Growers, Inc., known for both its oranges and its Sunkist brand orange soda, sponsors the Sunkist Fiesta Bowl. This is the first college sporting event to carry a corporate name. General Motors, Coca-Cola, Anheuser-Busch, and MCI Communications sponsored the 1985 Cherry Bowl, advertising in the game program and on television and radio spots promoting the game.

Further, corporations can link up with nonathletic, intercollegiate events that can attract student leaders from colleges around the country. Such events include the National Model United Nations Conference and other college model U.N. conferences; intercollegiate debate and public-speaking competitions; and conventions of members of national fraternities/

sororities and other major student organizations. These types of sponsorships are underutilized by corporations, despite the fact that (1) they are highly efficient at targeting student leaders, and (2) it usually is less expensive to link up with such intercollegiate conferences than with athletic events.

5. SPRING BREAK PROGRAMS

To most college students, the third week in March means just one thing: spring break. Although they travel to Vale, Colorado; Sugarloaf, Maine; Hilton Head, South Carolina; Los Angeles; Lake Tahoe; Viginia Beach; and various ski resorts in Vermont, the largest number of college students go to Florida. Each spring, over a half million descend on Daytona Beach and Fort Lauderdale. Although there are significantly more corporate sponsors at Daytona, all of these sites are excellent places to reach students from around the nation.

These vacationing students are a captive audience. They have a lot of free time to sample and to learn about new products through a wide range of advertising and promotional approaches. For example, *Rolling Stone* and *Newsweek on Campus* both sponsor expositions where many corporations can display their wares, and MTV runs free concerts on the beach with top musical performers. One of the most active sponsors is Miller; the company holds special events, provides free telephone calls home, and gives out free gifts in exchange for empty Miller beer bottles.

6. COLLEGE-ORIENTED CONTESTS

Contests, specifically aimed at college students, are important to establish a product presence on campuses. The choice of contest design and prizes will determine the product's image and the types of students who will be attracted to the contest.

For example, for the past thirty years, *Glamour* magazine has run a "Top Ten College Women" competition. Prior to

1967, the contest was principally a beauty and fashion contest. However, in the late 1960s, trends began to change among college women, who became much more serious about their careers and futures. As a result, *Glamour* itself was developing into more of a lifestyle than a fashion/beauty magazine. This change was reflected in the college contest, with beauty being replaced by success in academics and extracurricular endeavors as the principal selection criterion. As Wanda Bolton, director of career and college competitions at *Glamour,* notes, recent winners have included Rhodes, Marshall, and Truman scholars, student body presidents, and top college athletes.

The prizes offered are consistent with the career-oriented image of the contest. The winners are flown to New York City, where the magazine arranges meetings with top professionals in their fields of interest. Thus, the contest and its prizes dramatically demonstrate that, despite the name *Glamour,* the magazine is concerned with women's careers and social advancement—issues of great concern to college women.

7. SAMPLE AND POSTER GIVEAWAYS

Since most college freshmen are living away from home for the first time, they must make many purchasing decisions. By providing incoming freshmen with free samples or special discount coupons, a company can demonstrate how well its brand fulfills their needs. If students are satisfied, they will be encouraged to purchase that brand over that of its competitors. The 13–30 Corporation creates a "Good Stuff" box filled with samples of varied products for distribution to incoming freshmen.

Instead of giving away free samples, a company might provide an informational sheet or pamphlet for freshmen on how to survive college. The pamphlet could incorporate a product advertisement or other promotional information.

Some companies reach student through attractive posters that are given away free or even sold. College students love to hang posters on the walls of their apartments and dorm rooms.

These posters can serve as continuing advertisements for anyone who walks through that room. Budweiser beer, Dole pineapple, and Sun Country wine cooler are just a few of the products with posters. These approaches to college students will be most effective if they are part of an ongoing campaign to keep a company and its product prominent in their minds.

8. CREATING A CONTINUING PRESENCE ON THE COLLEGE CAMPUS

Besides student dorm rooms, there are two other potential display spaces found on campuses that companies should take advantage of. Over the past few years, for example, college stores have been transformed from mere booksellers into mini-department stores, even food/convenience stores. More than half of all college students go to the school store at least once a week. Since students do not have time to search for products, often the brand that is most commonly available is the one purchased. Also, the brand that is always before them, in their own college store, becomes the one they are most comfortable trying and using. For this reason, it is important for companies to get more point-of-purchase displays into college stores.

Another way a company can create a presence on campus is to advertise on college billboards and kiosks or through wall media produced by 13–30 Corporation. As well, IBM, Apple, AT&T and Commodore all provide discounts to students and universities to encourage use of their computers in the school curriculum. This strategy gets students into the habit of using a product everyday, making it part of their lifestyle.

9. GENERATING STUDENT APPRECIATION

In looking at the college market, companies must also consider medium-to-long term strategies that will encourage future purchases by these important consumers. Smart companies seek to develop student appreciation of their product—even if students are not their targeted consumers—during college, when young people are making important life decisions. This is the basis of the "Newsweek Approach."

For example, *Reader's Digest* has the largest circulation of any monthly magazine in the world: 30 million in seventeen languages, with U.S. circulation at an incredible 17 million. But, clearly, college students do not represent a significant segment of *Reader's Digest*'s current readership. Nevertheless, as its publisher, Richard McLoughlin explains, "We want college students to appreciate the *Digest,* to realize its impact and influence throughout the country." He noted three specific reasons for his interest in the college market: (1) It will be easier to sell the magazine to these individuals when they are are older if, as college students, they have a positive perception of the magazine; (2) as a major company, *Reader's Digest* wants this significant consumer group to appreciate its value; and (3) soon after graduation, some of these college students will be involved in making decisions about whether to place advertisements in the magazine.

To accomplish its goal of gaining attention among college students, *Reader's Digest* has run several programs. For example, in one campaign, each month it provided a kit of articles, anecdotes, and humorous pieces, in both print and audio formats, to campus newspapers and radio stations. Reprints or broadcasts of these materials by the campus media helped establish the fact that the magazine is interesting and informative, and thus worthwhile reading.

One final note: College students are a critical consumer group; they are intelligent, discriminating purchasers who seek quality in brand names. Since they live in close proximity to so many members of their peer group, they are especially concerned about using the "right" products. As a result, it is essential that any promotion directed toward college students, especially if placed on campus, be done well. A poorly designed or executed advertising or promotional campaign can be devastating to a product's popularity, but a successful campaign can have a dramatic, positive impact on the present and future buying patterns of these elite consumers.

Many young people, of course, do not attend college; and in the next section, we'll consider their purchasing power and special needs, as well as some effective ways to reach them.

The $100 Billion Nonstudent Young-Adult Market

There are over 21 million individuals, aged eighteen to twenty-five, who are not in college—almost three times the number of same-age college students. Many of these young people work full-time, and as a group, they represent a total annual income of over $100 billion. But despite the size and relative affluence of this "off-campus" segment of youth consumers, marketers rarely attempt to reach them directly. There are two reasons for this lack of initiative: First, it is difficult to target advertisements and promotions to noncollege young adults since they are are distributed throughout the general population and are not large consumers of television, radio, or print media. Second, many marketers feel that they do not understand this group as well as they do most other consumer segments.

LIFESTYLE AND SPENDING PATTERNS

The Census Bureau reports that 67 percent of the eighteen to nineteen-year-olds and 77 percent of twenty- to twenty-four-year-olds are members of the labor force, although many continue to receive some money from their parents. These noncollege young adults are the workers who type and file America's letters, drive its trucks, construct its buildings, grow its food, manage its stores, operate its machinery, clean its buildings and streets, assemble its durable goods, and fix those goods when they break down.

More precisely, based on Census statistics, just over half (55.8 percent) of the young adult males have blue-collar jobs as transport operators, craft and kindred workers, and manual laborers of various kinds; the rest are white-collar workers (30.5 percent), service workers (10.4 percent), and farm workers (3.3 percent).

In contrast, the large majority (67.5 percent) of the young adult females are white-collar workers, principally in clerical jobs. The rest are service workers (18.8 percent), blue-collar workers (13.0 percent), and farm workers (just 0.7 percent).

In the 1980 census, the median annual income of twenty- to twenty-four-year-old males was reported as $11,477; for females of the same age, it was $8,575. However, 25.1 percent of the young men and 5.6 percent of the young women reported annual incomes above $15,000. Certainly, since they have not attended college, the future incomes of these individuals will not be among the highest in their age group. However, at present and at least for the next few decades, the majority of American adults will not have attended college. Thus, this segment of the youth market represents and will continue to represent the larger American adult consumer market.

Unlike yuppies but like teenagers, most young adults do not have the financial burdens of rents, mortgages, and utilities; since 61 percent of the men and 47.8 percent of the women still live with their parents. Hence, although most are employed, the majority still depend on their parents to provide for some of their financial needs. As a result, the current disposable incomes of these consumers is relatively high.

The way they use that income and the durable goods they own more closely resemble those of college students than those of adults. Whether they purchase clothing or automobiles, soft drinks or beer, movies or records, their choices of brands and products reflect the commonality of tastes that we have labeled the F.L.Y.E.R.S. sensibility. However, unlike college students, this segment of the youth market has a substantial amount of money to spend right now. In addition their brand preferences will continue to be of great importance to the manufacturers of low- and medium-priced items, including brand name foods, household products, personal care items, fashion/clothing items, and even appliances, for decades to come.

INFLUENCE AND ATTITUDES

Many marketers find it difficult to empathize with the prob-lems, concerns, desires, and interests of the noncollege young adult consumer. Since most marketers and their associates are college graduates, these young adults seems more distant than other consumer groups, even teenagers. But it bears repeating that these noncollege young adults are not so different from college and high school students. The real distinctions develop when college students graduate and begin their careers, or when their noncollege counterparts marry and start families.

The stereotype of young adults is that after high school grad-uation, they immediately move into their own apartments, get married, and begin having children. This is incorrect, since the Census statistics confirm that most young men and women do *not* marry before age twenty-five, and most live at home with their parents. Like college students, most young adults do not assume the responsibilities of adulthood immediately after finishing high school.

Based on the research of our F.L.Y.E.R.S. Consulting firm, the social life of young adults revolves primarily around dating or going out with friends to night spots, to bars, to restaurants, to movies, or even to exercise clubs. Many young adults, espe-cially those in white-collar and service jobs, think about going back to school, but few of them or their friends get around to doing it. However, the college lifestyle remains something that appeals to them.

Many young adults have strong career-oriented training. Nevertheless, for most part, they consider their jobs routine and tedious. Not surprisingly, they view their social lives as a necessary release from unchallenging work, representing an opportunity to meet new people and to do exciting things. However, their work brings more than purely economic rewards; working is essential to their sense of self-worth.

Young adults do not spend much time discussing or even thinking about the future or about national/international affairs, but, still, they indicate optimism about the future of this country. They care about what happens to America, although feel there is little they can do to help solve the problems that exist. Noncollege young adults do spend time talking about the opposite sex, dating and marriage, music, entertainment, and what to do during leisure time. Of course, sports remains an extremely important interest for young men, and young women like clothing and fashion.

Regarding their own futures, many are concerned about whether their successes will live up to their expectations, whether they will get a fair share of the American dream. Yet they want to take advantage of as much of the "good life" as they are able. They look forward to acquiring all the visible signs of material success in the future, but they want at least some of those possessions right now. Having the "right" clothing and car and apartment, using the "right" products and services, going to the "right" events, and being involved in the "right" leisure pursuits are all important to these young consumers.

What follows are some special approaches to this young-adult consumer who is not college educated.

Targeting the Young-Adult Market

This segment of the youth market is probably the most difficult to target precisely. For one thing, they don't watch television or listen to the radio much more than their counterparts in college do. Moreover, unlike students on college campuses or in high schools, their population is not concentrated in specific, identifiable, and targetable areas.

Yet, these young adults will not respond well to advertising or promotional campaigns that are directed either at the middle-aged married couple or at the so-called yuppie. Why? Counter to the stereotype, most young adults are not ready to get married and to start a family; thus, the problems and concerns of the married housewife or husband seem distant to them. As for a yuppie-focused pitch, young adults envision young urban professionals as people wholly different from them in attitudes and lifestyles.

But there are ways to reach this segment of the youth market, and they are much too important to neglect. Here we'll present four methods that have been particularly successful at capturing the interest of young adults:

1. PUBLICATIONS

Certain national magazines are moderately successful in reaching this group. According to a 1985 report from the Simmons Market Research Bureau, the following are the eight most popular magazines among eighteen- to twenty-four-year-olds: *Sports Illustrated* (4.0 million average audience), *Cosmopolitan* (3.7 million), *Glamour* (2.9 million), *Playboy* (2.7 million), *Rolling Stone* (2.4 million), *Seventeen* (2 million), *Hot Rod* (1.9 million), and *Mademoiselle* (1.8 million). Not surprisingly, the top four publications for the eighteen- to twenty-four-year-old women are *Cosmopolitan, Glamour, Seventeen,* and *Mademoi-*

selle, while the top four magazines for the same age young men are *Sports Illustrated, Playboy, Hot Rod,* and *Rolling Stone* (listed in order from highest to lowest average audience). However, all the magazines listed have at least 100,000 readers of the opposite sex within this age category, with *Rolling Stone* having nearly a million young female readers and *Cosmopolitan* having over 400,000 young male readers.

Another, possibly more effective, avenue is young-adult publications. As Warren Guy, publisher of the 13–30 magazines, explains, just as college students have the college campus in common and teenagers have the high school, young adults have various places/events around which they congregate: bars, nightclubs, laundromats, concerts, health clubs, and professional athletic events. By examining the young-adult lifestyle and the product to be promoted, a link can be discovered and then translated into an appropriate publication.

For example, the 13–30 Corporation publishes *Moviegoer* and *Tables* magazines. The former publication focuses on the strong interest that young adults have in movies and entertainment. The five-year-old magazine is distributed monthly at no charge in movie theaters around the nation. It is entirely sponsored by R. J. Reynolds to promote its Camel and Salem cigarettes.

Tables magazine, by contrast, is targeted at an even more defined market niche: waiters and waitresses. This two-year-old monthly is distributed in five thousand restaurants and its sole advertiser is Seagram's. Thus, the company is able to advertise both its alcoholic and carbonated beverages to a group that serves those products to its patrons. The many publications of the 13–30 Corporation offer a special opportunity to companies who want to reach the specific types of young adults who are most likely to buy their products both at the present and in the future.

2. CONCERTS AND EVENTS

Music is a thread that unites young people, whether they attend college or not. Recognizing this fact, the number of companies providing support for major rock concert tours has increased dramatically over the last two years. Pontiac Fiero sponsored a nationwide tour for Hall & Oates; and Pioneer Stereo supported Blondie concerts. And, of course, Pepsi sponsored 1985's most celebrated rock concert series, the Jackson's Victory Tour.

These and other companies have also sponsored such philanthropic fundraisers as Live Aid, Hands Across America, and Farm Aid. Given the changing attitudes of young people who seek to improve society through constructive means, as opposed to violent demonstrations, corporate involvement in these events provides an opportunity for firms to communicate with young adults—as well as to boost youth perception of the sponsors and their products.

Athletic events, too, are a significant unifying force for non-college young adults, principally young men. Thus they also provide ample opportunities for product tie-ins. In addition, Michael Moore, director of media planning at D'Arcy Masius Benton & Bowles Advertising, notes that since young adults are so mobile and hard to reach through traditional media, these events are excellent chances for billboard advertisements.

Not surprisingly, many companies have stepped into the sponsorship of sporting events and top athletic performers. For example, Coors beer sponsored Bill Elliott, the hottest driver on the NASCAR (National Association for Stock-Car Auto Racing) circuit; a ten-man skydiving team; a thirty-lake fishing tournament; and its own Coors International Bicycle Classic. Interestingly, since the company wants to capture this noncollege young adult, Coors does not sponsor golf or tennis tournaments because it finds that the fans are too upscale.

For similar reasons, Dole Pineapple, which is interested in

attracting young women, sponsored Joan Benoit, who won the first Olympic Gold Medal in the women's marathon during the 1984 Los Angeles Olympics. Budweiser, along with all the major automakers, sponsors various car-racing events. And Wrangler Jeans, which wants to win a bigger share of the young-adult market from its vigorous competitor, Levi-Strauss, supports a range of sporting events including professional rodeos and stock-car racing.

3. LOCAL EVENT SPONSORSHIPS

Sponsoring events at local bars, nightclubs, resort areas, and other young-adult leisure spots parallels efforts made toward college students on the campus. By coming to where young adults live and play, corporations can vividly illustrate their concern for the individual young customer.

One of the most successful and extensive local programs is the Miller Brewing Company's American Rock Network, created for Miller by Gary M. Reynolds & Associates. Over the past five years, Miller has sponsored ninety local rock bands, each representing a different region of the country. Miller provides each band with a regional concert tour (consisting of 150 to 200 performances) and the necessary local radio publicity, as well as promotional posters, T-shirts, and jackets. These concerts link Miller with local musical groups that are popular with young adults. Furthermore, each event provides additional publicity for the product.

4. YOUNG-ADULT CONTESTS

Contests can be an important part of any company's youth campaign. But Donna Alda, director of promotions for MTV Networks, explains that typical contests are passé with today's young adult: "To create a successful promotion for youth, you must create a fantasy. You must devise a package of events that are unique."

Certainly, recent contests run by advertisers through MTV have fulfilled this goal. For example, to promote the 1985 release of a new album by the rock group Van Halen, MTV ran Van Halen Lost Weekend contest. The 1.2 million entrants each sought to win a weekend of partying with the band members. Even more people—3 million—vied for MTV's 1985 Nabisco Million-Dollar Give-Away. Advertisements ran on MTV for several months to announce the contest and to promote Nabisco's Baby Ruth, Butterfinger, Bonkers, and Bubble Yum products.

Unusual, extravagant contests probably are the only ones that can truly capture the imagination and excitement of young adults. Of course, any contest with reasonably sufficient advertising support will receive some attention. But with less inventive ones, it remains unclear whether running the contest contributes anything positive to the image of the product and whether advertising dollars spent to generate entrants could have been better utilized elsewhere.

14

YouthTrends: What's Coming in the Next Decade

*T*hroughout this book, we've discussed the growing social and economic clout of youth as one of the major trends of the 1980s. Companies that recognize the power of this trend have reaped not only great financial benefits but also enhanced their images as vital contemporary trendsetters among the larger adult market. But what will the 1990s hold?

F.L.Y.E.R.S. Consulting has conducted research studies to discover some directions for the coming decade. The results suggest that in the not too distant future, we will see the establishment of new social paradigms as well as some new developments in industry. The new social groups and trends we see emerging are:

1. The Increasingly Independent Teenager

2. The Coming College-Oriented Society

3. The Future Fun-Loving Professional

4. The Developing Disaffected Young Adult

5. An Even More Youth-Conscious America

And the new trends we envision for business include:

6. A Continuing Rejuvenation of Corporate Images

7. An Expanding MTV Revolution in Advertising

8. A New "Uniqueness" in Product Promotions

9. A Push for Even Younger Young Consumers

10. A Growing Connection between Youth Appeal and Mass Appeal

All of these trends already have begun to show their strength, to varying degrees. We'll examine each one here:

1. THE INCREASINGLY INDEPENDENT TEENAGER

The U.S. Census has projected three demographic trends that will dramatically change the lifestyles of future teenagers: (1) An increasing percentage of them will work while in high school; (2) a growing number will live with only one parent; and (3) an increasing percentage will live in households with two working parents. All these developments within the structure of the American family will make teenagers even more independent of their parents.

With more of their own money to spend and with decreasing parental supervision, teenagers will make a growing number of brand decisions—not only for themselves but for their households as well. Since 75 percent of all teenage girls already do at least some of the family shopping, during the next decade they will very likely rival their mothers as their families' primary shoppers.

2. THE COMING COLLEGE-ORIENTED SOCIETY

A growing percentage of high school graduates are deciding to go on to college. In addition, more adults are returning to school for a college education or for special career-oriented programs; today, more than 5 million college students are over the age of twenty-four. Thus, in the coming years an increasing number of Americans will have some type of post–high school education.

Clearly, such higher education will make American consumers more sophisticated and discerning. Moreover, more people of varying ages will share or identify with campus life. This will increase the youth consciousness of the general population, through their continuing connection to eighteen- to twenty-two-year-old college students.

3. THE FUTURE FUN-LOVING PROFESSIONAL

Today's college students, and even college-bound high school students, show growing dissatisfaction, even disgust, with the yuppie lifestyle; these future professionals see that there is more to life than work. The strong attraction to our F.L.Y.E.R.S. (*F*un *L*oving *Y*outh *E*n *R*oute to *S*uccess) trend by students around the nation clearly reflects their widespread desire to succeed not only in their careers but also in their social/personal lives.

This changing attitude among today's best students will have a great impact on the spending habits of tomorrow's most elite workers. Young professionals will still be making high salaries but will be increasingly concerned with enjoying the money they make. Thus, entertainment, family activities, and leisure pursuits will play an even greater role in the economy of the future.

4. THE DEVELOPING DISAFFECTED YOUNG ADULT

Even today, as we discussed in Chapter 13, young adults who have not attended college doubt that they will ever share in the American dream. They realize that they are not as financially secure as their parents' generation and that they may never reach a similar level of material wealth. Their jobs are not sources of challenge and excitement; they are dissatisfied with the quality of their life.

Therefore, like the future fun-loving professionals, noncollege young adults will continue to seek fulfillment in their social lives, instead of in their work. Products that support their sense of self-esteem, such as low- to medium-priced status symbols, as noted in Chapter 11, will be increasingly important. Owning the "right" products will help them see themselves as successful, amid other dissatisfactions.

5. AN EVEN MORE YOUTH-CONSCIOUS AMERICA

In the future, the American emphasis on youth will continue to grow, given three societal trends: (1) Even now, staying and looking youthfully vigorous is central to the lives of many Americans; (2) people are living longer and will want to remain healthy and active during their later years; and (3) with the rising divorce rate, the single, early-twenties lifestyle will remain common among people of all ages. These factors, coupled with young people's growing economic importance, will make it even more critical for industries to appeal to the youth sensibility in the 1990s.

6. A CONTINUING REJUVENATION OF CORPORATE IMAGES

More and more companies are using the YouthTrends Approaches to establish strategies to improve their images among young people, while strengthening their appeal to adults. Many will continue to favor the "American Express," the "Snickers," or the "Newsweek" approaches, allowing them to target each market separately. But increasingly, corporations are trying the "Pepsi," the "MTV," and the "Swatch" approaches, following the lead of such companies as General Motors' Pontiac Division, Colgate-Palmolive and the American Home Sewing Association, and the others noted in Chapter 5. These firms have already realized that, to compete successfully into the 1990s, it will be essential to focus on youth. Farsighted companies have begun to rejuvenate their images, to refashion themselves as contemporary, vigorous, and trendsetting to attract both young and adult consumers of the future.

7. AN EXPANDING MTV REVOLUTION IN ADVERTISING

Today's young people are just the first wave of the MTV Generation with a strong desire for powerful visual stimulation. Not surprisingly, they are bored with traditional print and television ads, and these higher expectations will remain as young people progress into adulthood. They will continue to demand greater creativity in advertising design, especially from such trend-conscious industries as clothing, fast foods, and cosmetics. Not only will television ads have to be compelling, they will also need stronger audio complements to satisfy young consumers. Print ads will have to show more animation and imagination if they are to compete for their share of young people's attention.

8. A NEW "UNIQUENESS" IN PRODUCT PROMOTIONS

Even today, to promote products to youth and to youth-conscious adults, it is essential to develop unusual contests and events. With the burgeoning of state lotteries and million-dollar giveaways, young people have grown tired of random drawings for typical prizes. And there are already so many corporate-sponsored events that it has become difficult to impress young consumers.

Hence, in the future, "unique" promotions will grow more important to establish a stronger link between manufacturer and consumer. Some of the MTV contests reviewed in Chapters 10 and 13 are the harbingers of this trend. In the future, the "me-too" attitude so many companies take toward youth promotions will no longer be adequate to attract the youth market.

9. A PUSH FOR EVEN YOUNGER YOUNG CONSUMERS

The income of young people continues to soar above the $200 billion mark. In addition, given the changing structure of the American family, young people will be making many more brand decisions at progressively earlier ages. Therefore, in the future companies who want to attract the teenage consumer will begin to target thirteen- to fifteen-year olds instead of high school students.

As for the college market, companies will abandon their fascination with graduating seniors and start to concentrate more on freshmen and sophomores, in the hopes that they will carry their brand preferences into their adult years.

10. A GROWING CONNECTION BETWEEN YOUTH APPEAL AND MASS APPEAL

As we have discussed throughout this book, the youth mindset is of growing importance to many industries, from soft-drink and entertainment companies (both television and movies) to even credit card firms and auto makers. These companies recognize that, to sell their products and services, they must appeal to youth. In essence, the youth mentality has so pervaded the consciousness of all Americans that selling an "image of youthfulness" has come, and will continue to serve as, a significant marketing tool for a growing range of industries.

Youth is the wave of the present—and the power of the future.

APPENDIX
THE BEST AND WORST CAMPAIGNS

*I*n this appendix, we review some of the best youth-oriented advertising and promotional campaigns discussed in the book. The six lists for the best and worst campaigns were determined through the following three-step process. First, a list of approximately five hundred television/radio commercials, print advertisements, and promotional campaigns aimed at young people and the youth-conscious adult was created based on the following sources:

(1) Suggestions from officers and account executives from ten of the largest advertising and public relations firms in the country;

(2) Suggestions from the publishers and editors of the magazines most read by young people; and

(3) Our own F.L.Y.E.R.S. Consulting survey of (a) ads that have run either on television programs or in magazines that are popular among youth and (b) youth-oriented promotional campaigns (including events, contests, etc.) that have been sponsored by corporations in various regions around the country or at a significant number of high schools or college campuses.

All the campaigns must have been for national brands and must have run after January 1984 but before June 1986. Television and radio commercials are combined into one category because of the local character of radio stations.

Second, the advertisements and promotions which received the strongest reactions from our own poll of young people (considered highly appealing/convincing or highly unappealing/unconvincing) were compiled into a brief composite list. Attempting to choose approximately ten to fifteen campaigns for each list, our selection was guided by the desire to present diversity in product category, size of the corporate sponsor, style of presentation, and illustration of effective youth-appealing marketing techniques.

The Best Television/Radio Commercials

Product/Sponsor	Campaign Name/Ad Slogan
1. American Home Sewing	"Be an American Original"
2. Budweiser	"You Make America Work and This Bud's for You"
3. Colgate Toothpaste	"Colgate Pump Dance"
4. Del Monte Vegetables	"You Work Hard for Your Body"
5. Farah's Generra Sportswear	"I Love You 'Cause You're My Style"
6. Levi's 501 Jeans	"501 Blues"
7. Lipton Cup-a-Soup	"After the Game"
8. Pepsi-Cola	"Choice of a New Generation" (celebrity ads)

9.	Pioneer Stereo	"Be a Pioneer"
10.	Sprite	"High School"
11.	Tostitos Tortilla Chips	"Classic Reruns"
12.	U.S. Army	"Be All That You Can Be"
13.	Wendy's	Humor Campaign: "Where's the Beef" and "Russian Fashion Show"
14.	Maxwell House Coffee[1]	"Young Comedians

[1]Although only on the air in test markets, this advertisement merits inclusion in this list because of its uniqueness in the coffee industry and its effectiveness in reaching young people.

Below we examine significant details of these commercials and suggest why they have been so effective at communicating their messages to the youth market.

1. AMERICAN HOME SEWING—"BE AN AMERICAN ORIGINAL"

As was discussed in Chapter 5, the American Home Sewing Association's commercial has the exceptionally difficult job of trying to convince young women to sew their own clothing. But this rock-video-style commercial successfully explodes the negative stereotype that sewing is old-fashioned by showing exciting and fashionable clothing that can be sewn at home. By repeating the musical phrases "One of a Kind" and "You Can't Buy It; It's Not for Sale," the ad also emphasizes that young girls can sew unique, trendsetting items that their favorite rock stars would wear. Thus, the commercial is notable for its ability to rejuvenate the industry's image in the eyes of young women.

2. BUDWEISER—"YOU MAKE AMERICA WORK"

The campaign for Anheuser-Busch's Budweiser beer is an excellent combination of appealing images and a stirring, original musical theme. The ad presents varied scenes of working life in America. Its memorable song "You Make America Work— And This Bud's for You" draws out strong feelings of pride in one's work and in one's country. Thus, the ad especially appeals to the noncollege, young adult—an important segment of the youth market, which is frequently ignored by advertisers.

3. COLGATE—"THE PUMP DANCE"

Colgate Toothpaste's "Pump Dance" commercial was groundbreaking in its use of the rock-video style to sell a product often viewed by advertisers as mundane. The ad presents the traditional copy points of a toothpaste ad (fights cavities, contains fluoride, etc.) in a visually exciting manner, which attracts both the product purchaser (typically, the parent) as well as the end user (young people).

4. DEL MONTE—"YOU WORK HARD FOR YOUR BODY"

This Del Monte commercial links its vegetables with being vigorous and physically fit. The theme is sung to the tune of Donna Summer's hit "She Works Hard for the Money" while scenes of sexy, athletic young men and women are shown. Thus, like the "Colgate Pump Dance" this commercial makes an everyday household product seem new and interesting to young viewers, here through the use of an adapted musical theme and sensual images.

5. GENERRA—"I LOVE YOU 'CAUSE YOU'RE MY STYLE"

Farah's Generra Sportswear is one of three clothing brands whose commercials were rated as particularly appealing by youth. The Top Forty, easy listening sound of "I Love You 'Cause You're My Style" combines with pictures of fashionably dressed young men and women to create very sensual commercials without any display of skin.

6. LEVI'S 501 JEANS—"501 BLUES"

The campaign for Levi's 501 Jeans uses scenes of city life and varied types of young people. Its theme song sometimes has an upbeat, contemporary sound while at other times, jazz or "the blues" provides the musical backdrop. Thus, the ads appeal to the wide-ranging musical tastes of young people and have made the product one of the trendiest and most successful for Levi-Strauss in recent years.

7. LIPTON CUP-A-SOUP—"AFTER THE GAME"

"After the Game" demonstrates excellence in slice-of-life advertisements targeting youth. The ad revolves around two teenage brothers, preparing and then eating the soup for lunch. The conversation and its style is extremely realistic. This sensitive portrayal of a relationship between young men/brothers is so rare in television commercials that it really hits home with young consumers.

8. PEPSI—"CHOICE OF A NEW GENERATION"

In the use of celebrities in its advertisements, Pepsi-Cola is unequaled. With superstars Michael Jackson, Lionel Richie, Don Johnson, and Michael J. Fox each appearing in one of its "Choice of a New Generation" commercials, the soft drink manufacturer gained both tremendous entertainment value for its advertisements as well as a major public relations boost.

9. PIONEER STEREO—"BE A PIONEER"

Pioneer Stereo demonstrates its superiority in the use of non-celebrity spokesmodels with its "Be a Pioneer" campaign. The ads correctly recognize that today, young people think of themselves in many different ways—from Preppy to F.L.Y.E.R.S., from Punk to Career-Oriented—and show them coming together through music. But the ads further realize that, beyond music, the connection among all these types of young people is that they pride themselves on their individuality. Thus, the theme "Catch the Spirit of a True Pioneer" fits perfectly with this self-image.

10. SPRITE—"HIGH SCHOOL"

The Sprite soft drink commercial also presents a realistic slice of life, but this time among groups of teenage students. The students look and act so true-to-life that the ad could have been shot in the hallway of almost any public high school. Such an accurate portrayal effectively links Coca-Cola's Sprite to this important teenage consumer.

11. TOSTITOS—"CLASSIC RERUNS"

The Tostitos campaign is the only one selected from the entire snack food industry, which depends greatly on its sales to the youth market. These "Classic Reruns" are humorous, visually unique, and technically superb. The black-and-white ads intersperse footage from old episodes of TV programs, such as "The Adams Family," "The Lone Ranger," "Leave It to Beaver," and "Mr. Ed," to make it seem as if the characters are part of a conversation about the tortilla chips. These ads are especially appreciated by young adults, who enjoyed these shows from their childhood or from recent television syndication.

12. ARMY—"BE ALL THAT YOU CAN BE"

The "Be All That You Can Be" campaign includes some of television's most familiar commercials. Its memorable theme song and exciting images of soldiering emphasize what young people believe are the most positive career and lifestyle qualities: pride, duty, service, hard work, challenge, and achievement. The ads' great success in helping to maintain an all-volunteer Army is true proof of their ability to reach out to young people.

13. WENDY'S—HUMOR CAMPAIGNS

"Where's the Beef" and the "Russian Fashion Show" are classic uses of contemporary humor. The ads were hip, trendy, and entertaining to watch, but also forcefully presented the point that only Wendy's could satisfy the taste requirements of consumers.

14. MAXWELL HOUSE COFFEE—"YOUNG COMEDIANS"

Humor is also well-demonstrated by the youth-oriented ad for General Food's Maxwell House Coffee. In the "Young Comedians," a young stand-up comic tells humorous stories related to coffee drinking. The commercials make the youth-appealing point that that drinking coffee is a right of passage into adulthood. Thus, the campaign combines the best qualities of advertising humor: jokes are both funny and make a convincing, attractive point about the product.

The Worst Television/Radio Commercials

Product/Sponsor	Campaign/Ad Slogan
1. Chips Ahoy	"Boxer: Betcha Bite a Chip"
2. Cherry Coke	"Outrageous"
3. Chunky	"Chunky's Back"
4. Coffee Industry	"Coffee for the Young Achiever"
5. Combos	"Combos Really Cheeses Your Hunger Away"
6. Dow	"Dow Lets You Do Great Things"
7. McDonald's McDLT	"Romeo and Juliet"
8. Michelob	"Where You're Going Its Michelob"
9. Oxy-10	"Zitzo"
10. Panasonic Portable Stereo	"Take the Music with You"
11. UltraBrite	"The UltraBrite Supergirl"

1. CHIPS AHOY—"BOXER"

Nabisco Brands' Chips Ahoy commercial shows an awkward, skinny teenage boy alone in his bedroom caught up in a fantasy world. He imagines that he is in a "boxing match" where he must bite into a cookie (the "Champion") without biting a chocolate chip. In the match, the boy gestures wildly and jumps around the empty room. Clearly, the ad is uncomfortable to watch. Moreover, it does nothing to make young people believe that the snack is good to eat.

2. CHERRY COKE—"OUTRAGEOUS"

Cherry Coke uses a surprisingly juvenile presentation of strange animated-like scenes in this commercial. Its theme "New Cherry Coke—Outrageous" seems forced, even ridiculous. Typically, soft drinks create lifestyle ads that are exciting and trendy. But this ad makes the product seem weird, quirky, and out of fashion.

3. CHUNKY—"CHUNKY'S BACK"

Chunky candy uses 1950s-looking cartoon characters singing "Chunky's Back" to the tune of "My Boyfriend's Back." The animation and the old-fashioned song makes the ad appear childish, cheap, and silly.

4. COFFEE INDUSTRY—"COFFEE FOR THE YOUNG ACHIEVER"

The Coffee Industry attempted to respond to a negative image problem, which was causing young people, especially young adults, to turn away from the product and remain drinking carbonated beverages. However, its "Coffee for the Young Achiever" could have been produced by the soft drink industry or even by the people who do spoofs of commercials on "Saturday Night Live." In the end, this confusing ad seems to emphasize the most negative aspects of the product by showing coffee drinkers as nervous, aggressive, and compulsive.

5. COMBOS—"REALLY CHEESES YOUR HUNGER AWAY"

Combos uses some of the most patronizing "gatekeeper" advertisements in the snack food industry. Instead of speaking directly to the youth audience, a spokesmodel parent pitches the snack food to parents by explaining how good "real cheese" Combos are for their children and how much "the kids" enjoy it. Their out-dated slogan "Combos *Really Cheeses* Your Hunger Away" (emphasis added) amplifies the youth-alienating features of this campaign.

6. DOW—"LETS YOU DO GREAT THINGS"

Dow's image continues to suffer from the company's involvement in the Vietnam War and its recent commercials to encourage recruitment are doing little to help improve young people's perceptions. Just a brief sample of the ad's dialogue amply illustrates this point: A student during her graduation ceremony thinks to herself, "I can't wait! I never understood when mom made me eat my vegetables because 'there were places where kids were starving.' Now . . . in two weeks I walk into a Dow laboratory and begin working on new ways to help grow more and better grain for those kids who so desperately need it. I can't wait!" For today's sophisticated, sometimes cynical young adults, this dialogue is corny, naive, cliched, and unbelievable.

7. MCDONALD'S—"ROMEO AND JULIET"

The McDLT campaign included a slew of terrible commercials, but certainly the chain's attempt to compare the smashing of lettuce and tomato onto a slab of hamburger with the first secret meeting of Romeo and Juliet ranks as one of the worst. Young people found the ad exceptionally precious and felt it took itself a tad too seriously to be effective.

8. MICHELOB—"WHERE YOU'RE GOING"

From 1980 to 1984 Michelob beer experienced a annual volume decline of 5 percent. And with commercials like "Where You're Going You've Always Known It—Where You're Going It's Michelob" this is no surprise. Young adults do not want to associate themselves with the repulsive yuppie lifestyle that seems to be glorified in the campaign's scenes and the musical theme.

9. OXY-10—"ZITZO"

Oxy-10 Acne Medication ads present a teenage boy, whom an unseen announcer insults with names like "zitzo." Humiliated by this harassment and his problem, the boy puts a bag over his head. Like the boy in the commercial, young people, who not surprisingly do not think of acne as hilarious comedy, were embarrassed and insulted by the ad.

10. PANASONIC—"TAKE THE MUSIC WITH YOU"

Panasonic Portable Stereo's commercial certainly takes the award for one of the most condescending characterizations of young people in a television commercial. In the ad, a preppy-looking young man is seemingly unconcerned when a barber shaves off a long strip of hair across his head revealing a bare strip of scalp in the middle of an otherwise full head of hair. In this same barber shop, other young people with bizarre, multi-colored hair styles seem to be on "acid trips." The ad concludes with the preppy boy moronically jumping and skipping around the barber shop with his portable stereo in hand. The point of this ad and the image it is trying to create still remains a mystery.

11. ULTRABRITE—"SUPERGIRL"

Colgate-Palmolive's UltraBrite Toothpaste tries to use slice-of-life commercials to make its point; but fortunately no one's life is like the one presented. In the ads, one character is ignored by an attractive member of the opposite sex. But after using UltraBrite (represented by a blonde girl in blue spandex tights who "zaps" the person with a light flash from her UltraBrite gun), the person has no problem finding his or her true love. If the ad is trying to make youth believe that toothpaste can solve their love life problems, the ad failed. If the ad is supposed to be humorous, young people missed the joke.

The Best Print Advertisements

Product/Sponsor	Campaign/Ad Slogan
1. Swatch	"Switch Me to Swatch"
2. Ford Mustang	"Spring Break"
3. U.S. Navy	"Dress for Success"
4. Lucky Strike Cigarettes	"Light My Lucky"
5. Oxy Skin Cleanser	"Oxyology"
6. Benetton Clothing	"United Colors of Benetton"
7. Nike	"Mysterious Athlete"
8. General Foods Coffee	"Recipe"

| 9. Maybelline/Caress/
Dr. Scholl's | "Teen Advertorial" |
| 10. Honda Scooters | "Grace Jones" |

1. SWATCH—"SWITCH ME TO SWATCH"

This is an eight-page full-color ad that began with a green headline "Operator, switch me to Swatch!" The campaign promoted the new Swiss-made plastic watches, as well as introduced other Swatch products like sunglasses (they call them "shields"), umbrellas, sweatshirts, writing pens, army knives, shavers, and tote bags.

Action, color, and outrageously risqué sarcasm are the elements that made this print ad (that ran in such youth-oriented magazines as *Mademoiselle* and *Seventeen*) so popular. Unlike many companies, Swatch seems to understand that young people like print ads that "move" or tell a story. Instead of photographing their products lying flat on a table, they feature all of the products in use. The umbrellas are being carried by two models during a rain shower; the watches (four on an arm) are worn by a funky model as she talks on a car phone; and the tote bag is thrown over the shoulder of a young executive who is *skateboarding* his way through midtown traffic.

What makes the ad memorable to young people is that while it shows off the products, it doesn't take itself too seriously. Nobody is posing for the camera. The ad makes one think that Swatch products will turn normal situations into absolute fun.

2. FORD MUSTANG—"SPRING BREAK"

This two-page ad ran in college magazines like *Business Week's Guide to Careers,* and featured a giant map of the United States with twenty different cities highlighted across the page. The main headline was "The 20 Hottest Places to Go During Spring Break."

This Mustang convertible ad easily could have fallen on its face with its corny looking cartoon characters who frolic at the bottom of the page, but the piece succeeded because it provided information that students want: suggestions on where to spend their vacation. Since it was rather colorful *and* provided at least a paragraph of details on twenty vacation cities, the ad became a poster for many students' walls.

3. U.S. NAVY RECRUITMENT—"DRESS FOR SUCCESS"

The line for this full-page ad is "Dress for Success" and shows a head and shoulders shot of a young man dressed in a white naval hat and jacket.

If there was ever a way to make the armed forces look like good, clean fun, the Navy has done it here. They appeal to the young person who wants financial and career success by talking about decision making, management, and training, and by listing naval salaries ranging from $17,700 to $31,000. It used to be taboo to talk about money in a recruiting ad, but the Navy knows that it takes more than just patriotism to attract the interest of today's young people. Money and success speak much louder.

4. LUCKY STRIKE CIGARETTES—"LIGHT MY LUCKY"

There are several versions of this print ad, but the copy is always the same—simply "Light My Lucky." In all of them, there is a cool-looking person staring at the reader. He or she is holding a cigarette in hand or mouth.

Although all cigarette makers claim they don't try to sell to young people, several have managed to create campaigns that young consumers like. This one uses sexually suggestive copy and a young model who stares seductively at the reader.

5. OXY SKIN CLEANSER—"OXYOLOGY"

This two-page ad has a lot of copy and a sub-head that reads "An introductory course to skin care. And Oxy." Two students are featured, as are several of Oxy's cleansing products.

You couldn't find a topic more depressing than acne pimples, but Norcliff Thayer's Oxy skin cleanser ad literally makes the subject seem like a fun course. The ad talks about the causes of acne, the fact that it affects adults, and how the Oxy product affects pores, oil, and skin. The ad is educational and memorable.

6. BENETTON CLOTHING—"UNITED COLORS OF BENETTON"

Almost none of these ads has the same models, but they all utilize young people of different nationalities. Sometimes the models are draped over each other, crowded together, or standing separately. These ads were a big favorite because they captured a bohemian, international flavor that goes against the typical staid, blond-haired, blue-eyed American ads that fill magazines. In addition to featuring a large number of Asian, black, Hispanic, Scandinavian, and European models, the ads include peace signs, colorful globes, maps, and flags from countries around the world.

7. NIKE—"MYSTERIOUS ATHLETE"

We used the above term to describe these ads because they have absolutely no copy. The Nike name is usually displayed in the bottom left-hand corner or the upper right-hand corner, leaving almost 75 percent of the ad empty except for a dark, shadowy background. At the edge of the ad, there is an athlete who looks as though he or she has just worked out.

If you've seen any one of these Nike ads, you probably looked twice at it because of its mysterious quality. These ads create a mood. It's a mood athletes experience after they've performed—it's one that makes you remember Nike and its fitness wear.

8. GENERAL FOODS INTERNATIONAL COFFEE—"RECIPES"

These ads ran in many young women's magazines and featured recipes that used the coffees being advertised as ingredients. There is a ad for each of the different General Foods flavors (Mocha Mint, Orange Cappuccino, Amaretto, etc), and although the ad shows no people, written dialogue explains that the speaker and a friend have made a special coffee dessert to eat next to the swimming pool or the fireplace.

The ads use color quite effectively—a deep blue swimming pool that splashes near two glasses filled with ice cream and coffee in the "Summer Mocha Mint" recipe and deep orange shadows that reflect from the flames of a fireplace onto glasses mixed with coffee, brown sugar, and cinnamon in the "Winter Cappuccino" recipe. The ads cleverly display all six of the colorfully decorated tins of coffee and the recipes cause young people to think of coffee not just as an adult drink, but as a sweet youthful dessert.

9. MAYBELLINE/CARESS SOAP/DR. SCHOLL'S—"ADVERTORIAL"

This is a new and unusual advertising method that combines commercial products and editorial copy, thus making a six- or eight-page advertising spread look like the magazine's editorial copy. This particular four-page spread combined three different products and gave information on skin care and foot care while also displaying the products. *Teen* and *Young Miss Magazine* commonly use advertorials.

Teens who see these ads enjoy reading them because practical information is given in a nonobtrusive manner. Because these advertorials look like magazine copy, the readers are less skeptical of the fact that a company is trying to sell them a particular product—even though the product is shown several times. The models used look no different from the models typically used in the editorial sections of the popular magazines; as a matter of fact, most of these advertorials have to carry the word "Advertisement" in the bottom corner of each page so readers realize they are not a part of the magazine's copy.

10. HONDA SCOOTERS—"GRACE JONES"

This ad and its similar TV ad bring together the unusual, but popular singer/actress Grace Jones with the sleekly-designed, metallic colored Honda motor scooter. These provocative ads appeared in magazines like *People* and *Rolling Stone.*

While Grace Jones is very recognizable, she has a funky, bohemian-based popularity among young people. Here, Honda uses a serious New Wave star to lend credibility to a serious, New Wave product.

The Worst Print Advertisements

Product/Sponsor	Campaign/Ad Slogan
1. Panasonic Typewriter	"Letter to Mom and Dad"
2. R. J. Reynolds	"Peer Pressure"

3. Head & Shoulders Shampoo	"Gorgeous Models"
4. Casio	"Music on the Subway Train"
5. Calvin Klein	"Obsession for Men"
6. Ralph Lauren	"Polo Clothes"
7. Canon	"Power Tool Typewriters"
8. Converse	"This Performance Made Possible"

1. PANASONIC TYPEWRITER—"LETTER TO MOM AND DAD"

This ad promotes a typewriter that prints in color. It focuses on a letter typed to Mom and Dad from a student named "Ginnie." Also featured in the ad is a lock of hair and a Polaroid photo of Ginnie with her new haircut, her new typewriter, and her new boyfriend named (what else) "Moose."

Although Panasonic uses the line "just slightly ahead of our time," they obviously took ten steps *backward* when they ran this corny "kids will be kids" print ad. Words and phrases like "real hot," "super," "stuff," "hint hint," and "so-o-o creative" are used in the copy and make the ad sound like a bad teen movie.

Young people take offense to these ads because they create laughable stereotypes with which no young person identifies. It was bad enough to show Ginnie's enclosed lock of hair and her school stationery, which was embossed with the school name "Tech," but what young person can really take the accompanying photo seriously? Why is Ginnie posing with Moose on his fraternity's front steps—with a typewriter in her lap?

2. R. J. REYNOLDS TOBACCO—"PEER PRESSURE"

This full-page ad is run in teen magazines and professes to teach young people how to avoid cigarettes at an early age. The ad is without color and includes no graphics. A clever concept, it features five different conversations between students. An example: "Go ahead and take a puff—what's the matter, are you chicken?" Another example: "Do you want everybody to think you're a nerd?"

Wasn't it kind of the R. J. Reynolds cigarette company to run a series of ads in teen magazines, telling teenagers not to smoke cigarettes? Not only did the people at Scholastic Inc. turn their noses up at this ad, but so did many young people.

The dialogue in this ad truly sounds as though a sixty-year-old copywriter was trying to remember how young people spoke when he was twelve years old. Today's young people don't say things like "getting teed off" or "You must think I'm pretty dumb to fall for that one" or "Come on, all the cool kids smoke" or "Friends are people who like you for who you are . . . back off." Yes, R. J. Reynolds—back off.

3. HEAD & SHOULDERS SHAMPOO—"GORGEOUS MODELS"

These print ads featured a large black-and-white photo of an incredibly good looking male or female model and a quote like, "Would I trust my oily hair to a dandruff shampoo?" The ads were seen in magazines like *People* and *Us,* as well as on billboards and in trains and announced the two new formulas of Head & Shoulders that Procter & Gamble produces for different types of hair.

Most advertisements feature good-looking models, but the worst mistake a marketer can make is to remind consumers that the good-looking people in the ads *really are* models. These ads look like glossy black-and-white publicity shots from a professional model's portfolio—they seem too gorgeous to be honest. The average consumer knows he or she will never measure up to the model in the ad—no matter what type of shampoo is used. The ad is eye-catching, but the chiseled features, the moussed hair, and the sexy stare are too contrived to win over the average person trying to control dandruff.

4. CASIO—"MUSIC ON THE SUBWAY TRAIN"

Kids will be kids. This full-color print advertised Casio's portable keyboards, which you can take and play just about anywhere—even on the subway. The ad ran in magazines like *Glamour* and *Spin* and featured a wild-eyed boy in a wornout sleeveless jean shirt who is playing on the keyboard and screaming at two outlandishly dressed, overly made-up teenage girls who are dressed in black brassieres, fishnet tops and stockings, black lace gloves, and white high heels.

This is one of the most unrealistic portrayals of young people that has appeared in the musical instrument business. Not only is the bug-eyed boy catching the attention of a disturbed subway policeman in the background, but the girls look like high school-age prostitutes. Every possible stereotype was dumped into this ad, which seems to praise those brazen, counter-culture, colorfully rebellious young people. And if you look closely, you'll find stereotypes for other generations as well. In addition to the middle-aged policeman, there is a white-haired grandmother and a female yuppie who is sporting a bow-tie, vest, and page boy haircut. To follow up the whole parade of caricatures, Casio ends the ad with their own company tagline: "Casio—where miracles never cease."

5. CALVIN KLEIN—"OBSESSION FOR MEN"

This memorable ad was designed for all men, but has received a lot of attention on college campuses. It promotes the Obsession cologne for men and shows a photo of three naked female bodies draped over each other. The ad is yellowed and there are scratches running across the whole photo.

Many college students refer to this ad as "the rape scene" or "the lesbian orgy." Calvin Klein may not realize it, but young people spend a great deal on fragrances, and young men are looking for a cologne that conveys an image they are comfortable with. This ad does not promote a masculine image. It is very troubling and very violent; to quote several young people who commented, the ad looks "queer."

6. RALPH LAUREN—POLO CLOTHING

This critique refers, in general, to all of the Polo ads. The brand, especially the pull-over shirts, is immensely popular among young people, having almost replaced the old Izod alligator. The ads promoting this American-made brand seems to feature beautiful photographs of only white, Anglo-looking people with blonde hair, blue eyes, and rosy cheeks.

The reason why clothing ads from Benetton, Pierre Cardin, Esprit, Calvin Klein, and many other companies are appealing to young people is because they can look at an ad and say "That could be me in that blouse or those pants." The Polo ads are a turn-off for many because they all reinforce the WASP stereotype. This may be comforting to a certain sector, which falls into or aspires to the delineation, but it is disturbing to many more who feel that the clothes are only for the types of people shown in the ads. Young people are actually quite aware of the absence of ethnic groups in advertisements and it works to the detriment of manufacturers guilty of it.

7. CANON—"POWER TOOL TYPEWRITERS"

This full-color ad is an aerial shot of seven young people who are sitting outside on the grass with typewriters in their laps. The product is the Canon Typemate 10 electronic typewriter. The bold headline at the top is "Power Tool for the Class of '89."

There is a very simple problem with this ad and it has to do with word usage. Canon used the term "power tool" to describe their wonderful new machine, just as one would refer to a drill. What Canon should have realized is that "power tool" is used in most high schools and college campuses as a derogatory term for someone who acts like a nerd. A "tool" is someone who is serious, hardworking, and cutthroat. A "power tool" is someone who is even worse. This term has had negative connotations for the last four or five years. Canon should have done a little research before attempting to use this slang term.

8. CONVERSE—"THIS PERFORMANCE MADE POSSIBLE"

This particular print ad promoted Converse's leather sneaker called Aerodyne. The top half of the ad is a black-and-white photo of a woman with a tank top, button earrings, thick hair down to her shoulders, long, glossy white fingernails, and heavy wet lipstick. The photo is very dark and shows the woman sitting on the floor in a guarded position, with her arms stretched out defensively and one leg extended as though it is kicking someone. We cannot see her feet.

The photo looks like a shot of a woman who is about to be sexually attacked. The shadows, the protruding bust, flexed leg, wet lipstick, and wide eyes look sexual and frightening. It is not until one reads the several lines of copy on the bottom half of the ad that one realizes that the woman is an athlete in the middle of a workout. Although Converse is supposedly advertising her athletic shoes, we don't see her feet. We see every part of her body *above* her ankles. Although the woman is an athlete, the reader looks at her long nails, earrings, heavy lipstick, and the dark, eery surroundings and comes to a much different conclusion.

The Best Promotions

Product/Sponsor	Campaign/Slogan
1. Pontiac Fiero	"Hall & Oates Concerts"
2. American Express	"Real Life Planner"
3. Miller Brewing Co.	"Skiing/Rodeo/Films/Bands & Comedy Shows"
4. *Glamour* Magazine	"Top 10 College Women"
5. Milton Bradley	"Twister–Guinness Book of Records Contest"
6. Nabisco	"MTV Million Dollar Give Away"
7. Seagram's	*"Tables* Magazine"
8. Nissan/Datsun	*"America* Magazine" sponsor
9. Daniel Hechter Clothes	"Search for the Adventurous Man"
10. *Rolling Stone* Magazine	"Florida Spring Break Events"
11. Swatch	"F.L.Y.E.R.S."

| 12. General Foods | *"Seventeen* Magazine Cooking Contest" |
| 13. McCall's Patterns | "Sew 'n Show Contest" |

1. PONTIAC FIERO—"HALL & OATES CONCERTS"

With the help of the ad agency D'Arcy Masius Benton & Bowles, Pontiac created a tie between its new youth-oriented sports car, Fiero, and the biggest record-selling duo in U.S. history. GM's Pontiac Division sponsored the sixty-five-city national tour of singers Daryl Hall and John Oates in late 1984 and early 1985. In conjunction to the tour, there were sweepstakes and poster, T-shirt, and bumper sticker give-aways at local Pontiac dealerships.

Since the Hall & Oates duo appeals to the same youthful audience (eighteen to thirty years old) that the Fiero was trying to capture, the sponsorship was an effective move for Pontiac. It was a well coordinated campaign that brought the young Hall & Oates fan into the Pontiac showroom with the hopes of filling out a local dealer's Fiero/Hall & Oates Sweepstakes entry form. Not only were there Hall & Oates tickets at local Fiero dealerships, but there were Fiero car displays at each of the Hall & Oates concert sites.

2. AMERICAN EXPRESS—"REAL LIFE PLANNER"

For several years, American Express has created a major presence for itself on college campuses. The company most recently created a student guide which ran monthly in the college magazine *Newsweek On Campus.*

What appeared to be a serialization from a guidebook for

graduating students was actually an eight- to ten-page advertisement. The well-written text was entitled "The American
Express Real Life Planner" and included a new subject each
month. Such practical areas like networking, job-hunting, interviewing, money management, and office politics were covered
over a period of several months. There was so much practical
information here, students were likely to save each installment
and remember that American Express really does care about
the young consumer.

3. MILLER BREWING—"SKIING/RODEO/FILMS/BANDS & COMEDY SHOWS"

Miller Brewing Company has programs to promote Miller
High Life, Miller Lite Beer, and Löwenbräu. In addition to a
well-designed Spring Break Guide, which they publish for
Florida-bound students, they organize "Lite Beer Comedy"
shows, the "Miller Music Series," ski competitions, and film
series just for college students and their campuses.

This company understands the importance of creating a presence on campus. Not only are its activities and sponsorships
conducted on a national level, but they are run locally as well.
And to complement the activities, special merchandise like
posters, painter's caps, jackets, bandannas, and T-shirts are
given away to further promote each of the individual events.

4. GLAMOUR MAGAZINE—"TOP 10 COLLEGE WOMEN"

Realizing that today's college-educated woman is interested in
a lot more than her appearance, *Glamour* magazine runs a
contest where it selects high-achieving college students who
have displayed leadership abilities on their campuses or in their
communities. The applicants must write essays and the winners
are flown to New York to meet with influential politicians,
business people, and anyone else that they might select.

Glamour not only gets real involvement out of its applicants, but because it typically selects young women who are Rhodes Scholars and class valedictorians, the image of the magazine improves constantly. *Glamour* is seen not only as a fashion monthly, but as a magazine for the ambitious, well-educated, and successful woman, a fact not lost on advertisers. Another important aspect of this promotion is that the prizes are highly unusual and much more meaningful to the contestants. The prize is the opportunity for each winner to meet with a top professional in her intended career.

5. MILTON BRADLEY—"TWISTER-GUINNESS BOOK OF RECORDS CONTEST"

Ketchum Public Relations came up with a creative way to bring back the popularity of Twister, the "hands and feet" game, which is played on a giant map with different color dots. The promotion was a challenge to different college campuses, as well as to students who came to the Florida Spring Break activities, to set up the largest possible Twister game, with the greatest number of participants.

The idea of creating enough enthusiasm over a game so as to try and break a world's record is brilliant. Not only does such a contest create publicity on TV news and talk shows (as this did), but it also makes a product seem current and popular. Milton Bradley scored a hit with this promotion because it made a childhood game seem acceptable to young adults.

6. NABISCO—"MTV MILLION DOLLAR GIVE AWAY"

Many companies have finally come to accept the significance that MTV holds within the youth market. This highly popular promotion was a year-long project which was concluded on New Year's Day 1986 and promoted such Nabisco products as Lifesavers, Baby Ruth, Bonkers, Butterfinger, and Bubble Yum

Bubble Gum. Advertisements about the $1 million give away were not only on the popular MTV channel, but were also on the wrappers of the various Nabisco products.

The fact that a young person could pick up a Baby Ruth bar and see that green MTV logo on the wrapper was an immense asset for Nabisco. The popularity and reputation of MTV rubbed off instantly when a product was associated with it.

7. SEAGRAM'S—"TABLES MAGAZINE"

Twelve times each year, the 13–30 Magazine company publishes a magazine called *Tables.* It is designed for and paid for by Seagram's, the beverage company, and is distributed to waiters and waitresses, aged twenty to thirty. It contains fiction and nonfiction pieces, and all the ads promote Seagram's beverages.

Both Seagram's and 13–30 understand there are many young people who are in school or in jobs where the traditional media forms do not reach. They realize that specialized, targeted media is the secret to reaching and appealing to various groups.

8. NISSAN/DATSUN—"AMERICA MAGAZINE"

Following the same logic as Seagram's sponsorship of *Tables* magazine, the Nissan automobile company sponsors another 13–30 magazine called, *America: The Nissan Student Travel Guide.* Distributed twice a year, this slick seventy-page magazine features stories about ideal vacation or activity spots for young people. All the ads feature Nissan/Datsun autos and the publication is sent to college campuses throughout the country.

Here is another innovative idea for creating a presence for one's name brand even though the product is not sold on the campus. Any student who reads *America* begins to relate the Nissan name with excitement and adventure as the Nissan name is in the title and the ads run throughout the magazine.

The magazine also fills an important need as there is no other travel magazine tailored for young people.

9. DANIEL HECHTER CLOTHES—"SEARCH FOR THE ADVENTUROUS MAN"

The largest manufacturer of men's fitted clothing runs a very ingenious promotional campaign that is aimed at the young man who is buying suits and dress clothes. The clothing company created a national contest in which entrants wrote essays on why they represented the Adventurous Man. The promotion was run in the men's departments of several major stores throughout the country and the finalists spoke and modeled in front of the judges. The winner received clothing and the chance to appear in an upcoming Hechter ad.

Not only did the essays provide Hechter with a chance to see what today's young man saw in himself, but they also told what he saw in the Hechter label. As the finalists competed and spoke before highly publicized judgings in department stores, their presentations were taped. These tapes seemed like outrageously original commercials, each young man getting up and telling why he fits the "Hechter Adventurous Man" image. They were creating the image as they spoke, thus making the brand seem like a gold standard.

10. ROLLING STONE MAGAZINE—"FLORIDA SPRING BREAK EVENTS"

The activities that take place in Daytona Beach and Fort Lauderdale, Florida, during March and April attract thousands of college students who are on Spring Break. Like many other companies, Rolling Stone magazine uses the opportunity to sponsor live concert performances, athletic events, and an Expo Hall, where various student-oriented products can be sampled by young people.

Rolling Stone believes in marketing through music. Not only does their name appear on T-shirts and caps, but also on broad banners that welcome young people to the Spring Break concerts on the beaches They and many others realize that students will visit Florida during this period and sample new products for the first time. The sponsorship is relatively easy, since the students are all along the beaches, just waiting for events to take place.

11. SWATCH—"F.L.Y.E.R.S."

When Swatch Watch was about to introduce its new line of watches, its very first line of clothing, and such trendy accessories as tote bags, pens, and sunglasses, they wanted youthful, upbeat media exposure. Realizing that we (as creators of the new F.L.Y.E.R.S. term to describe the youth generation) commonly make many speeches on college campuses and appearances on television, they asked us to wear and use their items whenever we made public appearances.

According to both Max Imgruth, president of Swatch, and Carol Mamone, public relations associate at Jody Donohue Associates, the response to our public appearances with Swatch paraphernalia was incredible. Articles and photos appeared in papers throughout the country; the media and the public found the whole campaign outrageous—both because we are young ourselves and because Swatch fashions were something they wanted to try as well.

12. GENERAL FOODS—"SEVENTEEN MAGAZINE COOKING CONTEST"

For three years General Foods has been the sole sponsor for *Seventeen* magazine's cooking competition. There are "official ingredients" which include such General Foods products as:

Birds Eye frozen vegetables, Shake 'n Bake mixes, Stove Top Stuffing, Minute Rice, Maxwell House coffees, and so on. The entrants are male and female and range in age from fourteen to eighteen. The prizes are college scholarships and the winners are judged on creative use of ingredients, good nutrition, menu planning, and use of official ingredients.

Unlike many food companies, General Foods realizes that young people are not only cooking at home or in school, but that they are buying their family groceries. This contest encourages young men and women to try General Foods' many products at an age when brand loyalty hasn't been garnered by another product. The concept is a good one and recognizes the fact that the stereotypical forty-year-old housewife is not the only one in the supermarket and the kitchen.

13. MCCALL'S PATTERNS—"SEW 'N SHOW CONTEST"

For six years, McCall's has sponsored this sewing contest aimed at young people aged fourteen to eighteen. Working with Kodel Fabrics, McCall's developed a clever way to attract young people to both the sewing as a hobby and to their own line of unique sewing patterns. The rules require applicants to use a McCall's pattern and create a piece of clothing.

The people at McCall's utilize a marketing plan that could benefit the entire sewing industry, as well as other industries that have not traditionally captured the youth market. McCall's contest convinces the young consumer that sewing is not just for older people. Even the prizes are carefully chosen: the chance to have lunch with a teen celebrity, a tour of Universal Studios, and a photo in *Teen Magazine.* The contest follows *all the rules:* getting the entrants involved, requiring the use of a McCall's product, and offering an unusual prize that could not be purchased or won elsewhere.

The Worst Promotions

Product/Sponsor	Campaign/Slogan
1. Burger King	"Find Herb"
2. Gillette/Maybelline Ups 'n Downs Stores	"*Teen*'s Great Model Search"
3. *Wall Street Journal*	"Promotional Brochure"
4. Ford Mustang	"Rick Springfield Concerts"
5. Coty Cosmetics	"Ingenious Solutions Sweepstakes"
6. Oreo Cookies (Nabisco)	"Oreo Super Sounds Sweepstakes"
7. K-Mart/Kraco	"Custom Cab Giveaway"
8. Mars Candy/Twix Bars	"Twix Keep on Winning Game"

1. BURGER KING—"FIND HERB"

This outrageous campaign cost the second largest hamburger chain $40 million and drummed up an incredible amount of publicity. The whole program focused on a fictional nerdlike character called Herb. As the print ads, billboards, posters, TV/radio commercials, and cardboard display units explained, Herb was the only person on earth who hadn't yet eaten at Burger King. The contest explained that the "Herb" character would make surprise appearances around the country in different Burger King restaurants. In order to become a winner,

Burger King patrons had to spot Herb and announce that he was in the restaurant.

It has already been documented that the Herb campaign was a flop. Neither the industry, nor the Burger King people were impressed with sales that followed the Herb campaign. But consumers knew the chance of winning such a contest was completely out of their hands. It was up to Herb to appear in the restaurant. Young people were not about to travel the country, stalking Burger King dining rooms. People laughed, but no one took it seriously.

2. GILLETTE/MAYBELLINE/UPS 'N DOWNS STORES—"TEEN GREAT MODEL SEARCH"

For the last eight years, *Teen Magazine,* a monthly for teenage girls, has been running a promotional campaign that promises to discover and launch teen models. The concept is very appealing to young people and well-organized. The main problem with the program is that it is not beneficial to all those companies that participate.

Although this contest is based on a common interest of many young women—modeling—it combines too many company sponsors and product brands. In addition to *Teen Magazine,* Gillette, Maybelline, and Ups 'n Down Stores are all competing for attention. Because of all these companies, young contest entrants don't associate the campaign with any particular company. Furthermore, there is a fifth brand name product involved. The winner gets a *Mazda* Luxury sedan. And this prize is not entirely appropriate since many of the contestants are not even old enough to drive.

3. WALL STREET JOURNAL—"PROMOTIONAL BROCHURE"

In an effort to attract young readers to their paper, the *Journal*'s education department produces a brochure that describes the paper and why students should want to read it. While the paper is indeed beneficial to young readers, the promotional information does not work. First of all, the cover of the brochure is a reduced photo of the *Journal*'s front page. The target market for this piece is young people who have been raised on magazines and papers with color photos and entertainingly designed graphics. And here is a paper that has no photos, almost no white space, and few graphics. The *Journal*'s reputation and appearance are sufficiently threatening without being reduced three times and then used as the cover of a promotional brochure.

4. FORD MUSTANG—"RICK SPRINGFIELD CONCERTS"

Ford created a disaster for themselves because they didn't do their homework when deciding to sponsor pop singer/soap opera star Rick Springfield for music concerts to promote their sporty Mustang. Yes, they were correct in noting Rick Springfield's great popularity. But they didn't recognize the fact that his popularity was divided between two entirely different groups: those who knew him as a singer (aged eleven to fifteen) and those who knew him as an actor on the daytime soap opera *General Hospital.*

Unfortunately, for the car company, the young people who liked Rick's music were twelve- to fourteen-year old girls. They came to hear him sing, but they couldn't afford cars and were too young to drive.

5. COTY COSMETICS—"INGENIOUS SOLUTIONS SWEEPSTAKES"

Coty announced their sweepstakes in a five-page layout, which promoted four different Coty fragrances: Wild Musk, Sophia, Nuance, and Emeraude. The first page mentioned four grand prize trips and showed photos of Egypt, Paris, Venice, London, and the Riviera. Also on the page was a poem that seemed to give instructions on how to enter the sweepstakes and how to analyze the following four pages that featured models with each of the four fragrances. Here is an excerpt from the confusing poem/instructions:

> *"Discover your fragrance personality*
> *By solving this puzzling mystery.*
> *The next four pages have hidden clues*
> *So take your time to peruse.*
> *You must first uncover by coloration*
> *The key to adjective identification . . ."*

What on earth do they mean by "coloration" and "adjective identification"? Whomever designed the contest instructions must have either planned to launch a poetry career or plotted to prevent people from entering the contest.

6. OREO COOKIES—"OREO SUPER SOUNDS SWEEPSTAKES"

This is a very simple sweepstakes, which only requires entrants to give their name and address. The prizes are fairly ordinary—portable stereos, cassette players, and turntables with speakers. The contest was used to promote Nabisco's Oreo cookie.

What is the connection between Oreo Cookies and music? Absolutely none. The fact that Oreo is the sponsor of a "Super Sounds Sweepstakes" does not benefit the cookie brand at all. As a matter of fact, the name of the sweepstakes—"Super Sounds"—is derived from the fact that the prizes are music and sound equipment. Furthermore, Oreo does not get the entrants involved in an activity, only requiring a name and address. And to top it off, the prizes are ordinary and inexpensive.

7. K-MART/KRACO—"CUSTOM CAB GIVEAWAY"

In this promotional contest which was advertised in such college-oriented magazines as *Newsweek On Campus,* K-Mart Stores and Kraco car stereos sponsor sweepstakes where entrants have the chance to win one of seven Custom Cabs. A Custom Cab is one of those sooped-up, high performance, wide-tired pick-up trucks. In the ad, there is a photo of a truck, four Kraco car stereos, and race car driver Michael Andretti. In all, the ad displays the following different name brands: Toyota, Kraco Car Stereos, K-Mart, *Newsweek,* BF Goodrich, Bosch lamps, and Turtle Wax.

This contest is a complete mess. First of all, the prizes are ridiculous—considering the audience. Not many college students want to win a high performance pick-up truck. Next, there is the brand-name confusion. The only redeeming feature of this contest is that it offers an toll-free number to dial Kraco if one needs to get information or order their car stereos. It is doubtful that K-Mart benefited from this poorly designed contest at all.

8. MARS CANDY/TWIX BARS—"TWIX KEEP ON WINNING GAME"

Even if you had the patience to collect all of the wrappers in order to spell out "Keep on Winning," this contest is hardly worth the effort. The odds of winning the *grand prize* (two Honda Scooters) are 1 in 6,666,667. The odds of winning the instant prizes are a little better. One's chances of winning the Schwinn bicycle (value: $200) are 1 in 200,000. The other instant prize is another pair of Honda Scooters and your chances for that are 1 in 10,000,000. The numbers and odds of winning are all listed on the inside label of every Twix candy bar.

Young people who read the contest rules and see their odds of winning such meager gifts will walk away from this contest.

The Honda company and the Mars Candy company come off appearing incredibly cheap, offering such prizes as a $10 check or a free Twix candy bar (value 35 cents) with impossible odds like 1 in 12,500.

Index

269

ABOUT THE AUTHORS

*H*ailed by *Fortune* magazine and *Advertising Age* for their consulting advice to corporate America on reaching the youth market, Lawrence Graham and Lawrence Hamdan are the spokesmen of American youth. They are graduates of Princeton University and are now students at Harvard Business School and Harvard Law School. They are co-founders and partners of F.L.Y.E.R.S. Consulting, which has given advice and lectures to numerous corporations, including 6 in the Fortune 500, on how to better target their products and services to the 13–25 year old market. Their previous book, *FLYERS: Fun Loving Youth En Route to Success* (Simon & Schuster) examined the styles and trends of America's youth.

Graham, is currently a student at the Harvard Law School. In addition to his books with Mr. Hamdan, he is the author of 7 other non-fiction books and 3 television movies—all aimed at the youth market. A popular lecturer to both corporate and student audiences, he has appeared and given advice on over 350 TV and radio shows including *Phil Donahue* and *The Today Show* as well as in publications such as *The New York Times* and *People Magazine.* He has been hailed by *Mademoiselle* as one of "The 10 Most Interesting Young Men in America." He has held positions at NBC, The Ford Foundation, and The White House.

Hamdan, a magna cum laude graduate in Economics from

Princeton University where his thesis was written under Nobel Laureate Sir Arthur Lewis. He is presently a student in the J.D./M.B.A. program at Harvard Business School and Harvard Law School. In addition to his international consulting work in the Middle East and South America, he has edited three books on industry developments, has been published in the field of corporate taxation, and has worked in market research and financial analysis on Wall Street. His marketing advice has appeared in the *The Boston Globe* and *Los Angeles Times.*

SEND FOR THE YOUTHTRENDS NEWSLETTER

*K*eep up to date with tomorrow's YouthTrends by reading the monthly marketing newsletter, YouthTrends. Based on
the continuous research, interviews and polling of F.L.Y.E.R.S.
Consulting, authors Lawrence Graham and Lawrence Hamdan
provide on-going information and advice on understanding and
selling to the 13- to 25-year-old youth market. Monthly features
include information on what young people are talking about,
what they are purchasing, their current attitudes on what's in
and what's not, as well as profiles on what certain innovative
companies are doing in the areas of advertising or marketing to
the F.L.Y.E.R.S. age group. Each issue also features an interview with a marketer, as well as a strategy column from the
authors which offers new methods for reaching out to the young
consumer.

To begin a year-long subscription to the *YouthTrends Newsletter,* send a check or money order for $300 (payable to
F.L.Y.E.R.S. Consulting) to:

> YouthTrends Newsletter
> F.L.Y.E.R.S. Consulting
> P.O. Box 968
> Cambridge, MA 02238